The Politics of Economic Power
in Southern Africa

RONALD T. LIBBY

The Politics of Economic Power in Southern Africa

PRINCETON
UNIVERSITY
PRESS

Published by Princeton University Press, 41 William Street,
Princeton, New Jersey 08540
In the United Kingdom: Princeton University Press, Guildford, Surrey

Library of Congress Cataloging in Publication Data will be
found on the last printed page of this book

ISBN 0-691-07723-1 (alk. paper)
ISBN 0-691-02256-9 (pbk.)

This book has been composed in Linotron Melior

Clothbound editions of Princeton University Press books
are printed on acid-free paper, and binding materials are
chosen for strength and durability. Paperbacks, although satisfactory
for personal collections, are not usually suitable for library rebinding

Printed in the United States of America by Princeton University Press
Princeton, New Jersey

To Kathleen Christina and Kathleen Elizabeth
who gave me the confidence to write this book

CONTENTS

LIST OF MAPS

LIST OF TABLES

FOREWORD

RONALD LIBBY'S BOOK is an exemplary analysis of the use and limits of political and economic power in Southern Africa. Appearing at a time when the Republic of South Africa's racial order faces widespread internal resistance, and when the South African government has undertaken generalized military intimidation of its neighboring states, the book merits careful attention for its knowledgeable dissection of the region's political economy.

This is the mature work of a scholar who has spent many years on the ground in Southern Africa and who has a good nose for the way the political leaders in the region understand their political challenges and opportunities. In Libby's pages real people fight real battles for what they think are important goals. This is not a blow-by-blow account, however, nor a passionate tale of moral combat. Libby's political nose is disciplined by his skeptical analytic eye. His book is not for those who want to separate out the good guys from the bad guys, nor for those who seek, in Southern Africa, the unfolding of a historical drama pointing toward some inevitable end, be that revolution, resolution, or a racial bloodbath. It is a book for those who want to understand, and there is much here that should be understood by those who would shape policies toward the region.

The book's central analytic message is announced in its subtitle. Libby demonstrates that even in such economically penetrated and dependent states as those of Southern Africa, political leaders retain significant margins of autonomy with which they pursue their own political and economic goals. Certainly South Africa's economic power constrains its neighbors' actions, but that power does not permit Pretoria to call the tune in the region. South Africa's generalized military aggression should be seen not as the culmination of a campaign of economic coercion but as a desperate recourse when such coercion failed to achieve the political results desired. If one pushes Libby's central point a bit further, it suggests that Western nations desiring to bring about fundamental change in South Africa should not expect to rely on economic pressures to do the job, whether those pressures come through the "modernizing" effect of capitalist investment or through punitive economic boycott.

Beyond its substantive and topical interest, Libby's book makes a major contribution to the theoretical literature of the burgeoning international political economy field. The work is situated on the boundary between the traditional fields of international relations and comparative government; it is concerned with the domestic consequences of international economics and the international consequences of domestic politics. Along with the work of Peter Gourevitch, Miles Kahler, and others, Libby's book usefully undermines the intellectual wall that has kept these fields apart, without succumbing to the "world systems" school's temptation to eliminate the national state as a significant analytic entity. As is immediately apparent the book provides a sharp challenge to much of the "dependency" school writing. Libby's thoughtful engagement with that literature provides a central leitmotif for his analysis.

Although this is not an explicit concern of the book, I suggest that the work has much to teach those scholars busily engaged in rediscovering "the state." In Libby's analysis the state is no blind and bloodless collective actor; rather it appears in at least four important guises. First, however weak and harassed, the state is a legal entity buttressed by an international order that somehow works to preserve its component units. For all its power South Africa can neither eliminate even the weakest of its neighbors nor create legitimate new states out of its so-called homelands. Second, the state appears as a bounded political arena with its own distinctive sets of competitors and rules of engagement. The reader of Libby's case studies cannot fail to be impressed by how different those political arenas are one from the other. Third, the state is a structure of domination through which power is exercised. In even the weakest state that power can be decisive. Finally, in all the Southern African cases the state is the ultimate prize. The head that wears the crown may rest uneasy, but it has reason to rest more easily than those who are denied control of the state. Libby's intensely political analysis of Southern Africa's political economy elegantly suggests *en passant* just how rich and complex must be anything that aspires to call itself a "theory of the state."

Whether read primarily for its contribution to social science theory, or for its substantive analysis of Southern Africa's political economy, Ronald Libby's work stands as a stimulating challenge to accepted patterns of thought.

WILLIAM J. FOLTZ

THE IDEA for this book emerged during the course of six years of teaching and research in Southern Africa in the turbulent and exciting decade of the 1970s. During this time, I was privileged to witness firsthand profound changes in the region that were set in motion in Mozambique in 1975 and in Zimbabwe in 1979. As a member of the academic staff at the now defunct University of Botswana, Lesotho, and Swaziland between 1973 and 1975, I had a unique window into South Africa while being able to associate with an exceptional group of European scholars and African intellectuals and activists from all over the region whose understanding of the relationships between South Africa and other states in Southern Africa was unrivaled. I also had the opportunity to observe the importance of South Africa and Zimbabwe to one of the poorest and yet most fiercely independent and eccentric governments in Southern Africa—Malawi. While on the academic staff at the University of Malawi during 1976, I began to understand the political limits of economic power and the scope of a "weak" state's independent political action in the context of severe economic constraints. The shrewd and effective political rule of Malawi by Hastings Kamuzu Banda made a lasting impression on me.

I subsequently served on the academic staff of the University of Zambia in Lusaka from 1977 to 1979. Here I had access to senior Zambian officials and politicians who provided insights into the unique diplomatic activities of the five original Frontline States of Africa (FLS) in their efforts to cope with mounting security threats, initially from Rhodesia and then from South Africa. This helped me to understand how the political leaders of Zambia, Tanzania,

Mozambique, Angola, and Botswana assessed the threats to their governments. It drove home to me the overriding importance of domestic-national concerns to these leaders both in terms of assessing the importance of their countries' economic ties with South Africa and in terms of the limits of cooperating (economically and politically) with one another in order to cope with the threat posed by South Africa.

My conventional training as an American political scientist did not adequately equip me to interpret events I observed in Africa. Ironically, however, this turned out to be something of an advantage insofar as it forced me to undertake a learning process. I began a study of the vast political economy literature that was in vogue in African intellectual circles and among a younger generation of European scholars who were struggling to understand the failure of newly independent African governments to bring democracy and prosperity to their people.

While I found much of the political economy literature on African politics to be an improvement over the conventional North American social science approach, it also had its limitations. It had the advantage of bringing economics and class structure to the forefront of analysis, and it seemed to explain the persistent poverty and corrupt and, in many cases brutal rule of African governments. However, it failed to accord to politics a sufficient importance to account for its subversion of democratic institutions and its role in shaping and transforming class structures in society. The Southern African area, in particular, seemed to be dominated by a rather narrow orthodoxy that emphasized the importance of economic relationships over politics to the point where factors such as leadership, ideology, organization, and political mobilization were treated simply as epiphenomena of "dependent economic relations" or class forces. However, my experiences in Africa did not square with this narrow view of politics.

Dissatisfaction with both the approach to the study of politics that my training imparted and with the political economy literature led me to elaborate a syncretic fusion of these two streams of scholarship. The reader will recognize in my framework of analysis the contribution of, for example, interest group politics, which is popular among North American scholars, and state theory and class analysis, which is popular among many African and European scholars.

While I have had the advantage of living and working in a number of countries in Southern Africa, it is virtually impossible to remain current and in touch with developments in these countries from a distance. Furthermore, it is an ambitious undertaking simply to achieve a genuine expertise in the politics of one of these countries let alone the eleven countries that I have included in my study.

I therefore, have incurred a rather large number of debts to outstanding authorities in the field in the process of writing the book. In this regard I have been fortunate to have the suggestions, criticisms, and patient indulgence of leading economists, historians, political scientists, and sociologists in correcting errors of fact and interpretation and in encouraging me to sharpen and refine my arguments. While it is clearly impossible to list the names of the many colleagues and students who have without knowing it profoundly influenced my thinking on the subject, I can acknowledge colleagues who have directly contributed to the evolution of the book.

William J. Foltz and Douglas Anglin read the entire manuscript and made valuable and helpful suggestions for improvement. I owe William Foltz a special debt of gratitude for making research facilities and accommodations at Yale University available during the crucial revision stage of the work. I am also grateful for his support and encouragement in completing the project, for the title of the book, which was largely his suggestion, and for his generous foreword.

I also owe a special debt of gratitude to James Cobbe and George Dalton for their comments on the first chapter on the regional economy and to Cobbe for his comments on the section pertaining to Lesotho. Roger Southall and Hermann Giliomee went far beyond the call of professional colleagues in making detailed observations and suggestions for improving the section on South Africa. Heribert Adam and Philip Bonner also provided in-depth and penetrating criticism and suggestions for improving the section of the book on South Africa. Ann Seidman and Colin Stoneman were very informative in their comments and suggestions for revising the section on Zimbabwe. Thomas Callaghy, Michael Schatzberg, René Lemarchand, Nzongola-Ntalaja, Jean-Claude Willame, Benoît Verhaegan, and M. Crawford Young provided helpful recommendations for refining the section on Zaire. Special thanks also go to Thomas Callaghy for his detailed observations. Reginald Green, Cranford Pratt, and Harry Goulbourne read and commented on the section of the book on Tanzania, and Reginald Green offered extensive suggestions on the chapter on Namibia. Jonathan Crush provided insightful comments on the section on Swaziland, and André du Pisani was most helpful in his observations on the sections on Namibia and South Africa. T. David Williams, John Mc-Cracken, Alifeyo Chilivumbo, Robin Palmer, and David Hirschmann aided with revisions of the section on Malawi. Hirschmann also made helpful suggestions for revising the section on Lesotho. The section on Botswana was improved by the observations of William Tordoff, John Taylor, and Christopher Colclough, and the Mozambique section benefited from the recommendations of Barry Munslow, Thomas Henriksen, Allen Isaacman, and Norrie MacQueen. Special thanks to T. David Williams, John McCracken, and Barry Munslow for their careful observations.

I should also like to express my gratitude to Sandy Thatcher for listening to my proposal to publish an unconventional book and for guiding the manuscript to its completion. In times of straightened economic circumstances it is unusual to find an editor who is willing to consider an innovative work by a relatively unsung author. I should also like to express my gratitude to Mrs. Elizabeth Wessels of the Africa Institute for providing maps 3 and 12 plus additional maps used for preparing other maps in this volume. I am also grateful to Moore Crossey, the African curator at Yale University for his assistance. Hans E. Panofsky, the curator, and Maidel Cason, the documents librarian of the Melville J. Herskovits Library of African Studies of Northwestern University Library provided invaluable assistance in making final revisions of the book manuscript. Faith Mkhonta, the documentist at the University of Swaziland, also provided useful data on Swaziland. I wish to express my appreciation to the Centre of African Studies at the University of Edinburgh for allowing me to use conference papers on Malawi that will be published under the title *Malawi—An Alternative Pattern of Development*. I am grateful for the skillful work of my cartographer, Jeffrey Harley, and to my graphic artist, Wycliffe Ho-Shing, who prepared the diagrams, figures, and some of the individual country maps. J. Edward Greene, the acting director of the Institute of Social and Economic Research (ISER) at the University of the West Indies, Mona, arranged financing for my trip to Yale, and while in New Haven I had the benefit of competent research assistance from Jeffrey Herbst. My appreciation also goes to Kathleen Miles for expertly typing the entire manuscript with her usual selfless dedication. I am also grateful for Cathy Thatcher's superb job of editing the book.

Finally, I owe the biggest debt of all to my wife Kathleen Christina and my little daughter Kathleen Elizabeth for their faith in me and for their patience and understanding during the long hours I was shut away in my study. My wife also proofread the entire manuscript and offered valuable editorial suggestions and advice. To my daughter belongs a special note of appreciation for helping me to maintain my sanity during hectic and stressful periods of writing and rewriting by forcing me to take her for long walks and sharing the joyful simplicity of her happiness.

LIST OF ABBREVIATIONS

ANC (African National Congress of South Africa)
BCP (Basutoland Congress party)
BDP (Botswana Democratic party)
BNF (Botswana National Front)
BNP (Basutoland National party)
CONSAS (Constellation of Southern African States)
CP (Conservative party of South Africa)
FAPLA (People's Armed Forces for the Liberation of Angola)
FLNA (Front for the National Liberation of Angola)
FLNC (Front de Libération Nationale du Congo)
FPLM (Mozambique People's Liberation Force)
Frelimo (Frente de Libertação de Moçambique)
HNP (Herstigte Nasionale party)
Inkatha (Inkatha Yenkululeko Yesizwe Movement)
INM (Imbokodvo National Movement of Swaziland)
MCP (Malawi Congress party)
MFP (Marematlou Freedom party)
MPLA (Popular Movement for the Liberation of Angola)
MPR (People's Revolutionary Movement of Zaire)
NP (National party of South Africa)
PFP (Progressive Federal party of South Africa)
PTA (Preferential Trade Area Treaty)
RSA (Republic of South Africa)
SACU (Southern African Customs Union)
SADCC (Southern African Development Coordination Conference)
SWAPO (South West Africa People's Organization)
UDI (Unilateral Declaration of Independence)
UNIP (United National Independence party)
UNITA (National Union for the Total Independence of Angola)
ZANU (Zimbabwe African National Union)
ZAPU (Zimbabwe African People's Union)

The Politics of Economic Power
in Southern Africa

INTRODUCTION

THIS BOOK represents an effort to reconceptualize dependency relationships among states in the southern African region, an area of the world that is undergoing revolutionary political change while essentially remaining within a unified regional economy. My approach differs from conventional treatments of the subject insofar as I assume that the states in Southern Africa are economically interdependent with, rather than simply dependent upon, South Africa as the dominant national economy in the region. In taking this position, I am challenging the conventional orthodoxy that South Africa dominates the economies of other states in the region without, however, experiencing corresponding influence upon its own economy.[1]

I will argue that every state in the region—including South Africa—is to some degree able to manipulate regional economic ties to serve its own domestic and foreign policy objectives and at the same time is itself affected by these changes. Therefore, while South Africa's domination

---

[1] South Africa's domination of states in the regional economy is a theme running throughout the literature on the subject. The usual assumption is that South Africa dominates regional states, subject only to the pressures of world public opinion (Grundy 1973:285; Grundy 1979:311; Bowman 1971:16; Bowman 1968:253; Shaw 1974:648; Shaw and Heard 1977:82). Neo-Marxists take a similar position, arguing that since South Africa has economic control of the "inputs" of the economies of regional states such as labor and raw materials, this enables South Africa to manipulate the states (Amin 1972, 1976; Gervasi 1971; Emmanuel 1972; Nyathi 1974; and Frank 1981:56-57). Recent attention has focussed upon the nine-member regional Southern African Development Coordination Conference (SADCC), which has been interpreted as an attempt to decrease regional states' dependence upon South Africa (Cliffe 1980:240-261; Leys and Tostensen 1982; and Munslow and O'Keefe 1984:25).

of the regional economy enables it to exert great economic leverage over other states, in doing so its own domestic economy and politics are affected.

The study attempts to place the region's economic relationships into the context of the domestic national politics of states in the region. Instead of inferring the costs and benefits to ruling groups stemming from their economic relationships with other states in the region, I will evaluate the political significance of these relationships in terms of their impact upon the ruling party, class, or group and the political opposition to them in each state in the region.

In the absence of this important insight, we are left with only ad hoc inferences about the likely impact of changes in economic relationships on the various states of the region. This has the added handicap of assuming, for example, that increases or decreases in regional trade, labor migration, or investment have the same consequences for all states in the region. These and other economic relationships must first and foremost be evaluated from the perspective of the domestic politics of each state in the regional economy in order to understand their actual significance.

However, the study does not attempt a comprehensive discussion of all or even most of the economic relationships among states in the region. Such an undertaking would not only fill several volumes but it would tend to obscure the central purpose of the study. Because I am primarily interested in understanding how regional economic ties affect the ruling groups and their political opponents, I have selected for examination only those economic linkages that have a significant impact upon state power and have omitted from discussion other less important economic ties.

LIMITATIONS OF THE DEPENDENCY APPROACH

In an influential article by Larry Bowman in 1968, the shortcomings of the scholarly writing on Southern African politics was discussed. Bowman argued that there was a failure to appreciate the existence of an extensive network of economic linkages binding regional states together. Since South Africa was the principal source of the region's economic wealth, regional ties were said to strengthen the South African regime. It was pointed out that the failure to appreciate this fact led analysts to underestimate the strength and resilience of South Africa in the face of international condemnation and pressure. An important implication of this observation is that South Africa's policy of separate development was also strengthened by regional economic ties.

Bowman's insight concerning the necessity of viewing Southern Africa as a unified economic region was widely accepted by writers and commentators. Ironically, however, the uncritical application of his formulation has tended to stultify political analysis of the region.

There are two reasons for this. The first is that the regional economy came to be viewed solely from the perspective of South African hegemony. In other words, the region's economic ties were evaluated in terms of how they strengthened the South African state. There was no consideration given to how these ties might weaken the regime. Equally, there was no consideration given to how they might strengthen other states in the region (the exception being Rhodesia). The odious nature of apartheid, it appears, was sufficient to discourage scholars and commentators from investigating the positive side of black African states' economic relationships with South Africa. Economic ties with South Africa were solely regarded as being detrimental to their developmental goals and were seen as opening the states up to intimidation, pressure, and blackmail by South Africa. Hence, writers became preoccupied with utopian strategies and plans for "disengaging" black African states from their ties with South Africa and Rhodesia and with visionary proposals for creating de novo a new regional economy that excluded South Africa.

As a result, political analysis of Southern Africa was

largely undeveloped. What discussion there was, was reduced to cataloging economic relationships between South Africa and other states in the region. Inevitably authors would note that the particular relationship under discussion was asymmetrical and that South Africa could more easily forego the benefits derived from the relationship than its partner. From that it was inferred that South Africa derived political leverage or power over other states in the region. An indication of the inadequacy of this approach is the fact that despite revolutionary political change in the region since 1974 writers have continued to observe the same asymmetrical relationships with South Africa and have arrived at the same conclusions regarding South Africa's domination of states in the region.

While this suggests a remarkable continuity of regional economic networks, the observation contributes little to an explanation of the profound political changes occurring in the region. This indicates either that an understanding of the region's economic ties contributes little to our understanding of political change within the region or, as seems more likely, suggests an undeveloped political analysis of the economic relationships.

Indeed, a wide range of often conflicting state action is attributed to these asymmetrical relationships without any political analysis at all. In the case of Mozambique, for example, its economic dependence upon Rhodesia for rail and port fees, trade, labor remittances, and employment opportunities was said to have given the Smith regime political leverage over the country. It was assumed that if Mozambique challenged Rhodesia it would risk its own economic survival. However, in 1976, shortly after Frelimo took power in Mozambique, they closed the border with Rhodesia and thereby cut off Mozambique's important transit traffic and trade with Rhodesia. Likewise, Mozambique's nonaggression pact with South Africa in 1984, as well as the decision to curtail the operations of the African National Congress (ANC) in southern Mozambique, were attributed in part to South Africa's economic leverage over the country. However, there has been no attempt to explain why Mozambique challenged the Rhodesian regime at great economic cost and yet has not challenged South Africa, except to suggest that the costs are higher.

The answer to this question lies in an understanding of the importance that Mozambique's ruling party, Frelimo, attached to its economic ties with Rhodesia in 1976 compared to the importance of its economic ties with South Africa in 1984. While the economic ties have remained largely unchanged, Frelimo has undergone profound political transformation. Therefore, in order to understand the differences in Mozambique's assessment of its economic relationships with Rhodesia and South Africa, it is necessary to understand the changes in Frelimo's party politics.

Botswana, Lesotho, and Swaziland are treated in the literature as if they are so completely dependent upon the South African economy that politically they are "hostage" states. This is attributed to the fact that they are geographically encompassed by South Africa, they lack resources, and they need to export labor to the Republic of South Africa (RSA). The prevailing view is that these governments could not survive a disruption of their economic relationships with South Africa. The implication is that they also could not afford to challenge the South African political regime.

The difficulty here is that the logic is based upon the assumption that South Africa is able to use its economic ties with these countries as political leverage over them. There is reason to doubt that it can—or at least with the predicted results. For example, in the most extreme case, Lesotho, over one-half of its food requirements are supplied by South Africa, all of its industrial inputs come from RSA, an estimated 70 percent of rural income, 60 percent of governmental revenues, and almost all foreign exchange are derived from Lesotho's economic links with South Africa. In the light of this extreme economic dependence writers have been led to observe that Lesotho must have the good-will and support of the South African government under any foreseeable circumstance (Bowman 1968:239) and that Lesotho's policy is an extension of South African foreign policy (Grundy 1973:133).

However, despite the fact that Lesotho's economic relationship with South Africa has remained largely unchanged, events since the 1976 Soweto uprisings in South Africa have thrown into question these assessments. The head of Lesotho's ruling Basotholand National party (BNP), Chief Leabua Jonathan, became a vocal critic of South Africa's policy of separate development. As a result, his government refused to recognize the Transkei homeland as an independent state despite South African threats of economic reprisal, and members of the outlawed South African ANC were allowed refuge in the country. Jonathan's government also established diplomatic relations with communist countries, which was anathema to the South African government.

A clear indication that South Africa's economic ties with Lesotho did not provide the predicted political leverage over its government was the fact that South Africa was forced to resort to armed intervention against Lesotho for harboring exiled members of the ANC. South Africa also supported the exiled Lesotho opposition leader, Ntsu Mokhehle, and his Lesotho Liberation Army (LLA) against Jonathan's government.

South Africa has had similar difficulty in attempting to use its economic ties with Botswana and Swaziland as political leverage over them. The ruling groups of Botswana and Swaziland are ambivalent about the political consequences of their economic ties with South Africa for their tenure of power. The reason for this is that while the governments of Botswana, Lesotho, and Swaziland (BLS) depend economically upon the South African economy for trade, transportation, investment, customs revenue, employment, and remittances, their linkages with South Africa also constitute the social base of political opposition to these regimes. This has forced the BLS states to take a defensive posture toward their economic ties with South Africa.

Zambia has achieved the status of *cause célèbre* as a successful example of a black African state that severed its economic ties with Rhodesia after it declared Unilateral Declaration of Independence (UDI) in 1965. The usual explanation for Zambia's decision to break off trading relations with Rhodesia in 1973 by closing its border is that Zambia's president, Kenneth Kaunda, was committed to upholding United Nations' sanctions against trading with the unlawful Rhodesian regime. However, such a characterization of the importance of high-minded principles in Zambia's foreign policy cannot explain the reversal of the 1973 decision when the Zambian border with Rhodesia was reopened in 1978. The unlawful Rhodesian government was still in place.

In order to understand the Zambian decision to reopen trading relations with Rhodesia, it is necessary to understand the political pressures on the ruling United National Independence party (UNIP) both at the time of the 1973 decision and in 1978, prior to the border reopening. While the ostensible reason for the border closure, the unlawful government of Rhodesia, had not changed, what had changed was the state of the Zambian economy. In 1974, the world price for Zambia's major export commodity, copper, was high, and the large urban middle class and the powerful trade unions were prospering. By contrast, in 1978, the country was experiencing its deepest decline since independence, with four straight years of depressed world copper prices. In this dramatically changed climate UNIP was obliged to hold constitutionally mandated national presidential and general elections. The large urban electorate and Zambia's trade unions were in no mood to suffer further from the consequences of policies (such as the border closure) that had contributed to the deterioration of the economy. Therefore, public pressure on UNIP on this issue was intense. Growing concern within UNIP about public opposition to Zambia's policy toward Rhodesia was sufficient to force the reopening of the border with Rhodesia just prior to the 1978 elections.

Writers have tended to single out Malawi's labor migration (primarily to the mines) as the principal economic linkage between Malawi and South Africa. In the late 1960s, as many as eighty thousand Malawians were estimated to be working in the mines in South Africa. One of the largest South African labor-recruiting agencies, Wenela, was said to have remitted £2 million to Malawi out of total export earnings of £22 million in 1969. Conventional wisdom was that this source of revenue plus South African aid and favorable trading arrangements were too important for a poor country like Malawi to jeopardize by politically challenging South Africa.

However, in 1974, Malawi's life president, Dr. Hastings Kamuzu Banda, suspended all recruitment of Malawians for work in the South African mines, allegedly because of an airplane accident involving Malawian miners who were in transit to South Africa. Undaunted, however, writers and commentators have continued to point to Malawi's labor migration to South Africa (resumed in 1977, albeit on a smaller scale) as evidence of South Africa's political leverage over Malawi. Labor remittances from South Africa plus Malawi's famous "trade with the devil" agreement and labor agreements with South Africa in 1967, for example, led writers to conclude that Malawi was simply a client state of South Africa.

However, this approach to understanding the political significance of Malawi's economic ties with South Africa tends to obscure its real importance. To understand that, it is necessary to consider the economic relationship from the point of view of the Malawian leadership, particularly after the so-called cabinet crisis of 1964 when President Banda emerged as the unchallenged leader of the country after being opposed *en bloc* by his cabinet colleagues. The ministers who challenged Banda were the leaders and founder-members of the country's ruling Malawi Congress party (MCP). Banda only returned to Malawi to lead the MCP during the final stages of the independence struggle after living abroad for almost forty years. Hence, when his cabinet colleagues challenged him, it meant that the leadership of the MCP had also challenged him—or at least Banda saw it that way.

After surviving the initial crisis and surveying his political options, Banda set out to establish his own personal base of political power. Economic ties with South Africa were central to his strategy. Banda was able to secure substantial loans, investment, aid and technical assistance, trade, and labor remittances from South Africa for the purpose of creating a personal base of domestic political power. He did this by transforming Malawi's political elites into prosperous agricultural estate owners whose wealth and economic security depended upon their unqualified personal loyalty.

Rhodesia provides yet another example of South Africa's supposed political hegemony over a state in the regional economy. Writers claimed that South Africa had virtual "life or death control" over the Rhodesian government by virtue of its domination of the economy. However, the Smith regime's stubborn refusal to accept British conditions for granting independence to Rhodesia in the face of intense pressure from South Africa raises serious questions about this supposed control.

Nevertheless, the same logic has been applied to the newly independent Zimbabwean government. Since Zimbabwe inherited Rhodesia's economic relationship with South Africa, by implication South Africa is presumed to have life and death control over Zimbabwe. However, comparable with the other "targets" of South African military "destabilization" in the region, there is a failure to explain why it was necessary for South Africa to resort to armed attacks and support for insurgency against the Zimbabwean government. Yet writers have continued to assume that South Africa dominates Zimbabwe politically through its economic leverage, tending to focus upon strategies for reducing the country's economic relationship with South Africa. Hence, there is a penchant to enlarge upon Zimbabwe's potential role as the core economy in a new regional economic group, the Southern African Development Coordination Conference, which excludes South Africa.

This approach once again entirely ignores the actual political significance of Zimbabwe's economic ties with South Africa. From the perspective of the country's de facto ruling party, the Zimbabwe African National Union (ZANU), the relationship is a major source of domestic political controversy. The state has given high priority to restoring the highly lucrative trading relationship that Rhodesia enjoyed with its exfederation partners, Zambia and Malawi, prior to UDI and to ensuring the competitiveness of Zimbabwean exports in South African markets. However, state support for this competitive economic relationship with South Africa clashes with the ruling party's populist, socialist ideology: the party was installed in power through democratic elections on a platform promising to transform the country into a socialist state emphasizing rural cooperatives and communes.

As the center of the regional economy it was assumed that South Africa benefits from all of its economic relationships with states in the region. Similarly it was assumed that South Africa's highly favorable regional trading relationships and its high profitability from investment returns strengthened the ruling National party (NP) and its commitment to the policy of separate development. While there is no doubt that transnational corporations based in South Africa enjoy high profits from their operations in regional states, what is in question is the political significance attached to them by the ruling party and its following in the white electorate.

The transnational corporations had a strategic role to play in National party policy under the government of President P. W. Botha. In the context of the NP's "constellation of Southern African states" policy, transnational corporations were to be used to increase the economic dependence of "hostile" bordering African states upon South Africa. The policy was designed to increase South Africa's political leverage over these states so that they would be more cooperative and would be prevented from supporting liberation movements that would attack South Africa from their territories. The domestic counterpart of this policy was to use the transnationals to control black urban opposition to the regime. The NP's objective was to stratify the black urban population by dividing it into one group of highly paid workers and successful black commercial businessmen and another group of unskilled or semiskilled urban blacks. The latter and their dependents were to be sent to the homelands. In this way the NP hoped to stabilize the black work force in townships near "white (urban) areas."

However, the NP's transnational alliance strategy backfired and instead contributed to political divisions among the party's traditional Afrikaner political constituency, the principal source of opposition to the NP's political alliance with transnational corporations. Therefore, the regime's efforts to use transnational corporations to exert political leverage over regional states and to help defuse the explosive black urban threat has contributed to, not mitigated, domestic political opposition to the ruling party.

Most writing on Southern Africa tends to exclude Tanzania from the regional economy. However, with the establishment of southern transport routes to Zambia in the 1970s, Tanzania became involved (albeit marginally) in the region's economy. The irony of the southern route is that it was expressly designed to "disengage" Zambia from the regional economy, whereas it has had the inadvertent effect of pulling Tanzania into the regional economy.

Tanzania's ruling party, the Chama Cha Mapinduzi (CCM), has sought to use the country's southern route to cope with some of the adverse consequences of a prolonged agricultural crisis the country has been experiencing. They have attempted to reorient the country's manufacturing exports away from East Africa and toward Southern African markets. Likewise, the ruling party has sought to stimulate development projects and expand cash crop production in southern Tanzania alongside the southern route.

Zaire has receive little consideration in discussions of Southern Africa. Other than noting the fact that the country ships some of its mineral exports through South African ports and receives some loans and investment from South Africa, scant attention is given to Zaire. However, its involvement in the regional economy has an important political significance to the regime. From this vantage point Zaire's economic ties with South Africa are crucial in guaranteeing the operation of the country's important mining industry. Mining constitutes about one-fourth of the country's GDP, provides one-half of governmental revenues, and about three-fourths of the total foreign exchange. President Mobutu has used economic ties with South Africa (and Zimbabwe to a lesser extent) to stabilize the economic surplus derived from mining. These earnings are essential for the political patronage the regime needs to ensure the unity of, and support for, Zaire's ruling class.

The recent writing on Namibia has tended to focus upon the economic costs to a newly independent government of severing its economic ties with South Africa. This approach is primarily conditioned by writers' abhorrence of separate development in South Africa rather than by an appreciation of the internal political consequences to the new government of altering these ties. However, any government of a unitary state of Namibia must inevitably consider how the economic relationship with South Africa will affect its domestic base of political power. In this regard, if the new government of Namibia is led by the South West Africa Peoples' Organization (SWAPO), as seems likely, then a crucial decision facing them will be whether to retain the country's South African-integrated commercial ranching industry. Since SWAPO's major domestic political rivals have a historic claim to Namibia's grazing and ranching land, SWAPO's handling of this issue is likely to be extremely sensitive. If SWAPO severs the commercial ranching connection with South Africa, nationalizes the land, and carries out a socialist land reform policy, as advertised, it is certain to alienate the groups who feel they have an exclusive claim to the land.

This discussion of the shortcomings of the conventional dependency analysis of Southern Africa suggests the need for an alternative approach. What is needed is a framework that takes into account both the constraints and opportunities that economic ties present to regional countries and to the regimes in power.

CONTRIBUTION AND ORGANIZATION OF THE STUDY

The study represents an attempt to rehabilitate the political needs and aspirations of ruling groups as the principal explanation for state behavior in Southern Africa. It does not, however, challenge the conventional assumption that South Africa dominates the regional economy. No one can doubt that. As the center of the regional economy, the South African regime clearly commands great economic leverage over other states in the region, with its control over trade on South Africa's transport and port system, the migration of labor into South Africa, and the provision of critically needed food aid and other economic requirements.

However, it does not necessarily follow from this that South Africa's domination of the regional economy is simply a one-way affair in which the regime uses its economic leverage over regional states without incurring domestic political costs. Likewise, it does not necessarily follow that under certain circumstances the leaders of black African states in the region may not rationally choose to engage in economic relations with South Africa in order to increase their range of independent political action.

In an attempt to analyse these two related propositions, I have examined the political strategies of the ruling groups of eleven states in the regional economy,[2] including South Africa, Zimbabwe, Botswana, Lesotho, Swaziland, Malawi, Mozambique, Zambia, Tanzania, Zaire, and Namibia.[3] These states have been classified on the basis of the

[2] Bowman (1968) argues that there are nine states in the regional subsystem; Grundy (1973:xiv) includes thirteen states. In determining state involvement in the regional subsystem, Bowman adopted the six conditions for a subordinate system advanced by Brecher (1963) in his study of the Southern Asian subsystem. Grundy, on the other hand, followed the more conventional method of drawing the boundaries of the regional subsystem. He defined the regional system to include all states and territories south of the Zambezi river and its tributaries plus all states that share borders with "white governed territories" (that is, Angola, Mozambique, and Rhodesia). Palmer and Parsons (1977:1) define Central and Southern Africa as lying south of 8° latitude from north of Luanda on the Angolan coast, through southern Zaire, passing across the southern tip of Tanzania to the north of the Mozambique-Tanzania border. My designation of the regional political economy is thus far more limited and specific, including only those states whose ruling groups and political opponents are significantly affected by changes in the regional economy.

[3] Two states that are frequently included in discussions of the region, Madagascar and Angola, have been excluded from the study on the grounds that while they may be involved in diplomatic and military issues that are central to the region, their ruling parties and opposition groups are not significantly affected by changes in the regional economy. In Madagascar, for example, except for a brief flurry of negotiations with the government of Prime Minister Vorster in the context of South Africa's "outward-looking" policy that led to trade between Madagascar and South Africa, increased tourism, and the establishment of plants to assemble semifinished goods on the island, economic relations between these countries have all but disappeared. The overthrow of President Philibert Tsiranana in 1972 resulted in the severing of economic ties with South Africa.

way that ruling parties or groups have sought to exploit or counter regional economic influences in their own political and economic interests. A crucial dimension of the analysis is an assessment of the impact that these strategies have had upon the domestic political support for the regimes.

An examination of state involvement in the Southern African regional economy reveals four major categories of state action and response to change.[4] The first category includes South Africa and Zimbabwe, where the state's most politically significant participation in the regional economy has tended to divide rather than strengthen the regime. In the second category are Botswana, Lesotho, and Swaziland, states that have had to employ defensive strategies to cope with threats South Africa's economy poses to domestic sources of power. The third category, comprised of Malawi, Mozambique, and Zambia, encompasses states where the regimes have, for the most part, effectively used their regional economic relationships (with South Africa

---

Likewise, in the case of Angola, economic ties with Southern African states are relatively unimportant. The Cabinda operations of Gulf Oil Corporation have provided practically the entire source of income for the state. In 1984, oil contributed an estimated 80 percent of Angola's total exports by value, and 90 percent of the country's nonmilitary imports came from Western industrial countries. By contrast, state farms and the peasant sector have stagnated, and production is sharply down. While South Africa grew in importance as a supplier of Angola's industrial needs at least until 1975, it can easily be replaced as a supplier country with little or no cost to Angola's ruling party. In 1974, South Africa supplied approximately 11 percent of Angola's imports and purchased less than 1 percent of its exports. Although there are no published reports on South African-Angolan trade since independence in 1975, it almost certainly has declined.

[4] For present purposes I will employ a minimal or narrow conception of the state that includes such formulations as Weber's (1983) notion of the state as an agency exercising a "monopoly of legitimate force" in society, Gramsci's (1968, 1973) "narrow" state as a "politico-juridical organization" or apparatus that does not coincide with the political system, and Skocpol's (1979) conception of the state as an "administrative and coercive organization."

and Zimbabwe) to enhance their domestic political power. In the fourth category are those states, Tanzania and Zaire, that are only marginally involved in the regional economy. The ruling groups in these states are seeking to increase their countries' participation in the regional economy in order to bolster their eroding domestic base of political support (see Table 7.1, p. 317).

In addition to these main categories Namibia is examined as a country in a transitional stage of political independence that is faced with the prospect of change in the nature of its state involvement in the regional economy.

CHAPTER ONE

The Development of the Southern African Regional Economy

THE FORMATION of a Southern African regional economy with the industrial centers located in South Africa and Zimbabwe originated during the nineteenth century with the development of the mining industry. The enormous capital investment in the mining industry and its support- ing infrastructure created transportation, communication, farming, commercial, and land use patterns that constitute the basis of the contemporary regional economy.

The Southern African regional economy has the charac- teristics of a classical, colonial economic relationship with Western industrial powers. Western countries provide the bulk of foreign investment in the area, furnishing technol- ogy and capital equipment, while the Southern African economy supplies Western countries with semiprocessed raw materials, agricultural products, ore, and precious metals and stones.

South Africa and Zimbabwe (potentially) are exceptions to this pattern, however, having formed their own manu- facturing industries and secured markets for their prod- ucts in the regional economy. These countries have thereby managed to establish an economic relationship with other countries in the regional economy comparable to that of the Western countries with RSA and Zimbabwe. South Africa and Zimbabwe (potentially) enjoy a trade sur- plus with other regional countries, while the latter run large deficits with RSA and Zimbabwe.

HISTORY

The discovery of diamonds and gold in South Africa transformed it from a white colonial settlement of only marginal importance in the British Empire to a regional center of mining industry.[1] Table 1.1 illustrates the change in the Composition of South Africa's exports from being predominantly agricultural prior to 1880 to being dominated by the mining industry after 1884.

Both diamonds and gold were highly valued commodities that were dependent upon Western markets, especially the United States (the chief market for diamonds and after 1935 the fixer of the price of monetary gold). The effect of the mineral revolution in South Africa was to link its economy to that of Great Britain and other Western cap-

Table 1.1 South African Exports, 1860-1914
(in thousands of pounds)

Period	Annual Averages			Total Exports
	Wool	Diamonds	Gold	
1860-1864	1,551	—	—	2,321
1865-1869	1,886	5	—	2,626
1870-1874	2,787	1,027	3	5,246
1875-1879	2,679	1,905	34	6,317
1880-1884	2,583	3,418	28	8,578
1885-1889	2,446	3,717	653	8,982
1890-1894	2,545	3,816	4,447	15,099
1895-1899	2,251	4,516	11,440	21,208
1900-1904	1,803	5,137	8,236	19,159
1905-1909	2,931	7,231	28,753	45,027
1910-1914	4,494	8,689	32,666	59,046

SOURCE: Christopher (1976:154).

[1] This section relies heavily upon Christopher (1976).

italist economies through the London capital market, which was the center of world finance during the nineteenth century.

The exploitation of South Africa's mineral wealth was made possible by large-scale capital investments—mostly from Great Britain. For example, between 1870 and 1936, Great Britain invested 92 percent of a total of £523,000,000 invested in South Africa and 85 percent of the total of £480,000 invested between 1946 and 1951 (Farnie 1956:127). Almost immediately after the mineral discoveries South Africa became the center of world production in diamonds, surpassing both India and Brazil. She also exceeded Russia in 1892 and America in 1894 in the production of gold, becoming the dominant world producer of gold in 1920, with 51 percent of total output.

From 1870 to 1900, South Africa functioned as an integral part of the British economy, becoming Britain's principal supplier of gold. Gold was particularly important to Great Britain since it was during this period that British economic supremacy was being challenged by the rise of Germany and the United States as industrial powers.

The flow of large-scale British capital to South Africa made possible major exports from Britain to its colony. During this period, Britain monopolized trade with South Africa; in the peak year of 1898, an estimated 97.5 percent of the country's exports went to Britain (Farnie 1956:133). This massive flow of capital had a profound impact upon Southern Africa, providing the material and financial basis for the formation of two powerful international economic interests based upon diamonds and gold. British financier-entrepreneurs such as Rhodes, Barnato, Robinson, and Beit gained a virtual monopoly over these industries with the help of legislative support from the South African colonial government and the Republic of the Transvaal (for example, through the diamond trade acts of the 1880s and the Transvaal Consolidated Gold Law of 1885).

The mineral discoveries in the interior of the region created an urgent demand for efficient and reliable regional transportation. The mines required machinery and goods from Europe, and this provided the impetus for a rapid expansion of railway construction, which began in 1876 (see Table 1.2). The Cape Provincial government financed railway lines linking the Kimberley mines with the ports of Cape Town, Port Elizabeth, and East London. The Witwatersrand (Rand) gold fields were opened in 1886, and the Transvaal government financed the construction of a railway line from the gold mines to Lourenço Marques (Ma-

Table 1.2 Railway Construction in Southern Africa, 1860-1915

Period	Mileage Completed in Period					
	Cape of Good Hope	Natal	Orange Free State	Transvaal	Rhodesia[a]	Total
1860-1865	57	2	—	—	—	59
1866-1870	—	3	—	—	—	3
1871-1875	91	—	—	—	—	91
1876-1880	765	95	—	—	—	860
1881-1885	697	77	—	—	—	774
1886-1890	170	123	121	41	—	455
1891-1895	123	72	262	524	96	1,077
1896-1900	198	145	59	309	653	1,364
1901-1905	895	249	241	193	798	2,376
1906-1910	341	176	307	639	55	1,518
1911-1915	760	231	278	775	146	2,190
Total to 1915	4,097	1,173	1,268	2,481	1,748	10,767

SOURCE: Christopher (1976:175).

NOTE: [a] Includes the line through Bechuanaland (Botswana) and the Cape Colony, north of Fryburg.

puto) in Mozambique. By 1897, the British South Africa Company (BSAC; a British chartered mining company with a monopoly over parts of Central and Eastern Africa) had constructed rail lines from Kimberley to Bulawayo (in Zimbabwe), by 1899, from Beira (in Mozambique) to Salisbury (Harare), and by 1934, between Bulawayo and Salisbury and Victoria Falls. The BSAC also financed rail lines linking Katanga (in Zaire) to the Northern Rhodesian Copperbelt (in Zambia) and to Salisbury and Bulawayo in 1909. The effect of this railway boom was to lay what is to the present day the basis of the region's transportation system.

The railway system also profoundly influenced European settlement patterns and urbanization in the region. The frontier of European settlement spread to Kimberley (in the Cape Province) first and then to the Witwatersrand in the Transvaal. This set in motion a process of regional urbanization at the ports, railheads, junctions, mining centers, and along the line-of-rail. Kimberley was the first industrial community in South Africa and the most populous settlement outside of Cape Town. In the twentieth century Johannesburg became the new mining center of South Africa and the center of finance and banking for the entire region.

Before 1900, few railway lines were constructed in Central or Southern Africa specifically to develop agriculture. Until then agricultural development in the region was essentially tied to the mining centers and to the line-of-rail for the purpose of exporting commodities overseas. For example, in the 1870s, a well-organized cattle industry was established in South West Africa (Namibia) and Rhodesia to supply beef to Kimberley and later to the Witwatersrand (Christopher 1976:122). Wool, mohair, ostrich feathers, and sugar emerged during this period as important export commodities because they could be farmed near the line-of-rail. Following the pattern set in Southern Africa, South West Africa's small railway system connects its two main ports with the mines and major towns. Its only interregional railway line runs to South Africa (see Map 1).

SOURCES OF ENERGY

South Africa and Zimbabwe have a virtual monopoly of the currently worked coal deposits in the region. The first coal was mined in the Cape Province in 1864. This overlapped with the discovery of gold and the development of mining and secondary industry, and supplied the fuel needs for the railway and bunkering trade. It made South Africa the foremost producer of coal in Africa, with enormous reserves of 75,000 million tons.

Coal has played a vital role in the growth of South Africa's economy. An estimated 10 percent of its total annual output is used by South African Railways and secondary industries. The urban centers take about 35 percent of the total output, and Electricity Supply Commission (ESCOM) alone uses an estimated 55 percent of South Africa's internal coal consumption to generate electricity. In addition, an estimated 40 percent of South Africa's total petroleum requirements are met from Sasol oil-from-coal plants.

South Africa has also exported large quantities of coal to Japan, Israel, and Europe. The country's coal exports rose from 2.7 million tons in 1975 to 30 million tons in 1981, and they are expected to increase to 44 million tons by 1987. In this regard South Africa ranks alongside the United States and Poland as the major supplies of coal to the European community.

Although Zimbabwe produces only 10 percent of South Africa's total output, its coal production has also played a vital role in the industrial development of Central Africa. The Wankie (Hwange) area of southwest Zimbabwe possesses an estimated reserve of 5,000 million tons of coal of high-coking quality that is necessary for the iron and steel industry. Because the deposits are close to the surface, mining costs are among the cheapest in the world. The coal production in Wankie began in 1903 and grew with the development of the Copperbelt and the railways. Zimbabwean Railways transports ore and other bulk materials for the Copperbelt, requiring about 25 percent of Zimbabwe's coal output for fuel. The Wankie mines and industries take another 10 percent of the coal, with the remainder going to the Copperbelt and to iron and steel plants in Zimbabwe.

Zimbabwean coal has played a key role in the industrial development of the Zambian and Malawian economies as well. Prior to 1973, an estimated 70 percent of Zambia's fuel needs for locomotives, thermal power stations, and copper smelters came from Wankie. Malawi has imported Zimbabwe's coal in large amounts for its major thermal power plant in Blantyre. The Shaban copper mines and refinery plants in Zaire have also been taking an estimated 100,000 tons of coal and coke annually from Wankie.

Infrastructure and Settlement

The Rand cities in South Africa and the cities on the Copperbelt grew on the sites of mineral deposits and expanded with continuous production and demand. Thus Johannesburg and the Copperbelt towns of Zambia and Katanga (in Zaire) originated with the mineral discoveries there. Johannesburg eventually merged with other mining settlements to form, along with Cairo, the only other major conurbation in Africa, the Witwatersrand. The other center of economic wealth in the region is the Zambian-Katangan Copperbelt of Central Africa. These two areas are the focal points of regional infrastructure, including transportation, communication, power, industrial plants, and urbanization. An understanding of the role of these areas in the economic unification of Southern Africa is therefore important.

The Rand extends sixty miles from Randfontein to Springs in the Transvaal. Its location and growth are largely due to the discovery of gold fields, local supplies of coal and iron ore, water, the ease of constructing lines of communication on the veld (open grazing areas), cheap labor, and the availability of numerous other important industrial minerals such as fluorspar, fireclay, dolomite, chromite, and magnesite. Thirty-five percent of South Africa's industrial establishments (employing 43 percent of all industrial workers) are located on the Rand (Pritchard 1971:182). In 1982, it was estimated that the Southern Transvaal, which includes Witwatersrand, Pretoria, and Vereeniging (PWV), alone was responsible for 37 percent of the country's total gross geographic product (Hanekom 1982).

As the economic center of South Africa the Rand is linked to subordinate industrial concentrations in the country, all based near major port cities: Cape Town, the Eastern Cape centered at Port Elizabeth and East London, and the Durban-Pine town region of Natal. Most secondary industries in South Africa are also concentrated in these areas. For example, the PWV plus Durban, Cape Town, Port Elizabeth, Bloemfontein, East London, and Kimberley combined produce an estimated 60 percent of the total gross geographic product of South Africa (Nedbank Group, Ltd. 1983:203).

The Zambian-Katangan Copperbelt of Central Africa is a mining zone 280 miles long and 160 miles wide that produces 20 percent of the world's copper and 66 percent of its cobalt. These metals are among the most sought after by advanced industrial economies. The belt is a complex of mining towns extending from Lubumbashi northwest to Kolwezi in Zaire, to Ndola, and south to the Broken Hill district in Zambia. Each of the major mining areas has large towns and cities, residential areas, shopping centers, and commercial zones. In addition to copper, the belt contains 150 other mineral deposits, such as radium and uranium, lime, manganese, tin, zinc, coal and iron ore. Including Lubumbashi, the chief city of Katanga (now Shaba), and the secondary regional city, Jadotville, the Copperbelt contains an urban population of over one million people.

With the exception of the port of Cape Town (which occupies a strategic position commanding ocean trade routes and functions as a naval base), port cities in the region have grown in their role as entrepôts for the hinterlands. Generally speaking, ports lie at a junction of sea and land routes and handle the produce of overseas territories and the produce from their own hinterlands. Because they are points through which exports and imports pass and become storehouses for raw materials, they often develop industries based upon these raw materials. Frequently they become regional capitals or route nodes for whole areas of countries. Map 1 shows the major ports in the region and the railway system that links the ports with the regional hinterlands.

Although the port of Cape Town serves South African and Zimbabwean traffic, its industry is based largely upon its own produce. Durban, on the other hand, serves as a regional capital and major entrepôt, having developed along with the growth of mineral production and agriculture in the Transvaal and Natal. Because of the bulkiness of the cargo they handle, Richards Bay and Durban import and export more than other South African ports. Their importance lies in the fact that they are entrepôts and collecting centers for the entire southeast of South Africa, which includes the Rand.

Maputo (formerly Lourenço Marques) developed as a port city in response to the growth of the vast Transvaal, Zimbabwe, Zambia, and southern Mozambican hinterland. The port handles Zambian copper, Swaziland ore, fruit and wool of the Transvaal, Zimbabwean tobacco and minerals, and Mozambique's cotton, sugar, cashew nuts, and copra. The port city has attracted a number of secondary industries and has major oil refinery and rubber processing plants. Its primary role of serving an international regional hinterland is evident in the fact that there is no

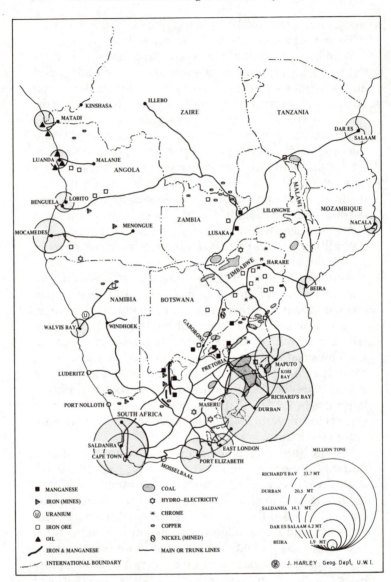

Map 1. Railways, Ports, and Minerals: Southern Africa

railway connecting it with northern Mozambique, and until recently there were no good road connections with Beira, Mozambique's second major port.

Beira also developed primarily to serve a wide hinterland beyond the borders of Mozambique. With the completion of the railway line to Harare (formerly Salisbury) via Umtali and later to the Copperbelt, Beira became the natural outlet for Zambia and Zimbabwe's mineral ores and agricultural produce. However, since Beira's harbor was unable to handle the huge increase in post-World War II traffic, much of this trade was redirected to Maputo.

Towns and cities tend to form at the focal points of regional transportation routes. Bulawayo in Zimbabwe is a good example of this, having developed from a small settlement in 1893 to the second largest city in the country next to Harare. Its rapid growth began when the South African Railway reached the town and constructed extensions beyond it to Salisbury and Beira, Wankie, Livingstone and Lusaka, the Copperbelt, and Lubumbashi. This placed Bulawayo at a strategic junction of major routes. Principal roads converge on Bulawayo from Beit Bridge on the South African border and from Umtali and Beira (in Mozambique), Ndola (in Zambia), and Lubumbashi (in Zaire). This has made Bulawayo the natural headquarters for Zimbabwean Railways and an ideal place to locate factories, iron and steel plants, and assembly plants.

Before 1950, the region's road system was based upon the railways that linked the major commercial centers with the ports. Postwar expansion of agricultural production led to the development of feeder roads in the main commercial agricultural areas leading to the main railheads. Hence the main flow of road traffic is from the interior to the coast rather than between countries. The only inter-country route that can be classified as long distance but that does not intersect industrial centers is between Zambia, Malawi, and Tanzania.

Air transport in the region underwent a major expansion

after World War II due to the growing use of air traffic for the transport of perishable exports and for the moving of supplies such as food to various regions of a country. The air transport system, however, paralleled the existing rail and road systems by connecting the major hinterland towns and cities with the ports. Until recently almost all interregional flights originated in Johannesburg, Harare, and Windhoek (in Namibia). A similar pattern obtained with respect to regional mail, telephone, and radio broadcasting flows, which tend to be concentrated in the Rand, on the Copperbelt, and at the ports (see Map 2).

DECLINE OF PEASANT AGRICULTURE AND INCREASE OF LABOR MIGRATION

From the beginning of the Cape settlement in the seventeenth century contact between Europeans and Africans was continuous and in the early years often mutually beneficial. As a case in point, in Rhodesia, although European settlers initially carved out large areas of land for themselves, they did so without seriously disturbing the indigenous population. Because European agriculture was at first inefficient and commercially unsuccessful, in many instances it was easier for the newcomers to buy from African farmers rather than to farm for themselves. In Rhodesia in 1903, for example, African sales of grain and livestock to Europeans was £350,000 (Christopher 1976:239). Similarly, in Botswana by 1875, the Ngwato Kingdom had emerged as an important "trading state" in Central Africa. And under Khama III, major commercial agriculture, including extensive marketing of cattle, wagons, grain, and tobacco, was being supported by the state for sale to Europeans.

The decline of commercial African agriculture came in the early twentieth century when the colonial settler states began to support the European commercial farmers' encroachment upon the best African agricultural land. Afri-

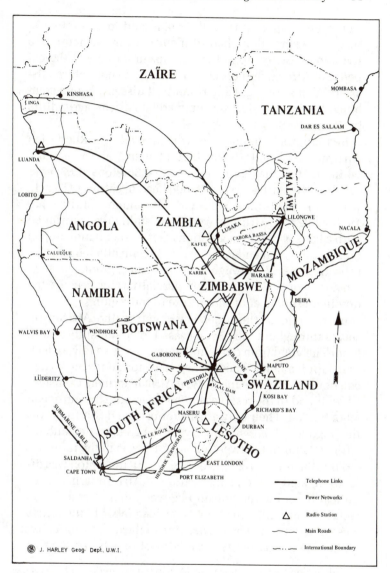

Map 2. Telecommunications, Power Networks, and Main Roads: Southern Africa

cans were displaced from their land and forced into "reserves" where they had difficulty even sustaining a livelihood. State support for European farmers at the expense of African farmers coincided with major natural disasters such as drought and rinderpest disease, which combined to virtually destroy commercial African agriculture by 1930.

In 1920, for example, it was estimated that Rhodesian Africans marketed 19,800 tons of maize at £5 per ton, while in 1921 the figure dropped to 4,360 tons at £2.5 per ton. In 1919, Africans sold 20,000 head of cattle at £8 each, while in 1922 they sold virtually none (Christopher 1976:239-240). Africans were also suddenly confronted with a battery of state regulations that further handicapped their commercial endeavors while specifically helping European farmers.[2] Through state subsidies, grants, and extension agents the white commercial farmer became the dominant producer of agriculture in the region.

By the end of the nineteenth century the African reserves throughout the region ceased to be self-sufficient in food. The yield from crops and animals was so low, in fact, that supplementary income had to be found for most African households. The inability of African farmers to sustain a livelihood in the reserves forced them onto the European labor market. Their only escape route from destitution was the migratory labor system. By far the greatest demand for African labor in the twentieth century was in the mines.

Thus the proletarization of Africans in the region was directly related to the pauperization of African farmers. An indication of the relationship between these trends is the fact that until 1977 the flow of African labor to the mines was not determined by the demand of the mining industry. Rather, there was an inverse relationship between the size

[2] Palmer and Parsons (1977) provide an excellent summary of the various laws and regulations that inhibited the development of commercial African agriculture in Central and Southern Africa.

of the maize crop (the staple food) and the flow of labor to the mines. The more successful the seasonal maize crop was, the smaller the flow of migratory labor. However, since 1977, the pattern has changed significantly. The South African policy of mine labor "stabilization" that established a ratio of 40 percent foreign African workers to 60 percent South African workers, together with the serious and prolonged drought in the region, have enabled the mining industry to determine the flow of African labor to the mines. The increase in average black earnings by 14.5 percent per head (6.6 percent in real terms) between 1960 and 1982 was an added incentive for African labor migration to the mines.

An important consequence of the migratory labor system is that South Africa and Zimbabwe have become perennial suppliers of maize and other foodstuffs to other states in the region. Table 1.3 shows the sale of maize by South Africa to Botswana, Lesotho, Swaziland, and Namibia from 1969 to 1985. Zimbabwe has also supplied maize and other food supplies to Zambia, Malawi, Zaire, and Mozambique.

South Africa has sought to reinforce the dependence of African states upon it for food by selling its maize during periods of serious food shortages at below government-guaranteed prices. For example, due to the abundance of maize on the world market the country has been forced to sell its exported maize at a price that is below the producer price paid to South African farmers by the Maize Board. Therefore, since South Africa cannot sell its maize on world markets for a profit, it must subsidize the cost of exporting its maize to states in the region. It was estimated, for example, that in 1981 the South African Maize Board would lose as much as forty rands for every ton of maize exported (Henderson 1983:43). South Africa has reportedly even bought maize and wheat abroad and resold it to Mozambique and other African countries at below cost.

Maps 3 and 4 and Table 1.4 illustrate the pattern of labor

Table 1.3   South African Maize Exports to African Countries, 1969-1985 (in metric tons)

Year	Botswana, Lesotho, Swaziland, and Namibia[a]	Other Africa[b]
1969/1970	104,000	12,224
1970/1971	202,000	46,439
1971/1972	70,000	28,929
1972/1973	83,000	5,853
1973/1974	139,000	—
1974/1975	60,000	5,121
1975/1976	73,000	10,977
1976/1977	131,000	23,179
1977/1978	171,000	49,613
1978/1979	248,000	25,566
1979/1980	250,000	296,034
1980/1981	189,000	348,992
1981/1982	214,000	45,385
1982/1983	222,000	62,111
1983/1984	248,000	14,279
1984/1985	408,000	NA

SOURCE: South African Maize Board, private communication, February 13,1986.

NOTES: NA = not available.

[a] Maize and maize products.

[b] Whole maize.

migration in the region. Maps 3 and 4 show the three major areas of labor demand: the Rand, the Copperbelt in Zambia, and the mines and farms in Zimbabwe. There is also a flow of labor to the tea and coffee plantations in Malawi. Table 1.4 shows the high levels of mine labor migration to South Africa primarily from Lesotho, Mozambique, Malawi, Swaziland, and Botswana.

In addition to labor migration to the mines, James (1978) has estimated that in 1977, forty thousand foreign-born African men were employed on South African farms (60 per-

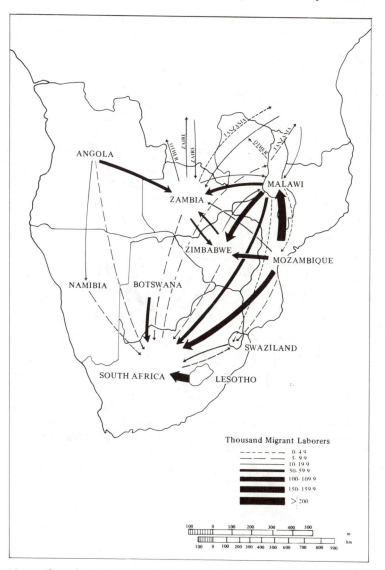

Map 3. Flow of Regional Migrant Labor, 1970: Southern Africa

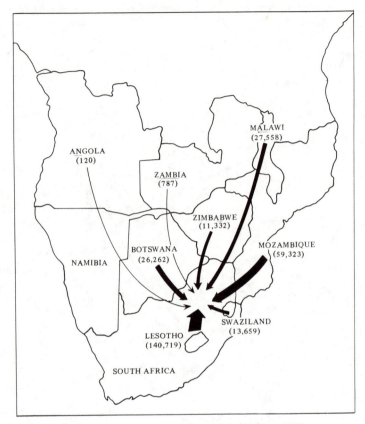

Map 4. Flow of Registered Migrant Labor to South Africa, 1982

cent from Botswana, Lesotho, and Swaziland and 17 percent from Mozambique). However, since 1977, South Africa's agricultural sector has been severely affected by the drought, resulting in the loss of an estimated 800 million rands in foreign exchange earnings, for example, during the 1983/1984 season. Consequently, the South African National Maize Producers' Organization (NAMPO) appealed to its members to cut their planting by half and to produce only for local consumption since it was uneconomical to grow for exportation (SAIRR 1984:160). It has been estimated that as a result of this action, fifty thousand Africans, including migratory workers, will lose their jobs.

According to Davies and Fransman (1978) the principal reason for continued labor migration is the absence of sufficient domestic wage employment in labor-supplying countries to absorb the working-age population. Their projections to 1988 are that only 64.7 percent of the working-age population of Botswana will be able to find domestic wage employment, 56.3 percent in Swaziland, 72.8 percent in Malawi, and 72.4 percent in Mozambique. Since these African governments cannot provide employment in the formal wage sector for large numbers of their working-age population, labor migration provides the only real employment alternative for thousands of Africans who must supplement their household income.[3]

[3] The Southern Africa Labour Commission (SALC), comprised of Zimbabwe, Mozambique, Tanzania, Botswana, Zambia, Swaziland, and Lesotho (all members of SADCC), was established in 1980 with the express purpose of breaking their dependence upon the migrant labor system. However, to date not only has the migrant labor system remained intact but individual member countries have sought to increase their national quotas within the South African migratory work force. For example, as part of the Nkomati Accord, the Mozambican government sought to have their quota of Mozambicans working in South African mines doubled. They also hoped to restore South Africa's payment of Mozambican mine workers' deferred wages to Maputo in gold valued at the official price or at a more favorable rate of exchange. In return for such a labor agreement Mozambique has agreed not to abruptly reduce their migratory labor to South Africa (*African Business* 1985:21).

Table 1.4 National Composition of Black Mine Labor Force in South Africa

Year	South Africa	Basuto- land (Lesotho)	Bechuana- land (Botswana)	Swazi- land	Mozam- bique	N+S Rho- desia + Nyasaland (Malawi)[a]	Total[b]	Non-South African Workers as a Percentage of Total Labor Force
1904	18,057	2,240	531	492	50,997	4,550	77,000	76.5%
1905	11,842	1,571	591	639	59,284	7,005	81,000	85.4
1908	58,303	4,604	1,221	1,509	81,920	1,266	149,000	60.4
1909	61,135	3,895	1,020	1,413	85,282	4,160	157,000	61.1
1912	64,710	9,970	1,146	3,705	91,546	2,941	191,000	66.1
1913	58,497	8,804	1,800	2,898	80,832	2,007	155,000	62.3
1915	93,396	12,355	2,950	4,910	83,338	1,148	198,097	52.8
1918	59,534	10,349	1,817	4,123	81,306	805	158,000	62.3
1920	59,269	12,680	1,435	2,802	96,188	605	173,000	65.7
1922	78,983	14,475	2,690	5,472	80,959	403	183,000	56.8
1927	84,495	12,264	1,483	3,655	107,672	430	215,000	60.7
1929	79,950	21,586	2,337	3,977	96,657	389	205,000	61.0
1931	112,548	30,781	3,367	5,062	73,924	316	226,000	50.2
1932	131,692	31,711	4,963	5,872	58,483	280	233,001	43.5
1936	165,933	45,982	7,155	7,027	88,499	3,402	318,000	47.8
1939	155,393	48,385	8,785	6,686	81,335	1,941	323,000	51.9
1942	214,243	—	—	—	74,507	21,656	310,406	31.0
1943	207,379	—	—	—	84,478	23,213	315,071	34.2
1944	185,658	—	—	—	78,950	26,770	291,378	36.3
1945	210,485	—	—	—	78,806	30,856	320,147	34.2

1951	108,000	35,700	9,100	5,600	106,500	41,200	306,100	64.7
1956	116,100	39,900	10,400	5,400	102,900	59,800	334,500	65.3
1960	150,900	51,400	16,000	5,600	95,500	82,800	402,200	62.5
1961	150,900	53,900	13,200	6,500	100,200	89,100	413,900	63.5
1963	153,800	56,500	15,300	5,800	88,700	74,200	394,300	61.0
1964	139,400	58,500	16,000	5,500	97,500	71,800	388,800	64.1
1965	130,500	64,300	19,000	4,300	109,000	56,300	383,400	66.0
1969	116,500	65,500	14,800	5,000	99,800	69,900	371,500	68.6
1970	96,900	71,100	16,300	5,400	113,300	98,200	401,200	75.8
1971	86,500	68,700	16,000	4,800	102,400	107,800	386,200	77.6
1972	87,200	78,500	17,500	4,300	97,700	129,200	414,400	79.0
1973	86,200	87,200	16,800	4,500	99,400	128,000	422,200	79.6
1974	90,100	78,300	14,700	5,500	101,800	73,100	363,500	75.2
1975	121,800	85,500	16,600	7,200	118,000	15,500	364,700	66.6
1976	142,100	85,300	18,800	8,300	44,100	30,300	331,000	57.1
1977	217,090	99,964	24,810	11,756	38,244	24,934	420,536	48.4
1978	253,320	107,296	17,652	8,951	35,234	30,241	456,678	44.5
1979	265,229	108,310	17,647	8,583	38,995	22,973	465,064	43.0
1980	282,843	108,699	17,764	8,681	39,539	19,632	480,024	41.1
1981	292,152	110,542	17,543	9,480	40,094	16,179	488,685	40.2
1982	290,421	107,554	16,667	10,015	42,544	13,910	483,727	40.0
1983	289,560	106,139	17,285	11,303	43,794	14,522	483,869	40.2
1984	300,131	105,189	17,265	11,467	45,472	15,337	495,080	39.4

SOURCES: Innes and Malaba (1978), and chamber of Mines of South Africa (1984:101, 1985:113).

NOTES: [a] Miners from Zimbabwe (formerly Southern Rhodesia) rose from 8 in 1974 to 18,658 in 1977 and fell to 9 in 1984.
[b] Total includes black miners from other unspecified African countries.

Labor migration also provides an important source of governmental revenue from the workers themselves and from the South African government in the form of deferred payments (see Table 1.5).

Historically Zimbabwe has also been a major importer of African labor. In 1973, for example, it was estimated that there were about 220,000 foreign Africans in employment in the country, the majority of them being Malawian and Mozambican. However, beginning in 1975, this situation changed, and Zimbabwe began to supply South African mines and farms with migrant labor. The change was due largely to the political uncertainty accompanying Zimbabwe's independence war and to growing unemployment in the country. In 1977, for example, the number of Zimbabwean Africans employed on South African mines was a record high of 18,653 workers. However, this trend was reversed by 1983 when the total number of Zimbabweans working on the mines in South Africa was only 603 (SAIRR 1984:137).

There is one additional important change in the pattern

Table 1.5   Deferred Pay and Remittances to Foreign Migratory Workers on South African Mines, 1983

Country	Rands[a]	Numbers Employed[b]
Botswana	22,139,421	18,620
Lesotho	154,167,720	99,740
Malawi	21,920,262	16,149
Mozambique	69,659,404	44,487
Swaziland	12,162,952	10,834
Total	280,049,759	189,830

SOURCE: SAIRR (1985:290-291).

NOTES: [a] 1 rand = U.S. $0.8955 in 1983.

[b] Average numbers of Africans employed in 1983 on gold, platinum, and copper mines that were members of the Chamber of Mines.

of mining labor migration reflected in Table 1.4. Beginning in 1975, the proportion of foreign migratory miners in South Africa declined in relation to the proportion of South Africans. By 1984, the foreign element was 39.4 percent of the total, down from a high of 79.6 percent in 1973. This change was due in part to the onset of economic recession in South Africa, but more significantly it represented South Africa's policy of shifting its reliance for unskilled and semiskilled black labor to South African blacks in the so-called independent homelands rather than relying primarily on foreign labor.

SOUTH AFRICA'S TRADING RELATIONSHIPS

Historically the United Kingdom has been South Africa's major trading partner, source of capital, and agent for the sale of its most important export—gold. This was due to the colonial relationship between the two countries and to the fact that Great Britain for over a century was the major world market for raw materials and agricultural products (Houghton 1976:177). Since 1970, however, the structure of South Africa's foreign trade has changed. While the market concentration of her exports has increased and the country's reliance upon a few supplying countries for its imports has remained the same, South Africa has managed to maintain a geographical spread of its major trading partners. Table 1.6 illustrates this.

While the country's six major export markets remain highly concentrated (constituting 59 percent of total export earnings in 1970 and 62 percent of the total in 1981), South Africa nevertheless maintained geographically dispersed trading partners. In 1984, the country's major export markets in order of importance were the United States, Japan, Switzerland, the United Kingdom, West Germany, and Africa.

South Africa's reliance upon a few countries for its im-

Table 1.6 South Africa's Imports and Exports by Area and Main Countries (in millions of rands)

	Imports[a]			Exports		
	1970	1977	1984	1970	1977	1984
Europe						
U.K.	560.6	844.7	2,416.1	466.4	1,315.1	1,060.9
W. Germany	372.4	933.2	3,425.8	109.1	517.0	977.7
France	89.0	239.6	820.0	40.2	213.5	561.8
Switzerland	49.6	120.1	388.2	51.1	211.4	1,679.3
Italy	104.4	212.4	761.1	180.6	148.9	648.0
America						
U.S.A.	423.8	974.6	3,403.0	129.3	787.5	2,106.7
Asia						
Japan	221.3	625.8	2,800.5	180.6	640.9	1,957.3
Africa[b]	131.2	287.3	404.2	263.9	520.9	891.2

SOURCES: Wiese (1981:35), and South African Commissioner of Customs and Excise, *Monthly Abstract of Trade Statistics* (1970-1985), Pretoria.

NOTES: Figures are for merchandise trade, excluding gold bullion but including krugerrands and all other mine output.

1 rand = U.S. $1.39 in 1970, $1.15 in 1977, and $0.695 in 1984.

[a] Oil and strategic materials excluded.

[b] Foreign trade statistics for Botswana, Lesotho, and Swaziland only.

ports is also highly concentrated. The six biggest supplier countries in 1984 in order of importance were West Germany, the United States, Japan, the United Kingdom, France, and Italy. These countries provided a combined total in excess of 75 percent of South Africa's total merchandise imports.

The significance of the structure of South Africa's foreign trade for an understanding of its position in the Southern African region lies in its large and persistent trade deficits (excluding gold)[4] with its Western trading partners and its large trade surpluses with African countries, particularly in its region. Table 1.6 shows that for the years 1970, 1977, and 1984, South Africa ran trade deficits with its five most important trading partners (the United States, the United Kingdom, West Germany, France, and Japan), which supply the bulk of South Africa's imports. Apart from Switzerland, which markets about 40 percent of South Africa's gold exports, Africa is the only major trading area where South Africa runs a large and continuing trade surplus—487 million rands in 1984 (US $338 million), including Botswana, Lesotho, Swaziland and Namibia.[5] The structure of South Africa's trade has an added significance because the country has one of the highest reciprocal trade flows—51.8 among major capitalist countries. This has made her economic growth highly dependent upon external trade.

In addition to helping South Africa balance merchandise trade deficits with its major Western trading partners, the African states provide a major external market for her important manufacturing industries. South Africa's imports of capital goods has been the largest category of im-

[4] The contribution of gold (South Africa's single most important source of foreign earnings) to balancing the country's trade deficits fluctuates with the free market price of gold bullion. For example, in 1977, the price of gold was low, and therefore gold sales contributed 26.2 percent to the country's total export receipts. However, in 1980, the price of gold reached a record high of U.S. $613 per ounce, and sales contributed 44.7 percent of South Africa's total export earnings. This indicates that the country is highly dependent (particularly in the short run) upon its gold mining industry (Nedbank Group, Ltd. 1983:123-125).

[5] SADCC (1984a:1.2) reported a two-way trade between South Africa and African countries of U.S. $1.5 billion in 1981, with about 75 percent (U.S. $1 billion) comprised of South African exports. In 1983, the South African government reported a trade surplus of over U.S. $413 million with African countries [excluding Southern African Customs Union (SACU) states] (New York Times 1985). The South Africa Foundation News (1985:4) has projected a record 1.8 billion rands in exports to Africa in 1985.

ports since the emergence of the manufacturing sector as the most important industry in the country. For example, during the period from 1969 to 1973, capital goods imports were 44.2 percent of South Africa's total merchandise imports. This trend has not only continued but it has increased. During the period 1976 to 1979, the imports of capital goods increased to 51.7 percent of the total, while all other categories of imports (primary, intermediate, and consumer goods) declined as a proportion of total imports (Nedbank Group, Ltd. 1983:127).

South Africa's capital goods imports are intended primarily for the country's manufacturing sector and supporting infrastructure, which dominate the economy. As Table 1.7 indicates, in 1960, mining was the most important sector of the South African economy. However, by 1970, manufacturing had emerged as the most important sector, constituting 21.2 percent of GDP and rising to 24.7 percent of GDP in 1983. Mining and agriculture declined to 10.9 percent and 6.2 percent of GDP respectively in 1983.

Since the 1950s, South Africa's dependence on the ex-

Table 1.7   South Africa's GDP by Economic Sector (in millions of rands)

Economic Sector	1960	1970	1980	1981	1982	1983
Agriculture, forestry, and fishing	1,402	1,753	2,572	2,584	2,371	1,861
	11.5%	8.3%	8.5%	8.2%	7.6%	6.2%
Mining and quarrying	2,576	3,893	3,465	3,430	3,375	3,312
	21.1	18.4	11.5	10.9	10.8	10.9
Manufacturing	1,965	4,490	7,729	8,248	8,009	7,478
	16.1	21.2	25.6	26.1	25.7	24.7

SOURCES: Nedbank Group, Ltd. (1983:85), and South Africa (1984:14.15).
NOTE: GDP in constant 1975 prices.

ports of unprocessed materials has declined in relation to total merchandise exports. During the same period, however, exports of semiprocessed and final manufactured goods increased. The growth in the exportation of final manufactured goods was particularly pronounced. During the 1950 to 1958 period, the growth rate was 3.1 percent per annum, during 1958 to 1966, it rose to 6 percent, and from 1966 to 1970, it increased to 16.8 percent (Reynders and van Zyl 1973:69). This was due to an expansion of the manufacturing sector and to the fact that South Africa replaced Britain as Rhodesia's main trading partner. It was also due to South Africa's increasing success in penetrating the markets of African countries.

For the period from 1956 to 1964, imported capital equipment constituted 70 percent of South Africa's fixed investment in manufacturing and 33 percent of the country's total fixed capital formation (du Plessis 1965). High levels of imported capital goods were necessary to sustain the growth of the manufacturing sector. However, this requirement poses a serious blockage to the continued growth of South Africa's manufacturing industry. The reason for this is that the country has been unable to gain access for its manufactured exports to the markets of its major Western industrial trading partners.[6]

Three reasons are usually advanced to explain this failure. The first is that of unequal exchange in trading relationships in which South Africa's costs of production have risen more rapidly than those of its major trading partners. Hence, the manufactured exports are simply not competi-

---

[6] South Africa still relies upon primary and intermediate products for most of its foreign exchange earnings. For example, during a ten-year period from 1969 to 1979, South Africa's capital goods exports declined from 7.9 percent of merchandise exports to only 5.3 percent (Nedbank Group, Ltd. 1983:119). South Africa's terms of trade also declined (excluding gold) from 115.8 percent in 1970 to 74.6 percent in 1982. And including gold, South Africa's terms of trade also declined from 111.7 percent in 1974 to 87.6 percent in 1982 (ibid., p. 116).

tive on international markets. The second reason is that South Africa's small domestic market has made it impossible for its manufacturers to take advantage of economies of scale; this gives major international firms a comparative advantage over South African manufacturers. The third reason is that increased domestic demand tends to coincide with recessions overseas. During these periods, South African manufacturing exporters tend to shift away from export markets toward satisfying domestic demand.

South Africa's inability to diversify its export base by increasing the proportion of manufactured exports is thus a serious constraint on economic growth since the country is industrialized and depends upon the exportation of its manufactured goods for economic expansion. This has become a serious concern for the government due to the small aggregate demand of South Africa's domestic market.

In light of this fact Southern Africa takes on an added significance (see Map 5), and its potential is even more important. For example, Southern Africa has a total geographical land area of 8.1 million square kilometers, or about one-fourth of the entire African continent. In 1982, it was inhabited by an estimated 118.7 million people, with more than one-fourth of them in urban areas and with a combined gross national product of U.S. $101.2 billion at 1982 market prices.

As a percentage of South Africa's total exports, the exports to Africa outside of the customs union area (excluding Namibia, Botswana, Lesotho, and Swaziland) were estimated to be approximately 14 percent in 1975.[7] When this figure is added to that of customs union countries, and taking into account the increase in South Africa's exports to African countries from 1975 to 1984, the exports to Af-

---

[7] Houghton (1976:178) estimated that in 1970 South Africa exported 17 percent of its total exports to African countries.

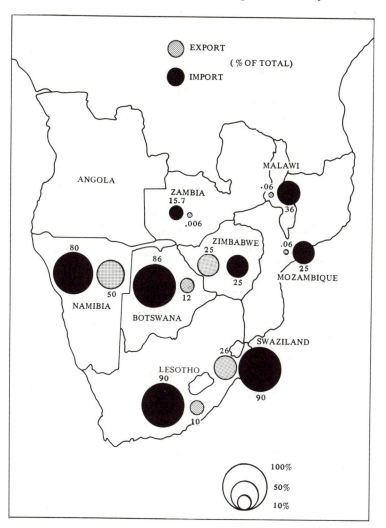

Map 5. Flow of Exports and Imports with South Africa, 1982: Southern Africa

rican countries could be as high as 25 percent of the total value of South Africa's merchandise exports.

Moreover, what is particularly significant about South Africa's penetration of regional markets (in addition, once again, to partially offsetting its trade deficits with Western countries) is that for important manufacturing industries Southern Africa is the only major external market. Table 1.8 contains data on South African exports to African countries outside of the customs union in 1983. These data indicate that 40 percent or more of plastics, resins, and rubber products, footwear and millinery, nonmetallic mineral products, and machinery, as well as 39 percent of chemicals and chemical products and 21 percent of miscellaneous manufactured goods, were marketed in African countries—primarily in Southern Africa. Therefore from the standpoint of these industries, at least, the maintenance and expansion of regional markets is integral to their continued growth and prosperity.

One explanation for the fact that South Africa (like Israel at present and Japan during the 1950s) tends to export capital-intensive goods to nearby countries whereas its more labor-intensive goods such as ore and unprocessed primary products are exported to major metropolitan export markets is what is termed a "two-tailed" comparative advantage.

Much of South Africa's rapid industrial growth has been based upon key, capital-intensive, high technology sectors. For example, the country's manufacturing sector as a percentage of GDP rose from 6.2 percent in 1916 to 25.1 percent in 1975. While the GDP increased at an annual rate of 4.5 percent in real terms, the average annual growth rate of manufacturing output during this period was 6.9 percent. The growth rates for agriculture and mining during this period were only 2.8 percent and 3.0 percent respectively.

The rapid rise of industries producing intermediate products and processed raw materials such as materials,

Table 1.8 South African Merchandise Trade with Africa, 1983 (excluding Botswana, Lesotho, Swaziland, and Namibia)

Commodity Group	Exports to Africa[a]	Exports to Africa as a % of Total Exports Per Group	Imports from Africa[a]	Imports from Africa as a % of Total Imports Per Group
1 Animal and animal products	39,396	18.3%	5,023	6.3%
2 Vegetable products	67,783	11.0	44,488	8.7
3 Animal and vegetable fats and oils	9,843	27.8	1,648	1.2
4 Prepared foodstuffs	53,845	11.2	53,539	13.7
5 Mineral products	39,788	1.9	17,140	7.4
6 Chemicals and chemical products	168,291	39.0	3,511	0.3
7 Plastics, resins, and rubber products	37,181	45.9	1,742	0.3
8 Hides, skins, and leather	1,518	1.2	4,074	7.4
9 Wood and wood products	6,056	10.8	15,618	13.1
10 Pulp, paper, and paperboard	31,288	11.7	1,996	0.4
11 Textiles	26,371	5.0	54,100	7.7
12 Footwear and millinery	2,745	42.3	3,895	4.4
13 Nonmetallic mineral products	16,915	46.1	642	0.4
14 Gems and jewellery	1,162	—	46,228	45.6
15 Base metals and metal products	138,157	7.3	43,758	5.7
16 Machinery	105,684	46.9	15,145	0.3
17 Vehicles and transport equipment	34,439	19.1	7,508	0.4
18 Optical and other instruments	7,240	21.8	1,454	0.2
19 Musical instruments	—	—	—	—
20 Misc. manufactured articles	4,486	21.4	3,678	2.3
21 Works of art, collectors' pieces	59	1.7	281	1.3
22 Unclassified	4,841	—	369	—
Total	797,091	3.9	325,658	2.0

SOURCE: *Monthly Abstract of Trade Statistics*, January-December 1983 (Pretoria: Government Printer), tables 2 and 3.
NOTE: [a] In thousands of rands.

parts, and capital equipment is evident in their high average annual growth rate of 8.6 percent. The producers of
metals, metal products, electrical machinery, paper and
paper products, and rubber goods also experienced a high
average growth rate of 9.0 percent. Processed raw material
outputs such as iron and steel, basic chemicals, oil, and
petrol had an average growth rate of 8.6 percent, and motor
vehicles grew at the rate of 9.9 percent a year.[8] From his
survey of South African industrial performance between
1916 and 1975, Marais (1981:30) concludes that there occurred a spectacular long-run expansion of the manufacturing sector relative to other sectors of the economy.
Concomitant with this rapid rise in the growth of manufacturing there occurred a significant trend toward accelerated growth in the science-based capital intensive industries whose continued growth and prosperity depends in
part, at least, upon exports to Southern African countries.

ZIMBABWE'S TRADING RELATIONSHIPS

Unlike Zimbabwe's commercial agricultural and mining
industries, which primarily supply Western European
markets,[9] the manufacturing industry is oriented toward
serving domestic and regional markets. The period of the

---

[8] Processed agricultural outputs grew at 6.6 percent, and consumer and
semi- and nondurables grew at an average annual rate of 5.8 percent and
5.5 percent respectively. The average rate of growth for all consumer
goods was 5.9 percent a year compared with the overall growth rate of 4.5
percent. For an extended discussion of sectoral growth rates see Marais
(1981).

[9] Almost all of Zimbabwe's mineral production is sold on world markets. Likewise, the preponderance of commercial agricultural output is
sold on European markets. For example, in 1981 tobacco exports earned
224.4 million Zimbabwean dollars, or 55 percent of total agricultural export earnings of 407.4 million Zimbabwean dollars. Fifty percent of total
tobacco sales went to Western Europe [46 percent to the European Economic Community (EEC)], 20 percent to the Middle East, 12 percent to the
Far East, and only 3 percent to the Americas (EIU 1981:115).

political federation of Northern and Southern Rhodesia and Nyasaland between 1953 and 1963 was significant because it was during this time that Zimbabwe's manufacturing industry experienced enormous growth.[10] While most industries were located in Salisbury (now Harare) primarily to serve the domestic market, they were also strategically placed to serve regional markets as well.

The establishment of a federal government regulating a single unified regional economy had a significant impact on Zimbabwe's manufacturing industry for a number of reasons. Prior to federation a manufacturer in any one of the three territories did not have automatic entree to the other territories. To the local manufacturer operating in one of the territories, the other territories were privileged export markets comparable with South Africa and thereby subject to bilateral governmental regulation. After federation, however, the federal government adopted a unified territorywide schedule of tariff duties. The federal tariff came into effect in 1955 (1957 in Nyasaland) and provided a common policy of industrial protection for local industries in the federation. The new federal government also negotiated a federal trade agreement with South Africa in 1955 in order to end South Africa's duty free access to federal markets and thus to end its competitive trading advantage.

The regional orientation of Zimbabwe's manufacturing industry was firmly set in place by the end of the federation in 1963. This is clearly illustrated in Table 1.9, which shows the geographic distribution of Rhodesia's exported manufactured goods and services in 1964. The data indicate that while the manufacturing industry in Southern Rhodesia was heavily dependent upon the domestic mar-

---

[10] During the "federal boom period," the number of manufacturing firms increased from seven hundred to an estimated thirteen hundred due to a massive inflow of private capital from Britain and South Africa. Wield (1981:154) estimates that over one-third of Britain's largest manufacturing firms invested in Rhodesia's manufacturing industry.

Table 1.9   Distribution of Products and Services of Southern Rhodesia's Manufacturing Industry, 1964 (in millions of pounds)

Rhodesia (Zimbabwe)	125
Zambia	30
South Africa	6
Malawi	5
U.K. and other markets	4

SOURCE: Association of Rhodesian Industries (1965:594).
NOTE: 1 Rhodesian pound = U.S. $2.80 in 1964.

ket, Rhodesia's export markets for manufactured goods were in the regional economy and primarily within the ex-federation territories—Zambia and Malawi—and South Africa. And, in fact, the production policies of firms that located in Southern Rhodesia were designed for the federation's regional market.[11] This development led the federal

[11] Most manufacturing firms were located in Southern Rhodesia, although their production was oriented toward the federation as a whole. B. N. Adams, the president of the Association of Rhodesian and Nyasaland Industries, gave the following explanation for the concentration of manufacturing production in Southern Rhodesia: "The agricultural and mining industries created the nucleus of a domestic market for manufactured goods and they earned the necessary foreign exchange to enable manufacturers to purchase capital goods to develop factories in Southern Rhodesia" (East Africa and Rhodesia 1964:563). Another important reason for the concentration of manufacturing industry in Southern Rhodesia was that the federal government was based there. This resulted in the transfer of a substantial portion of taxes paid by the Northern Rhodesian copper industry to Southern Rhodesia by the federal government, which retained 64 percent of federal tax receipts. Examples of the transfer of federal revenues from Northern to Southern Rhodesia were subsidies for European agriculture and education, budget items that were taken over by the federal government. Governmental expenditures for these services constituted an estimated 22 percent of current federal appropriations during 1956 to 1958. The preponderance of these expenditures went to Southern Rhodesia, where European agriculture was centered and where there was the greatest demand for skilled white labor. The federal government also invested heavily in Southern Rhodesia's infrastructure, such as

prime minister, Sir Roy Welensky, to warn the Rhodesian Front in 1962 against seceding from the federation on grounds that Southern Rhodesian manufacturers would lose about 30 percent of their markets (in Northern Rhodesia and Nyasaland) in the event of a break-up of the federation.[12]

The structure of Zimbabwe's trading relationships during the federation was as follows. Britain was Zimbabwe's principal trading partner, supplying 45 percent of its imports and purchasing 40 percent of its exports. South Africa was second in importance, supplying 33 percent of Zimbabwe's imports and purchasing 14 percent of its exports. Northern Rhodesia (Zambia) was next in order of importance, taking approximately 23 percent of Zimbabwe's exports while supplying a negligible proportion of its imports. Hawkins (1976:17) summed up Zimbabwe's trading relationships during this period by saying that Great Britain, South Africa, and Northern Rhodesia took approximately 80 percent of Southern Rhodesia's imports. Britain, Western Europe, and the United States purchased Southern Rhodesia's primary raw material exports, such as minerals and agricultural production, while most of Southern Rhodesia's manufactured exports went to Northern Rhodesia (Zambia) and to a lesser extent to Nyasaland (Malawi) and South Africa. Hence from the point of view of manufacturers in Zimbabwe their only important export markets were in the Southern African region.

Table 1.10 shows Zimbabwe's trading partners and changes in the direction of trade between 1965 and 1983. The data indicate a substantial decrease in trade with Great Britain as well as with Zambia and a corresponding increase in trade with South Africa as well as with the Far East and Europe. In effect, the United Kingdom and South

the Kariba Dam and the railway to Lourenço Marques (Maputo), which was necessary to attract the manufacturing industry. See Hawkins (1976:19).

[12] *East Africa and Rhodesia* (1962:285).

Table 1.10   Zimbabwe's Main Trading Partners, 1965 and 1983

	Exports[a]		Imports	
	1965	1983	1965	1983
South Africa	9.0%	18.6%	22.9%	24.5%
U.K.	21.9	11.6	30.4	11.5
Zambia	25.3	3.1	3.6	2.2
U.S.A.	2.4	6.7	6.8	9.5
West Germany[b]		7.7		7.4
Malawi	5.4	1.4	1.2	0.7
Botswana		4.0		4.2
Mozambique	0.8	1.5	1.1	0.9
Belgium[b]		2.2		1.0
Italy[b]		5.2		1.8
Netherlands[b]		3.5		1.8
Japan	5.2	6.3	5.5	4.7
France[b]		1.6		4.7
Zaire	1.2	2.1		
Switzerland[b]		1.3		2.0
Portugal[b]		1.3		
Other	28.8	20.7	28.5	25.8
Total	100.0	100.0	100.0	100.0

SOURCES: Zimbabwe (1984:tables 10.3 and 10.4), and EIU (1980:19).
NOTES: [a] Export figures exclude gold sales.

[b] In 1965, European countries took 16.5 percent of Zimbabwe's exports while supplying 15.2 percent of its imports.

Africa reversed roles as Zimbabwe's major trading partner. Zimbabwe's exports to Great Britain declined from 21.9 percent of the total in 1965 to only 11.6 percent in 1983, while her exports to South Africa increased from 9 percent of the total in 1965 to 18.6 percent in 1983. Likewise, Zimbabwe's imports from Britain declined from 30.4 percent of the total in 1965 to 11.5 percent in 1983, while her imports from South Africa increased from 22.9 percent in

1965 to 24.5 percent in 1983. An even more significant change in the direction of Zimbabwe's trade was the decline in its exports (mostly manufactured goods) to Zambia, from 25.3 percent of the total in 1965 to only 3.1 percent in 1983.

At the time of UDI in 1965, Rhodesia's manufacturing exports were at a high level of 40 percent of total exports. Manufactured exports were in two categories: processed primary agricultural and mining products for world markets (for example, cigarettes, ferrochrome, copper, sugar, and meats), and manufactures for export to regional countries such as Zambia, Malawi, and South Africa (clothing, textiles, radios, footwear, iron and steel, fertilizer, and others).[13]

Sanctions against Rhodesia from 1965 to 1980 had the effect of altering the flow of exports away from exfederation territories toward South Africa. Zimbabwe's Statement of External Trade for 1981, for example, shows that in that year U.S. $192 million (22 percent of Zimbabwe's total exports) were exported to South Africa.[14] Of these ex-

[13] Hawkins (1976:35) gave the export value of Rhodesia's manufactured goods in 1965 by commodity as follows: clothing—10.8 million Rhodesian dollars; meats—8.4 million dollars; pig iron—7.0 million dollars; sugar—5.0 million dollars; radios—4.1 million dollars; footwear—3.5 million dollars; ferrochrome—3.4 million dollars; passenger cars—3.1 million dollars; cigarettes—2.7 million dollars; and textiles—2.5 million dollars. One Rhodesian dollar equalled U.S. $1.40 in 1965.

[14] The Zimbabwean and South African Preferential Trade Agreement was extended beyond the expiration date of March 1982. The continuation of the agreement was critically important for Zimbabwe to ensure its access to the South African market for its manufactured exports. Under the terms of the original agreement the bulk of Zimbabwe's manufactured and processed food exports entered South Africa with duty rebates of between 5 and 35 percent, which is more favorable than most favored nation tariff rates.

Riddel has argued that if the agreement had not been renewed Zimbabwe would have lost U.S. $50 million in exports, and 6,500 people would have been thrown out of work. The agreement was also viewed by Zimbabwean businessmen as a definite advantage to Zimbabwe since it

ports approximately 60 percent included manufactured goods, which constitute 33.9 percent of Zimbabwe's total manufactured goods exports.[15]

The regional orientation of Zimbabwe's manufacturing industry has produced an industry with "excess capacity" for its domestic market. In fact, it was the excess capacity of Rhodesia's manufacturing industry that made possible the short-term rapid rate of growth in the economy during UDI.[16] Between 1968 and 1974, for example, real output grew at an average annual rate of 8.3 percent. The manufacturing sector was largely responsible for this high growth rate. The volume of manufacturing output more

---

allowed them to export consumer goods, radios, textiles, and footwear while only offering South Africa low tariffs on pharmaceuticals, which are already locally produced in Zimbabwe. The reduction in South Africa's surcharge levied against imports into RSA in 1983 also increased the competitiveness of Zimbabwe's exports in South Africa (*African Business* 1982:71, and *African Business* 1983a:28).

[15] However, since a large proportion of Zimbabwe's manufactured exports (in Standard International Trade Classification sections 6-9) consist of alloys and refined metals, most of which are sent overseas, the figure tends to inflate the actual value of manufactured exports. If alloys and refined metals are excluded from the manufactured goods export category, the proportion of Zimbabwe's goods that are exported to South Africa actually rises to three-fourths of the manufactured goods exports. For example, in sections 8 and 9 alone the proportion of manufactured goods that Zimbabwe exports to South Africa rises to over 80 percent of the total. I am indebted to Colin Stoneman for illumination on this point.

[16] The excess capacity of Rhodesia's manufacturing industry made possible the expansion of output through import substitution with static or falling unit costs. However, by 1975, this growth reached a point of diminishing returns. Rhodesia's tight balance of payments situation severely limited the replacement and renewal of capital equipment necessary for continued expansion of the economy. This led Hawkins (1976:25) to conclude that after a "sustained period of import substitution a shift back to exported growth is necessary—at least until the next 'plateau' of import replacement is reached." Ann Seidman has pointed out that this assumes the need to export manufactured goods without change or growth in the low-income mass domestic market (private communication 1984).

than doubled during the 1964 to 1974 period (Hawkins 1976:20). Riddell has estimated that during the period from 1965 to 1980, manufactured products in Rhodesia increased from 600 to over 6,200 items, many of which, however, were heavily dependent upon imported items, were labor-intensive, and thus were not export-oriented (*African Business* 1982a:12).

Nevertheless, during the 1965 to 1980 period, the value of Zimbabwe's exports increased 280 percent, while flue-cured tobacco exports went from being the country's largest export earner to being second to manufacturing. Manufactured imports to Zimbabwe, on the other hand, rose to 41 percent of Zimbabwe's total import bill in 1982 (supplied largely by South Africa). Hence, Zimbabwe became heavily dependent upon South African imports, especially for heavy machinery and transport equipment.

The "openness" of Zimbabwe's economy means that the size of domestic production and income distribution is strongly influenced by internationally traded goods. The country's exports and imports each constitute about one-third of Zimbabwe's gross domestic product. This means that the country's economic growth and income is extremely vulnerable to export earnings and to the terms of trade with other countries. Given the structure of its economy, therefore, in order for Zimbabwe to achieve high growth rates it is necessary for it to maintain high levels of exportation and to have favorable terms of trade with its trading partners.

In 1980, Zimbabwe's exports were valued at 902 million Zimbabwean dollars, which comprised 28 percent of total GDP. However, planners estimated that it was necessary to increase the country's export value to 30 percent of GDP in order for the government to achieve its high annual projected 8 percent real growth rate compounded each year to 1985 as targeted in the Three-Year Transitional National

Development Plan.[17] In order to meet this expanded export value it would have been necessary to increase export earnings to 1,053 million Zimbabwean dollars (at 1980 prices), which represents an increase of 17 percent over the 1980 figure. However, the projected total value of exports for 1981 was a disappointing 830 million Zimbabwean dollars, despite a very good year for tobacco exports. And Zimbabwe's three-year drought beginning in 1982, plus the depressed world prices for its primary commodities, have produced zero or negative growth rates since 1982.

The excess capacity of Zimbabwe's manufacturing industry and in particular its competitiveness in Southern African markets makes it a strategic sector for increasing the country's export value in order to begin to approach the government's planned rates of economic growth.[18] For

[17] Colin Stoneman has pointed out the fact that a growth rate of 8 percent during the period of the plan was never a real possibility unless the investment ratio were pushed from the existing 20 percent to over 30 percent (private communication 1985). However, Riddell (1984:464-465) has explained this "optimistic" growth target in terms of two immediate but short-lived benefits that the newly independent government of Zimbabwe enjoyed: a shift in the terms of trade strongly favoring Zimbabwe and the ability to sell export commodities that had been stockpiled by the former government. This combined with good rains and support from Western governments to produce an increase in real GDP of 26 percent during the first year of independence. Based upon these highly favorable economic conditions (albeit exceptional) it is not surprising that planners projected such a high annual growth rate during the period of the plan.

[18] Zimbabwe's recent accession to the Lome II Convention is expected to improve the country's terms of trade with EEC trading partners. However, Zimbabwe's competitive position in these markets is unlikely to substantially improve, especially in the light of protectionist pressures in these countries in the areas of clothing, footwear, tobacco, and textiles. For example, European trading partners might be pressured by their own national manufacturers to evoke the safeguard clause of the convention to prevent preferential rights from being granted to Zimbabwean exporters. Seidman has pointed out the fact that as a landlocked country Zimbabwe is at a comparative disadvantage in competing with Pacific basin countries such as Korea and Taiwan for European markets (private communication 1984).

example, Zimbabwe's manufactured and processed food products are regarded as being price competitive in the ex-federation territories that are members of the SADCC comprised of Angola, Botswana, Lesotho, Malawi, Mozambique, Swaziland, Tanzania, Zambia, and Zimbabwe.[19] While the volume of trade among SADCC countries is relatively small (an estimated U.S. $290 million in 1981, contributing only 5.1 percent of total exports and 3.9 percent of imports), Zimbabwe is the dominant exporting country within SADCC, accounting for 45 percent of total SADCC exports in 1981. This netted Zimbabwe a trade surplus of U.S. $20 million, which helped to offset her trade deficit with South Africa for that year of about U.S. $127 million (SADCC 1984a: sec. 1, p. 3).

Zimbabwe's manufacturing export industry may also be able to penetrate the markets of countries that have signed the Preferential Trade Area treaty for fourteen East and Southern African countries. In addition to the SADCC countries that signed the treaty by 1985 were Ethiopia, Kenya, Uganda, the Comoros, Rwanda, Burundi, Mauritius, and Somalia.[20] These countries constitute potential

---

[19] The reason that Zimbabwe's manufactured exports are price competitive in Southern African markets is that much of the sector's output is based upon domestic resources. Three major product groups combined—foodstuffs, beverages and tobacco, metals and metal products, for example—contribute approximately one-half of industrial value added (UNGA 1982:6).

One major implication of the full exploitation of Zimbabwe's comparative advantage in regional African markets is that since neighboring African states are trying to produce the same products, Zimbabwe's success in penetrating these markets will tend to undermine the industries of other states. This would undoubtedly threaten to undermine regional economic organizations such as SADCC and the Preferential Trade Area Treaty (PTA) in the same way that Kenya's manufacturing exports undermined the East African Community (see Anglin 1983).

[20] In 1985, there were still six holdouts from the desired twenty-member PTA: Angola, Botswana, Madagascar, Mozambique, the Seychelles, and Tanzania. The latter had signed but not ratified the treaty. PTA officials feared that the longer the six remained out of the organization the

markets for important manufactured products exported by Zimbabwe such as clothing, footwear, steel, and agricultural equipment.

In order to expand its manufactured exports in the Southern African region and beyond, however, two conditions must be satisfied. The first is that African countries which are potentially important markets for Zimbabwe's manufactured goods must dismantle their protectionist trade policies that discriminate against Zimbabwean products. The second condition is that Zimbabwe's products must be price competitive in the South African market and with South African exports in the region—the major source of manufactured goods.[21] This condition requires heavy state subsidies for Zimbabwean manufacturing exporters to match South Africa's heavily subsidized manufacturing industries.

One illustration of the importance of governmental subsidies to ensure the price competitiveness of Zimbabwean manufactured goods vis-à-vis South African manufactured goods in the regional economy is the case of the battery market in Zambia. In November 1980, the Zimbabwean government discontinued a 5 percent cash incentive scheme for its manufacturing exporters, while in May of that year South Africa inaugurated a major export incentive scheme for its exporters to countries in the region. This had the effect of cheapening South African goods vis-à-vis Zimbabwean goods. The consequence of this development with respect to Zambia's battery market was that Ever Ready batteries manufactured by South Africa became less expensive for Zambian importers than Zimbabwean-manufactured Kariba batteries.

---

lower the prospect of their ever joining. The concern was that this would handicap the organization and prevent it from ever reaching its full potential (*African Business* 1984g:32).

[21] Stoneman has made the observation that this condition would obviously not apply in the event that SADCC or the PTA excluded South African goods from their markets (private communication 1985).

EXAMINATION of the historical role of Western industrial states in the development of the regionally oriented manufacturing industries of Southern Africa reveals their importance in fostering a unified economic region with South Africa and Zimbabwe occupying strategic positions. The economic relationship of South Africa and Zimbabwe to other countries in Southern Africa is comparable to RSA's and Zimbabwe's relationship with Western industrial countries. South Africa and Zimbabwe's dependence upon Western countries for intermediate, capital goods, services, and investment has resulted in perennial trade deficits with these countries.[22] As a result, South Africa is only able to pay for a fraction (albeit substantial) of its imports from these countries by selling its gold. However, South Africa and potentially Zimbabwe are important manufacturing exporters in their own region, which enables them to partially offset their merchandise trading deficits with Western countries.

---

[22] As the major recipient of foreign investment in the region, South Africa financed only 66 percent of its investment from domestic savings until 1954. However, from 1954 to 1982 on average all but 2 percent of investment in South Africa was financed from domestic savings (Nedbank Group, Ltd. 1983:97). Out of South Africa's total foreign liabilities in 1983, the European Economic Community countries accounted for 55 percent, 13 percent by other European countries, 23 percent by North America and South America, 2 percent by Africa, 4 percent by Asia, and the balance by international institutions and Oceania countries. Foreign investment in South Africa has, in fact, been declining in real terms during the past decade, increasing at a slower rate than the growth in the country's gross domestic product. Much of the increase in foreign investment (which stood at 45.5 billion rands in 1983) was attributable to higher levels of retained earnings by foreign subsidiaries and not by new capital inflows. For example, it was estimated that there was not more than $100 million annually in new U.S. capital inflows to South Africa during 1981 and 1982 (SAIRR 1984:108-109, and Nedbank Group, Ltd. 1983:139-159).

CHAPTER TWO

State Strategies and Political Division: South Africa and Zimbabwe

THE FIRST CATEGORY of state involvement in the regional economy is one in which strategies for the political manipulation of regional economic ties have had the unintended consequence of producing major domestic political divisions. Instead of increasing state power, these strategies have tended to undermine or erode political support for the regimes in power.

States that fall into this category are South Africa, Zimbabwe, and Tanzania (discussed in Chapter 5). In these countries state strategies failed because they did not accurately assess the impact that the strategies would have upon state power. This was due in part to the extreme political pressures the regimes were under and in part to the fact that the regimes were forced to undertake risky action to cope with these pressures.

Because South Africa and Zimbabwe are the industrial centers of the regional economy, they adopted strategies that capitalized on their sources of economic power. They sought to politically manipulate nationally based transnational corporations in order to achieve domestic and foreign policy objectives. In the case of South Africa the ruling National party pursued political alliances with transnationals in order to cope both with the growing threat of liberation forces operating from neighboring countries and with black urban rebellion. In Zimbabwe the state sought to partially meet the post-independence demands of peasants, exguerillas, and other advocates of the ruling party for improved living standards by supporting the exports of manufacturing transnationals to countries in the region. In this regard SADCC and the PTA countries were targeted as important markets for Zimbabwe.

Both strategies failed, however. The South African regime miscalculated the degree and extent of white political opposition to the alliance with transnational corporations. And the failure of Zimbabwe's manufacturing industry to generate high levels of economic growth (necessary for improved living conditions) precipitated radical, populist opposition to the regime's plan. In both cases the strategies of these regimes not only failed to realize their political objectives but they inadvertently eroded regime support.

SOUTH AFRICA

From 1979 to 1984 the ruling National party of South Africa aligned itself politically with large-scale regionally oriented commercial and manufacturing industry in South Africa in order to cope with external and internal threats to the state. From the point of view of the NP cooperation with regionally oriented transnational corporations[1] was expected to advance the party's foreign policy objectives. By increasing "hostile" bordering African states' economic dependence upon South African-based transna-

[1] Unlike the mining or agricultural industries, the regionally oriented manufacturing corporations are of strategic importance to the NP. Manufactured industrial supplies to states in the region can easily be manipulated by the South African government by either providing efficient service on lenient terms of credit or by delaying delivery and requiring advance payment. In contrast, the mining and agricultural industries are less precise instruments of political pressure because of the lengthy time required for them to have an impact and in the case of food exports because of the adverse international reaction to the antihumanitarian implications of denying food supplies. For a discussion of the difficulties connected with any South African attempt to use food exports (or their denial) as an economic instrument of foreign policy, see Henderson (1983).

tional corporations,[2] the NP believed that it could increase South Africa's political leverage over these states so that they would be more cooperative and would curtail the operation of liberation movements against South Africa from their territories.

The NP's collaboration with transnational corporations was also designed to mitigate or defuse the explosive black urban threat to the regime by dividing black urban opposition to the National party. This was to be achieved by stratifying the black urban population into two groups: a privileged group of residential workers and businessmen who had the right to live and work in the urban areas and a nonprivileged group of migratory or commuter workers who did not have that right. In this way the NP hoped to create a black urban middle-class to "stabilize" the black townships in the "white (urban) areas."

An unexpected consequence of the NP's political alliance with the transnational corporations, however, was that it contributed to the most serious challenge to the ruling National party in its history. Conservative Afrikaner parties—the Conservative party (CP) and the Herstigte Nasionale party (HNP)—appealed to white trade unions, middle-class whites, and lower and middle echelon state employees for electoral support to defeat the party's alliance strategy.

[2] In the South African context, "transnational corporation" refers to South African affiliates of multinational corporations as well as to large South African conglomerates and firms that have investments in, produce for, or have retail outlets in South Africa and other countries in the region. Examples of multinational transnational corporations in South Africa are CALTEX Oil, S.A. (Pty.), Ltd.; British Petroleum Southern Africa; G.M.-South Africa (Pty.), Ltd.; General Electric Co. (Pty.), Ltd.; Masonite Africa, Ltd.; and American Hospital Supply Corporation of South Africa, Ltd. Examples of South African-based transnationals include Anglo American Corporation, Barlow Rand, Premier Milling, African Explosives and Chemical Industries, Fed Food, Ltd., and Pick 'n Pay.

Objectives of the National Party

The objectives of the National party in forming a political alliance with large-scale regionally oriented transnational firms based in South Africa were twofold—to deal with both the external and internal threats to continued white political hegemony. In the NP's strategy to manage the "total onslaught" against South Africa, the transnationals had a crucial role to play.[3] An alliance with transnationals was expected to help manage the external threat by increasing South Africa's leverage over so-called hostile bordering African states to moderate their antiapartheid rhetoric in international fora and to curtail the operation of anti-South African liberation movements from their territories. The alliance with transnationals was also integral to the domestic reform strategy of the NP under State President P. W. Botha, which was designed to deal with the internal black urban threat to NP rule. The NP's declared support for an incipient alliance between transnational corporations and a "permanently settled" black

[3] The basis of the political alliance between the government of P. W. Botha and regionally oriented industrial firms was part of the "four power bases" of the state's "means" in the total national strategy of dealing with the "total [communist] onslaught" against South Africa. One of the state's power bases was economic. Regionally oriented South African-based transnational corporations were for the first time given policy-making input into state security planning through the minister of industries, commerce, and tourism, who was a coopted member of the "keystone" agency in the National Security Management System (NSMS), the South African State Security Council. Transnational corporations were also represented on the prime minister's Economic Advisory Council and the Special Constellation Committee, which was established in July 1980 to assist the Office of the Prime Minister in planning regional economic cooperation across political boundaries. For a discussion of the role that the representatives of large industrial interests had in planning South Africa's total national strategy, see Geldenhuys (1984:140-141, 149-155, 160-165). For an elaboration on the theme of the NP's political alignment with monopoly capital, see Prinsloo (1984:20-42), Innes (1983:171-183), Wolpe (1983), O'Meara (1983:248-250), and Davies and O'Meara (1985).

urban labor force and businessmen had the objective of fostering the formation of a large black working and middle class in the white (urban) areas to act as a counterweight to black urban unrest.

EXTERNAL THREAT

The National party's "outward-looking" policy of the 1960s, détente in the 1970s, and the CONSAS (Constellation of Southern African States) concept of the 1980s were all designed primarily to mitigate the "hostility" of African states on South Africa's borders and to expand South Africa's markets for manufactured goods within the regional economy. The stated objective of CONSAS was to promote regional economic integration based upon the "growth-generating potential of the South African economy to be realized throughout the region and beyond" (Leistner 1981a:349). The policy envisaged the inclusion of the following states in CONSAS: Botswana, Lesotho and Swaziland, Zimbabwe, Zambia, Malawi and Mozambique, and possibly Angola.[4]

The principal means through which the NP expected regional integration to increase South Africa's political leverage over other states in the region was the African states' dependence on South African-based transnational corporations. The small individual markets of African states in the region (eight African states in the CONSAS concept had a combined GDP equal to one-third of South Africa's

[4] Geldenhuys (1984a:117-118) has argued that Botha's initial constellation plan had to be scaled down to include only an "inner constellation" of South African homelands—Transkei, Bophuthatswana, Venda, and Ciskei, the so-called SATBVC states—when the original targeted states refused to join and instead formed their own economic association designed to reduce their economic dependence upon South Africa. However, the nonaggression pacts that South Africa signed with Mozambique, Angola, Swaziland, Zimbabwe, and Lesotho undoubtedly revived the country's hopes for the at least partial achievement of the original constellation plan. For an elaboration of CONSAS see Botha (1979).

GDP) made the establishment of basic manufacturing industry uneconomic.[5] Thus, the close proximity of South Africa and the concentration of large-scale transnational firms there created a comparative advantage that enabled the firms to dominate the economies of regional states.

The oil industry provides an illustration of the domination of the economies of regional African states by South African-based transnationals. In the case of at least three states near South Africa—Botswana, Lesotho, and Malawi—South African-based oil companies supply most or all of their refined oil requirements. If this supply were interrupted and their storage tanks sabotaged, their economies would be seriously threatened. In the most extreme case, Lesotho, if South African oil supplies were cut off, the country would be in the position of relying upon oil supplies from Maputo, 650 kilometers away. Such a supply route would be prohibitively expensive and technically and politically unfeasible.

The advantage to regional states, therefore, of cooperating in CONSAS (albeit tacitly) was the guarantee of the continued operation of South African-based transnationals in their respective economies. South Africa's political

[5] An important consequence of South Africa's regional development strategy for Southern Africa as elaborated by Botha at the Good Hope Conference held in Cape Town in late 1981 was to pull investment away from neighboring countries and direct it toward the South African bantustans. A combination of low interest state loans, erection of buildings and subsidized rentals, tax incentives, direct subsidies, and railage and harbor rebates constitute a powerful incentive for firms to shift their investment from neighboring countries to the bantustans. Examples of this include the reorientation of the hotel and tourist industry away from the traditional centers in the region in Lesotho, Swaziland, and Botswana toward the homelands (Crush and Wellings 1983) and the transfer of manufacturing firms such as Swazi Carpets and Copperland that closed their operations in Swaziland and reopened in the Transkei and Ciskei (*African Business* 1983c:12). For a discussion of Lesotho's loss of competitiveness to the bantustans, see Wellings (1985).

leverage over states in the region is thus said to arise from the threat of interference in the operations of South African-based corporations in their territories.

South Africa's recent campaign of sabotaging industrial targets by raiding and supporting insurgency in bordering states does not depart from the NP's policy of encouraging cooperative economic relations with African states. The sabotage was primarily designed to increase South Africa's leverage over African states in the region by further increasing their economic dependence upon South African transnationals. Giliomee points out in this regard that these two strategies were being simultaneously pursued by different state bureaucracies (private communication 1985). The Ministry of Industrial Affairs, Trade, and Commerce as well as the Treasury were supporting expanded regional trade while the Department of Military Intelligence (MDI) was sponsoring sabotage.

In addition to raids into bordering countries, South Africa's support for opposition movements in bordering states was calculated to increase their economic dependence. For example, the actions of the Basutoland Congress party's (BCP) Lesotho Liberation Army, which blew up Caltex tanks in Maseru, and the anti-Frelimo Resistência Nacional Moçambicana (MNR), which blew up the British Petroleum storage tanks in Beira and which cut the oil pipeline to Zimbabwe several times, tended to increase the economic dependence of these states upon South African oil transnationals. MNR sabotage in Mozambique has had the effect of crippling the economy of a country already suffering the effects of a three-year-long drought that threatened starvation for an estimated seven hundred thousand people in the southern part of the country. The careful targeting for sabotage of key installations and projects by the MNR, for example, has resulted in reducing the volume of freight exported from South Africa through the port of Maputo (a major source of Mozambique's foreign exchange). According to South African Transport Services, the number of railway trucks that crossed into Mozambique in December 1983 was only one-fifth the number that crossed in December 1980. Likewise, MNR sabotage of the Cabora Bassa power lines leading into the South African power grid has forced Mozambique to use what little foreign exchange it had to purchase power from South Africa. Hence, MNR attacks have had a crippling impact upon Mozambique's economy that among other things has served to remind the Frelimo leadership of the crucial importance of its economic ties with South Africa (*Africa* 1984c:35-36).

Sabotage by the MNR of rail and road links connecting SADCC countries has not only increased their dependence upon the South African transport and harbor network but has produced something of a bonanza for South African-based manufacturers and commodity traders who have supplied emergency goods and food to United Nations, EEC, and voluntary organizations operating in SADCC countries to help them cope with the economic crisis created in part by insurgent operations. In effect, the disruption of neighboring countries' transporation networks has made South Africa the only feasible local source of supply and the South African transport system the only possible means of transport (*African Business* 1984s:49-50).

INTERNAL THREAT

In the wake of the widespread urban unrest of the 1970s and mid-1980s and the increasing frequency of mass strikes, the National party under the leadership of President Botha embarked upon a new strategy for coping with the major internal political threat to white political hegemony—growing black urban unrest and worker militance.[6]

[6] In addition to the urban rioting that swept the country and involved all "nonwhite" groups for the better part of two years from 1976 to 1978 and which resumed in late 1984, mass urban strikes by black workers have increased. The number of black workers in unions was estimated to

The Botha government viewed the politicization of the growing black urban trade union movement as being a potentially potent instrument of ANC power against the South African state (Geldenhuys 1984:166). The crucial element of Botha's declared strategy that involved stratifying the black urban population of roughly ten million (fifteen million by 1990) was to create a privileged group of depoliticized black urban workers in order to foster the formation of a black urban middle class.

Large manufacturing firms had a major role to play in the NP's strategy for coping with the black urban threat. The firms were central to the National party's plan for resolving the explosive situation in black urban areas with high unemployment, extreme overcrowding, and an absence of basic social amenities. They were expected to stratify the black labor force and thereby divide black urban opposition to the state. The NP's objective was to improve the working and living conditions of a "permanently settled" urban black labor force while "endorsing out" of the "white (urban) areas" the surplus labor and sending unemployed "migrant" laborers to the bantustans.[7] This objective was to be accomplished by producing a privileged stratum of black urban workers with an improved standard of living, including adequate housing, electricity, improved public education, and medical care.

---

have grown from 16,000 in 1969 to over 400,000 in 1984. Mass strike action by black workers has dramatically intensified from 69 strikes and work stoppages involving 4,067 black workers in 1971 to 394 stoppages in 1982 involving 122,481 workers (Nedbank Group, Ltd. 1983:50). It is significant that some of the most severely affected firms have been transnational corporations that for the most part have recognized and negotiated with black unions (Geldenhuys 1984:166).

[7] According to a July 1982 study by the Black Sash, more than three million people were forced to relocate over a twenty-year period with one million more scheduled for resettlement. In April 1982, the minister of cooperation and development, Dr. P.G.J. Koornhof, announced that all future information regarding resettlement would be confidential (Legum 1984a:B757, B796-797).

The large manufacturing corporations were strategically placed to facilitate the NP's policy. An estimated 81 percent of the country's total industrial production was produced in four metropolitan areas: southern Transvaal, western Cape, Durban-Pinetown, and Port Elizabeth-Uitenhage. Combined they account for 75 percent of net industrial output and employment, with the southern Transvaal responsible for more than 50 percent of the country's entire industry (Nattrass 1981:181; Hanekom 1982; *Africa South of the Sahara* 1984:788). It was precisely to these white (urban) areas that the flow of black workers has been the greatest.

For this reason the manufacturing sector, which was dominated by large-scale corporations,[8] preferred to have a permanently settled black labor force within close proximity of the white (urban) areas. In addition, the large manufacturing industries chose to recruit skilled black labor to fill critical shortages. They also sought to substitute expensive white labor with less expensive black labor whenever possible. The high cost and low productivity of skilled white labor was, in fact, regarded as a major factor contributing to the relatively low productivity of South Africa's manufacturing industry. The white unions to date have ef-

[8] The commercial and manufacturing industries of South Africa as a whole are highly concentrated and are strongly influenced if not controlled by large corporations. Tregenna-Piggott (1980:194-195) estimates, for example, that 2.7 percent of all firms command about 50 percent of the total turnover, and the largest ten public corporations control 40 percent of the total assets quoted by industrial companies. Lombard (1984:3) shows that only twelve groups of companies regulate 80 percent of gross assets of all companies listed on the Johannesburg stock exchange. These groups of companies are Anglo American Corporation, SANLAM, Barlow Rand, S.A. Mutual, Volkskas, Barclays, Stannic, Rembrandt, United Building Society, Liberty Life, S.A. Breweries, and Anglo-Vaal. Even the least concentrated industries (fabricated metal products and the food industry) tend to be highly concentrated. For example, in the food industry 10 percent of the ten largest firms control 72.1 percent of the total turnover and have 80.2 percent of the industry's fixed assets (du Plessis 1978:260-267).

fectively protected their members from the competitive threat from black labor through a variety of devices such as racial classification of skilled work and job fragmentation. Nevertheless, manufacturers recognize that the only solution to the skills shortage is increasing the proportion of high level manpower (that is, two years of post-secondary school training) among blacks. Hence, from the point of view of the NP, the manufacturing industry, which had the largest black labor force in the country (an estimated 800,500 in 1982), compared to the next largest employer of black labor—mining with 619,251—was strategically placed to help the party carry out its policy of stratifying the black urban labor force.

The National party also saw political capital in encouraging the largest manufacturing corporations to recognize, and deal with, black trade unions.[9] It was hoped that improving the wages of blacks would take some of the steam out of the campaign for disinvestment in South Africa that

[9] Foreign capital is more heavily concentrated in the manufacturing and business sectors than it is in the mining sector. In 1979, for example, it was estimated that 50 percent of foreign investment went to the manufacturing sector, 25 percent to the financial and business service sector, 15 percent to trade, and only 10 percent to mining. Foreign investment in South Africa's manufacturing sector was estimated at $11 billion in 1979. Foreign investment in the high growth or leading subsectors of the manufacturing industry—oil, automobiles, and electronics—was dominant. The subsidiaries of five multinational oil companies controlled 85 percent of South Africa's petroleum market and operated 91 percent of the petrol stations in the country. An estimated 80 percent of all electronic equipment and components was imported in 1977 (Myers 1980:199). In 1985, it was estimated that American corporations constituted about half of South Africa's petroleum industry, 70 percent of its computer industry, and a quarter of its automobile industry (The Economist 1985:29). With the exception of Sigma, Toyota, and United Car and Diesel Distributors, all the major manufacturers including Volkswagen, General Motors, Nissan, BMW, Alfa Romeo, and Leyland were subsidiaries of multinational corporations and were therefore subject to their control (Southall 1985:6).

was gaining momentum, particularly in the United States (*Africa* 1984a:21-22).

The large manufacturing firms have, in fact, recognized black trade unions, and most are prepared to negotiate labor contracts with them. For example, a firm of management consultants surveyed 152 large industrial and commercial firms in 1981 and found that 95 percent of all firms said they would recognize government-registered unions and 39 percent indicated they would negotiate even with unregistered unions (*X RAY* 1982). Volkswagen went so far as to accept the concept of a "living wage" in 1980 by acceding to strikers' demands for a wage of two rands an hour. In December 1984, Toyota agreed to raise the minimum "living wage" to three rands per hour by mid-1985. The increase in workers' wages was the result of bargaining with unions that belonged to the Federation of South African Trade Unions (FOSATU). Representing predominately black workers, FOSATU had a membership of 130,000 in 1985 in more than 350 factories around the country.

FOSATU, the General Workers' Union (GWU), and the Food and Canning Workers' Union (FCWU), along with the National Union of Mineworkers (NUM) and others, have formed a single massive black trade union federation, the Congress of South African Trade Unions, representing the basis of a politically independent black labor movement. However, the unions have maintained their autonomy from political movements in South Africa, such as the United Democratic Front (UDF), the Azanian People's Organization (AZAPO), and the Inkatha Yenkululeko Yesizwe (Inkatha) Movement, taking the position that as working-class organizations they should remain outside of the political organizations seeking black liberation in South Africa. They believe that the working class should not enter into alliances with political movements until they are strong enough to lead the struggle against the South African state, a position that has opened them to the charge that they are "workerist" because of their refusal to form political alliances with other classes.[10]

From the point of view of the NP, then, an independent worker movement that primarily follows an industrial strategy of advancing working-class interests meshed (intended or not) with the party's alliance strategy with large-scale transnational firms to stratify the black labor force and thereby control or defuse the black urban challenge to the National party.

Objectives of Transnational Corporations

State industrial corporations have played a crucial role in the penetration of regional markets by South African-based transnational firms. They have been instrumental in lowering the costs of production for transnationals, thereby enabling them to establish and maintain regional

[10] This is not to say, however, that FOSATU and the Congress of South African Trade Unions, for example, have not taken positions on important political issues. For example, FOSATU spoke out against black (that is, colored and Indian) participation in the August 1984 multiparliament election scheme designed to implement the government's constitutional reform proposals. The Congress of South African Trade Unions has called for the withdrawal of troops from black townships and the abolition of the pass laws. However, they have not joined any political movement. Chris Dlamini, FOSATU president, underscored the position of the federation in relation to Zimbabwe's recent independence. He pointed out that despite the socialist doctrine of the Zimbabwean government, the workers there were not liberated. This was attributed to the absence of a strong workers' movement in Zimbabwe prior to black majority rule and was given as the reason for the refusal of independent unions and federations to join political movements (Plaut 1984:121-122). However, the Botha government's strong-arm response to urban disturbances beginning in late 1984, which resulted in more than 2,300 deaths, is precisely the kind of action that may defeat the objectives of the government's alliance strategy. Because many of the union members live in the affected areas and have suffered the attacks of the riot police and military, continued repressive action will undoubtedly have the effect of forging a united front between trade union groups and black political organizations.

markets. For example, the massive state Iron and Steel Corporation (ISCOR), which is the basis of South Africa's manufacturing industry, did not raise the price of its steel between 1952 and 1970 (Saul and Gelb 1981:19). This substantially lowered the cost of production for plant and machinery producers in South Africa, which gave these firms a major comparative advantage in regional markets. Likewise, the South Africa (state) Coal, Oil, and Gas Corporation (SASOL) and the state Electricity Supply Commission (ESCOM) have subsidized South African-based industrial transnationals that supply markets in the Southern African region.

EXTERNAL MARKETS

The success that South African-based transnationals have had in capturing external regional markets is evident both in the concentration of regional manufacturing in South Africa (and secondarily in Zimbabwe) and also in the small and dependent manufacturing sectors of other states in the region. Table 2.1 shows regional manufacturing output by country as a percentage of GDP, exports, and employment.

The data in Table 2.1 illustrate the dominance of South African manufacturing in the region. The transnationals have located their headquarters in South Africa, from which they supply the entire region.[11] For example, trans-

---

[11] Large industrial corporations located their regional headquarters in South Africa because of its large settler population and hence sizable markets plus large capital resources earned by the country's enormous mineral wealth. These manufacturing enterprises were designed to service the relatively small and "truncated" manufacturing sectors in the other regional states. Transnational corporations expanded their operations throughout the region by supplying local manufactured goods for high income settler populations in preindependent African states in the region. The industries that did emerge outside of South Africa and Zimbabwe tended to produce luxury goods for the high income groups. The value added in the end product was low because the industries continued to rely heavily upon imported parts and materials from their regional

Table 2.1 The Manufacturing Industry in Southern African States in the 1980s

State	Output		Employment	
	As Per-centage of GDP	As Percentage of Exports	Numbers	Percentage of Economically Active Population[a]
South Africa (1983)	24.7%	25.5% (1984)	1,397,600 (1984)	15.6%
Zimbabwe (1984)	22.8	43.0[b]	167,000	15.7
Botswana (1984)	6.7	21.5[c]	9,531	1.9
Lesotho (1984)	7.0	36.0[d]	3,906	1.0 (1980)
Swaziland (1984)	22.1	23.8[e]	12,089	3.6
Namibia (1983)	5.3	21.5[f]	10,000	3.8 (1981)
Malawi (1985)	12.3	3.4 (1984)	30,300	1.3 (1982)
Mozambique (1981)[g]	10.0	NA	100,000	4.1 (1975)
Zambia (1984)	18.0	2.0	48,790	2.2
Tanzania (1984)	4.7	4.0	100,000	1.3
Zaire (1984)	6.1	3.0	150,000	3.8

SOURCE: Various Sources.

NOTES: NA = not available.

[a] Working age population between 15 and 65 years.

[b] Includes cotton lint, ferrochrome, copper, and nickel.

[c] Comprised of fresh and frozen beef, textiles, and miscellaneous manufactured goods.

[d] Comprised of wool, textiles, clothing, and footwear. Exports in 1984 were valued at 40.3 million molati (1 maloti = U.S. $0.514).

[e] Largely processed agricultural and forestry products (sugar, wood pulp, canned fruits).

[f] Half of this figure is processed meat, fish, and vegetables for export.

[g] After 1975, the Mozambican government changed its system of reporting, which makes comparisons with post-1975 figures impossible.

national oil companies have situated most of their African oil refineries in South Africa in spite of the fact that RSA itself has no known oil deposits. The United Nations estimated that in 1976, 82.3 percent of the region's total refined petroleum products were produced in South Africa. Less than 20 percent of the region's petroleum refining occurs in the region outside of South Africa. Even these refineries are small and operate at the final state of processing, which contributes little to the total value of the final product.

A similar pattern in regional manufacturing is evident in the iron and steel industries. While there are extensive deposits of iron ore in Tanzania, Zambia, and Mozambique, only South Africa and Zimbabwe have the large integrated iron and steel industrial complexes necessary to produce steel.[12]

INTERNAL MARKETS

In order for large-scale industrial firms in South Africa to operate their plants at economies of scale, they must have access to unified markets that are regional in scope.[13] This

---

headquarters in South Africa. The pattern has remained in force and, in fact, has been reinforced since the independence of African states in the region (Makgetla and Seidman 1980: 252).

[12] The same pattern of industrial production is evident in copper fabrication and hydroelectric power production. Makgetla and Seidman (1980:239-240) note the fact that the dominant commercial banks in the region—Barclays and Standard Bank—are also based in South Africa.

[13] Marais (1981:42-43) points out, for example, that for reasons of economy of scale, large capital-intensive industries producing processed raw materials require governmental assistance in the form of tariff protection in order to take control of the entire domestic market. However, even this form of state support will not resolve the problems of large industrial firms arising from economies of scale. A graphic illustration of this situation is the automobile industry. The economies of scale in the industry require sales of 100,000 units per model. However, in South Africa sales in 1978 were only 204,000 cars and about 100,000 commercial vehicles. Since there were ten major automobile producers in South Africa, it meant that approximately three-fourths of the models produced that year

means that large industrial firms cannot achieve economies of scale unless they can operate without interference not only in African countries in the region but also in the bantustans and in the so-called white (urban) areas. This situation has led industry analysts to conclude that the only real solution to the economies of scale problem (apart from expanding external markets) is to expand internal markets by increasing sales to blacks in South Africa.

Large industrial and commercial firms wish to encourage state intervention in black urban areas to build housing, provide electricity, and improve public services.[14] Similarly, the black commercial bourgeoisie—represented by the National African Federated Chambers of Commerce (NAFCOC), a South African umbrella organization of 14,000 members in 1984—is also interested in gaining state permission to operate in the white (urban) areas. Whereas the large industrial and commercial corporations do not pose a threat to black commercial interests because they are concentrated primarily in the small-scale retail and service sector, by contrast, the smaller white-controlled retail firms that have shown recent interest in the growing black urban market, estimated to be $4.5 billion in 1985, are of major concern to NAFCOC. The organization

---

were sold at below the break-even point of 5,000 units per year. This has led to vicious price cutting and a wide variation in models that has prevented any single company from controlling enough of the market to benefit from economies of scale (Myers 1980:256).

[14] The economic interests of large industrial capital would be well-served by state intervention on behalf of urban Africans. While the collective size of the black consumer market is growing (representing 40 percent of total personal income in 1983—SAIRR 1984:126), to date it has not been tapped by the large manufacturing firms. The reason for this is that black wages are too low to constitute a market for durable consumer goods and intermediate products in which large-scale industries specialize. Most African workers, for example, cannot afford to purchase a televison or automobile or to own their own home. And even if black workers could afford household appliances, most urban townships do not have electricity.

strongly defends the exclusion of white businesses from black urban areas on the grounds that whites have an unfair competitive advantage over them (*African Business* 1984q:25).[15]

In the aftermath of the upheavals of the 1970s, the National party made several important concessions to urban African businessmen and black urban workers. The transnational firms were regarded by the NP as being instrumental in implementing the changes,[16] which included modifications in the black urban land tenure policy and the removal of "racial discrimination" in the work place for skilled black workers.[17] Both of these concessions will increase market demand for industrial products.

Significant changes in black urban land tenure policy occurred in 1975 and 1979 when the government made it possible for the first time for blacks to purchase homes in Soweto and other black townships.[18] Indication of the im-

[15] Southall (1980:59) points out that in the retail sector (where black businesses are concentrated) black businessmen have opposed partnerships with white businessmen for fear of being taken over by them.

[16] The representatives of South Africa's major industrial corporations were not only involved in the implementation of the changes but also in actively lobbying both for revisions in the land tenure policy and for legislation for urban blacks to qualify for home loans (Myers 1980:73-74).

[17] Another action taken by the NP ostensibly designed to promote black businesses was the establishment of the Small Business Development Corporation (SBDC) in 1980. The SBDC is a joint venture (50-50) with private firms, the largest shareholders of which are the Sanlam group and Anglo American Corporation (the two largest conglomerates in the country). Under the terms of the amendment to the Group Areas Act, SBDC and its black clients are classified as being black when operating in a "black area" and white when operating in a "white area." At the end of 1984, it was estimated that SBDC owned property worth more than $38 million, with 900 tenants (80 percent black) who employed roughly 17,000.

[18] There are two ways in which this was to be achieved: a thirty-year home ownership scheme and a ninety-nine-year leasehold scheme. Under the terms of the home ownership scheme, which was introduced in 1975, registered tenants were entitled to purchase houses by making a 20 percent deposit and paying off the balance over a thirty-year period. In

portant role that the government expected the private sector to play in the provision of housing for blacks in urban areas was evident in the official estimates of the black housing backlog and the insufficient public financing available for this purpose. For example, the government's Viljoen Commission, which issued a report on black housing in 1981, estimated the black urban housing shortage to be 168,000 units in that year. The estimated cost of eliminating the backlog for black housing for the country as a whole (including the estimated shortage of 258,000 in the trust areas) was given as over 4.5 billion rands at 1982 prices, or 985 million rands for housing in the 1983 budget. However, the Department of Community Development, the ministry responsible for public housing schemes, allocated only 165 million rands for housing in its 1983 budget.

The private sector was expected to fill in this huge gap in the shortage of black urban housing. A further indication of the importance assigned to the private sector in helping the government to resolve the housing shortage was the housing scheme announced in 1983. Building societies, employers, and home owners were to be involved in a plan to sell an estimated 500,000 state-owned houses to low-income buyers during the 1983 to 1984 period. These houses were to be sold at a 40 percent discount and were expected to benefit primarily low-income blacks in urban areas (Nedbank Group, Ltd. 1983:247).

From the point of view of black urban businessman,

---

the case of the leasehold scheme, urban Africans who were outside of the homelands (that is, in the "white areas") and who already qualified for section 10 rights [that is, who were legally employed in "white (urban) areas"] were eligible to purchase a house and acquire a ninety-nine-year leasehold to the land. By August 1981, only an estimated 13,500 houses had been sold under the home ownership scheme, with another 1,000 registered, and 2,894 houses had been constructed and sold under the leasehold scheme (Nedbank Group, Ltd. 1983:246). The government has announced its intention to allow blacks who already have ninety-nine-year leases on property to own the land (New York Times 1985a).

home ownership made it possible for them to raise loans (with the lease as security) from commercial banks for business purposes. Likewise, for the well-paid black worker and professional it was possible for them to have a semblance of property ownership or equity rights in the white (urban) areas.

While state subventions for the purpose of building low-cost housing in these areas have been modest (in terms of the need), the large industrial corporations (particularly the TNCs) have allocated substantial sums for the construction of housing for blacks. They have also granted loans and loan guarantees for that purpose. The Urban Foundation (an association of the largest corporations, including major MNCs), for example, raised an estimated $100 million by 1980 (with an additional 43 million rands in 1983) to finance the construction of low-cost housing for urban blacks. The government has also made substantial outlays for improving the social infrastructure of African townships, such as the electrification of Soweto.

The second major concession made by the National party to urban blacks was an effort to restructure the labor market by giving urban "insiders" preferential access to jobs over contract workers from the homelands. This served the large industrial and commercial firms' goal of widening their markets in black urban areas. And, in fact, the Federated Chamber of Industries (FCI), one of the largest manufacturing employer organizations, as well as the (largely white) Association of Chambers of Commerce (AS-SOCOM), have been among the government's strongest supporters of restructuring the labor market.

The government's (partial) implementation of the Wiehahn and Riekert commissions of inquiry, which call for a "nondiscriminatory basis" for the work place,[19] will have

[19] The chief intended effect of the modifications for black workers was that it increase the rights of settled urban black workers provided the existing job reservation decrees affecting blacks were phased out. Under the new dispensation blacks may be trained as artisans and may seek em-

the inevitable result of creating a privileged urban black working class that should significantly expand the black consumer market. Such a modification of black labor law could also help resolve the transnationals' critical shortage of skilled and semiskilled workers. The National Productivity Institute of South Africa estimates, for example, that the economy requires 700,000 skilled professional and managerial personnel by 1987 if growth is to be sustained.[20]

From the point of view of large-scale manufacturing and commercial firms, such developments would be particularly salutary.[21] In addition to significantly expanding their markets and resolving their skilled manpower shortage, they would enable the corporations to deal with black trade unions, which are under stringent state control, rather than with the white trade unions, which have political leverage over the government.[22]

---

ployment in white areas. New labor laws, however, also increased the state's control over so-called black "migrants" or "commuters" (who comprised one worker in three in urban areas) and tightened the state's control over "recognized" black trade unions.

[20] Various methods have been tried to meet the critical skills shortage, especially during periods of economic upswing such as 1980 and 1981. For example, the government sought to increase both the inflow of skilled immigrants and the proportion of economically active white women and retired persons in the labor force. However, most industry analysts agree that these are only temporary stopgap measures to resolve a major structural deficiency in the available labor force.

[21] This is not to suggest, however, that areas of conflict do not exist between large corporate interests and government policy. For example, Hermann Giliomee points out the fact that large manufacturing firms want to do away with the government's influx control policy in order to be able to draw on black labor across the influx control boundaries. Business leaders are also less than enthusiastic about the government's policies of "economic decentralization," particularly for the development of the homelands for purely political or ideological reasons. (Private communication 1985.) For an elaboration of the reservations that large-scale capital interests have about supporting the NP's reform policies, see the *Financial Times* (1983).

[22] Such a development, however, does not necessarily imply either

Opposition to the National Party's Strategy

The white trade unions such as the Confederation of Labour, the Steelworkers' Union, the Construction Workers, the Mineworkers' Union, and others are vocal critics of the NP's strategy of relying upon transnational corporations to carry out a policy of stratifying the black urban labor force. The reason for this is that the plan involves hiring black skilled workers in place of white workers.[23] The strategy also threatens to end the privileged state support for white farmers and small white businessmen, and it places the burden of financing constitutional reforms upon the white working and middle classes.

White unions fear that the strength of black labor vis-à-vis white labor will increase without state intervention.

---

higher wages for skilled black workers nor increased job mobility. In fact, black workers have long been performing the skilled labor for which skilled white workers have been paid through job fragmentation and de-skilling. Moreover, even during periods of rapid growth in the economy, black workers in manufacturing industry only managed to increase their wages absolutely through overtime work, and they suffered a relative decline in their real earnings due to inflation (Keenan 1982). This would suggest that any significant improvement in the wages, working conditions, and job mobility of black workers is likely to come only from trade union bargaining with industrial firms. Moreover, the recession and the effects of the drought in the rural areas have tended to weaken the bargaining strength of black unions. This situation is unlikely to change at least until the economy recovers from the recession.

[23] Adam (1978:95) explains the government's "anti (white) union action" in terms of the state's "survival politics" in which national survival must come before avoiding class cleavages within the Afrikaner ruling group. Giliomee (1983:47) argues that the National party split of 1981/1982 can be explained in terms of class divisions. He attributes the split to the need for black skilled labor (presumably by the manufacturing industry), increased social services for urban blacks, support for the mining industry, and the withdrawal of state support for white agriculture. This was said to have eroded the economic position of lower-class Afrikaners. The Afrikaner working class thus supported the "right-wing opposition" (the CP and HNP), while the middle class supported the NP. According to Giliomee, the political contest between the NP and the CP is for the support of the Afrikaner lower middle class.

The extreme shortage of skilled manpower in such critical areas as electrical and chemical engineering, where gaps in personnel run as high as 22 and 16 percent respectively, adds to their concern. Another assault on white "job reservation" is that under the new labor laws some industrial unions that were previously restricted to white-only membership are now admitting blacks. The South African Boilermakers, the Iron and Steelworkers, and the Shipbuilders' and Welders' Society, for example, are integrating their unions.

It is hardly surprising, therefore, that conservative white trade union leaders have been among the most outspoken critics of the NP's policy of eliminating "racial discrimination" in the labor market. The opposition of white workers to the NP's limited implementation of the Wiehahn and Riekert proposals has found a political outlet in their support of the conservative opposition Afrikaner Herstigte Nasionale party. The April 1981 (white) general election and the October 1985 by-elections in South Africa revealed the electoral threat to the NP of blue-collar support for the HNP. Support for the party and its leader, Jaap Marais, by the white unions on the basis of "stopping the advance of blacks in industry" has produced an unprecedented degree of electoral support. It was estimated, for example, that one-third of all Afrikaners (which comprise 60 percent of the white electorate) voted for the HNP in the last general election of 1981. While the HNP has only a single seat in Parliament, the other conservative Afrikaner party, the Conservative party, holds 18 seats in Parliament of which 16 representatives won as Nationalists prior to the split in the party in 1982. Present projections expect the HNP/CP at this stage to win between 25 and 32 seats in a general election (which must take place before the end of 1989). The NP holds an unassailable majority of 126 parliamentary seats out of 178. However, it faces the danger of serious inroads on the right by the conservative Afrikaner parties and on its left by the official opposition party, the

Progressive Federal party (PFP, which has 27 seats). This could pose a threat to the NP's centrist position in the white electorate, which is the basis of its claim to being the only party capable of governing South Africa.

The second major source of opposition to the NP's alliance strategy with large commercial and industrial corporations is conservative Afrikaner civil servants and low-income state employees whose economic security and social status are threatened by the dismantling of the state institutions responsible for administrating and maintaining separate development (Adam and Giliomee 1979:186). Opposition is strong within the middle and lower echelons of the state bureaucracy, especially in the departments of Defence, Law and Order, National Education, and Cooperation and Development. Officials in these ministries have a vested interest in administering the approximately four thousand laws and six thousand regulations affecting the private sector (Coker 1981:239). An example of their opposition to the NP's labor reform strategy was the government's withdrawal of its legislative proposal embodying the recommendations of the Riekert commission, an action that it was forced to take when it was discovered that in the process of drafting the legislation (involving the repeal of sixty-two separate actions of parliament) the civil service had completely subverted the intention of the legislation.

The Transvaal is the seat of the state bureaucracy and is also where the leader of the CP, Andries Treurnicht, headed the Transvaal National party before his defection in 1982. This is where the CP has its stronghold of electoral support. For example, in national opinion surveys the CP has consistently polled 19 percent of the white electorate compared to as high as 40 percent in the Transvaal. However, following the CP's strong showing in the urban Primrose parliamentary by-election of 1984, Treurnicht claimed that the CP was now a political power capable of defeating the NP in any seat in the country. He argued that the CP's political support was no longer limited to the traditional strongholds of the Orange Free State and the Transvaal. Treurnicht asserts that the CP is now acceptable to Afrikaners as well as English speakers in the urban areas.

Conservative party supporters are strongly opposed to any modification of separate development such as the government's De Lange commission report, which recommended the phasing out of discrimination in education.[24] They also oppose the constitutional "power-sharing" reforms that include coloreds, Indians, and whites. However, the area where CP supporters converge with the HNP in their opposition to the NP is their condemnation of the ruling party's political alliance with transnational corporations.[25] For example, Treurnicht has attacked the relationship between "big business" and the government on the grounds that it placed the burden of financing "multi-racialism" upon whites.[26] He argues, for example, that

[24] The CP enjoys the support of the faculties of education and theology at the Afrikaans universities of Pretoria and Potchefstroom in the Transvaal. The influential Professor Hennie Maree, head of the Transvaal Teachers' Association and the rector of the Pretoria Teachers' College, also supports the Conservative party.

[25] Giliomee points out that most of the CP's support comes from marginal farmers, lower-income state employees, and small businessmen. He argues that the basis of their opposition to the NP is a defense of "ethnic political claims" embodied in the apartheid ideology. Hence, he asserts that if the NP had stuck to "political apartheid, the alliance with big business would not have cost it political support." (Private communication 1985.) However, while apartheid ideology, which is associated with Afrikaner rule, was undoubtedly an important factor in precipitating the political divisions within Afrikanerdom, this does not rule out the class nature of that conflict. The NP's strategy to reform the apartheid regime, which has the strong backing of large industrial firms, has undoubtedly contributed to these divisions.

[26] Constitutional development and planning for multiracial reform received the second largest budget allocation in the 1985 budget, second only to finance. Constitutional development received an allocation of over 5.3 billion rands (*Rand Daily Mail* 1985).

while this has imposed a massive burden on white taxpay-
ers, the rate of taxation on big business has fallen during
Botha's administration. Treurnicht has charged that under
Botha's government the building societies have been
"bleeding the middle class dry," the six largest banks have
paid less than 1 percent of their profits in tax in 1983/1984,
an estimated twenty thousand farmers have been forced off
their land for nonpayment of debt owed to the banks. The
principal beneficiaries of the dramatic fall in the value of
the rand are said to be the gold-mining companies who,
with the deepening of the recession, have been able to
"buy up South Africa" (The Star 1985). He points out, for
example, that the Anglo American Corporation alone controls 72 percent of the total listed companies on Johannesburg's stock exchange.

Leaders of the CP and HNP have attacked the "constellation of states" strategy of the National party for being
self-defeating. They argue that increased economic cooperation between South Africa and "Marxist states" on
South Africa's borders (Mozambique and Zimbabwe) is
counterproductive. Instead of heightening the costs to
"hostile" border states of supporting the operations of liberation movements against South Africa, it tends to reward
them.[27]

What is significant about conservative opposition to the
NP's alliance strategy[28] is that it has increased rather than

[27] For the results of a survey of HNP opinion on how best to cope with
"hostile" black states on South Africa's borders, see Geldenhuys (1982).

[28] Giliomee questions the argument that CP/HNP opposition to the NP
flows from the latter's political alliance with transnationals. Instead, he
argues that their opposition to the NP is based upon ending state subsidies for lower-income whites through inflated white salaries and job reservation. (Private communication 1985.) According to this logic, the state
undertook this change because of the recognition that it had to modernize
its form of "racial domination." However, there is evidence to suggest
that working-class whites were threatened by the NP's support for transnational corporations. For example, Geldenhuys (1984:219) notes the fact
that the NP launched the process of labor reform in the 1970s (leading to

decreased the ruling party's need to ally politically with transnational corporations if it is to carry out its reforms. The erosion of the NP's traditional Afrikaner electoral constituency has made it imperative for the ruling party to compensate for the loss by attracting white English-speaking voters who are needed for the NP to get a solid white mandate to carry out its reforms. In order to accomplish this the NP must have the political support of precisely the English-speaking industrial and commercial business class that, ironically, contributed to the conservative Afrikaner opposition in the first place. However, the apparent abandonment by the large corporations of the NP's reform strategy after the massive two-day strike in Johannesburg in November 1984 by an estimated 500,000 black workers has added to the government's dilemma.

Nevertheless, even if the NP had succeeded in its alliance strategy, there is serious doubt as to whether the black urban threat to white hegemony would have been resolved. In the best-case scenario (from the NP's point of view), the stratification of the black urban community into a small privileged labor force and a black commercial business class would have "stabilized" the black townships in the "white (urban) areas." On the other hand, the creation of a black urban middle class near South Africa's cities without the political rights to protect their newly acquired economic privileges and status could have set the stage for revolutionary resistance to any attempt to withdraw or eliminate these privileges. Therefore, even if the NP had been successful in carrying out its alliance strategy, it might have been faced with a potentially greater threat.

---

the Wiehahn commission inquiries), which the white working class regards as a major threat, partly in response to the disinvestment campaign directed at the transnationals. In other words, in order to protect the interests of large industrial corporations in South Africa, the NP was prepared to sacrifice the interests of the white working class.

ZIMBABWE

The Rhodesian state was primarily designed to serve the interests of a small white social economic elite (roughly 223,000 whites out of a total population of 7 million at independence in 1980) by fostering the growth of a dominant, regionally oriented manufacturing industry along with commercial farming and mining. The transition to Zimbabwe's political independence was achieved through peaceful democratically contested elections that ultimately transferred state power to the de facto ruling party, the Zimbabwe African National Union (ZANU).[29] However, ZANU's political support (particularly in the rural areas of the eastern provinces) is based upon a militant populist ideology advocating radical social, economic, and political reform of the state.

In the process of taking political control of the state the

[29] The February 1980 elections that preceded Zimbabwe's independence gave the Zimbabwe African National Union-Patriotic Front (ZANU-PF) 57 out of the 80 African seats in the new Parliament. The remaining 20 reserved seats went to the all-white Republican party (now named the Conservative Alliance party). ZANU-PF's rival nationalist party—the former Zimbabwe African People's Union (ZAPU), renamed the Patriotic Front party (PFP)—won 20 of the African seats, and the United African National Council (UANC) of Bishop Muzorewa won 3 seats. ZANU-PF was therefore the majority party and on that basis formed Zimbabwe's first black government. While the ZANU-PF formed a coalition government with the PFP, the long-standing bitter rivalry between the two parties erupted in armed conflict in November 1980 resulting in a steadily deteriorating political relationship between the parties (see *New African* 1980a). Since the outbreak of violent clashes between the rival parties, ZANU has declared itself the de facto ruling party. In August 1984, following the party's first congress in twenty years, ZANU reverted to its original name and dropped the Patriotic Front from its title. The congress also adopted resolutions declaring its intention to establish a one-party state (through constitutional means) and to follow "Marxist-Leninist principles" (*Africa Research Bulletin* 1984a:7,345). In the July 1985 elections the ruling ZANU party won 63 seats to the PFP's 15 seats in Parliament.

newly independent government appointed a group of technocratic elites whose principal task was to facilitate the maximum productive output of the inherited settler economy. However, this political objective conflicts with the populist goals of the rural supporters of ZANU who demand a significant restructuring of the economy to benefit them.

This has given rise to a major factional conflict within the Zimbabwean state between state technocrats and populist ZANU politicians. While both factions are represented in the cabinet and in the central committee, the technocratic faction is concentrated primarily in the economic and finance ministries and central bank while the populist faction is concentrated in the ninety-member central committee and the supreme fifteen-member politburo.

The outcome of the contest for control of public policy between the technocratic and populist factions will determine the extent to which the state continues to give priority support to the regional manufacturing industry as well as to farming and mining. Their continued priority treatment will probably involve major political costs to the ruling party. In the absence of high annual growth rates, priority treatment of modern sector industries will tend to seriously erode ZANU's political support in the rural communal areas among peasants, ex-ZANU guerillas, and urban workers.

Strategic Importance of State Support for the Manufacturing Industry

There are parallels between the structures of the Zimbabwean and South African economies. In both countries manufacturing is the dominant industry. Table 2.2 shows the industrial origin of the gross domestic product of South Africa and Zimbabwe. The data indicate that primary industries in both South Africa and Zimbabwe are subordinate to manufacturing and commerce in terms of GDP.

Table 2.2   Industrial Origin of GDP in South Africa and
Zimbabwe

	South Africa (1967)	Zimbabwe (1975)
Agriculture	12%	16%
Mining	12	7
Total primary sectors	24	23
Manufacturing	21	25
Construction	6	5
Electricity and water	3	3
Transport and communication	10	5
Wholesale and retail trade	13	14
Banking, insurance, and real estate	4	5
Public administration and services	10	11
Other services	9	9
Total secondary and tertiary sectors	76	77
GDP in millions of Zimbabwean dollars	9,032	1,909

SOURCE: *Africa South of the Sahara* (1981:1200).

Manufacturing and utilities in Zimbabwe contributed 28 percent to its GDP (the highest in sub-Saharan Africa, including South Africa), while agriculture contributed 16 percent and mining only 7 percent.

Another distinctive characteristic of Zimbabwe's economy is its regional integration. Unlike most African countries that exported on average only 8 percent of their goods to other African states in 1965, Rhodesia exported 38 percent of its commodities to African countries in that year. Since the bulk of Zimbabwe's regional exports are manufactured goods, it means that in order for the largest sector in the economy to grow, Zimbabwe's manufacturing industry must be competitive with its only regional manufacturing rival—South Africa. The domestic political significance of Zimbabwe's regionally oriented manufacturing industry is that the state must support the industry in order for the country's manufactured exports to remain competitive in regional markets.

One major reason that the Rhodesian economy continued to grow from 1965 to 1974 under UDI was precisely because of state support for the use of manufacturing industry's excess capacity, which had been underutilized after the breakup of the federation in 1963. The state provided tariff protection to guarantee local markets for Rhodesian manufacturers and assisted firms to expand into products that were no longer imported because of UDI. The excess capacity of Rhodesia's regional manufacturing industry made possible an increase in the number of new products from 1,059 in 1966 to 3,837 in 1970 (Wield 1981:155).

In addition, the state Industrial Development Corporation helped manufacturers to secure private foreign capital. Public loans were made for the expansion of the country's iron and steel industry, abattoirs, and meat-freezing industries. The state also became heavily involved in providing economic infrastructure, cheap energy, and transportation for manufacturers. Just prior to independence, an estimated 25 percent of the current budget and about 40 percent of the total capital budget was allocated to economic services for infrastructure and the productive sectors (Rhodesia Railways, Air Rhodesia, and the Electricity Supply Commission) (USAID 1977f:II, 4). As a result, the manufacturing industry experienced an overall annual growth rate of 9.6 percent by volume.

Table 2.3 shows the expansion of the manufacturing industry in the Rhodesian economy during the 1966 to 1975 period. Manufacturing increased from 122.9 million Rhodesian dollars in 1966 to 474.5 million in 1975, more than doubling. This was an increase from 18 percent of the total value of output to 25 percent, while European commercial agriculture and mining remained constant over the same period.

Table 2.3   The Manufacturing Industry in Rhodesia's Economy, 1966-1975

	1966			1975		
Sectors	Value	%	Volume Index	Value	%	Volume Index
Manufacturing	122.9	18	98.6	474.5	25	204.3
European agriculture	85.8	12	112.8	216.3	12	172.2
Mining	45.2	7	105.3	132.5	7	186.6

SOURCE: Riddell (1977:7).
NOTES: Volume index in millions of Rhodesian dollars.
1 Rhodesian dollar = U.S. $1.40 in 1966 and $1.60 in 1975.

After 1974, however, there was a decline in production volume of 27 percent between 1974 and 1978, and profit margins began to decline after 1974. While the onset of the worldwide recession undoubtedly contributed to the downturn in Rhodesia's manufacturing industry, another factor of equal importance was that import-substitution growth had reached a point of diminishing returns. Further growth in Rhodesia's manufacturing industry required export-led growth.[30] Moreover, what was required was not simply further export volume within existing trading patterns but rather the restoration of Rhodesia's highly profitable trading relationships with its former federation states to the north (Zambia and Malawi) plus the penetration of the markets of other states in the region.

[30] It is obvious that the pursuit of this policy ignores the issue of domestic income distribution and the desirability of restructuring the industry to meet growing domestic demands.

Technocratic Faction

Soon after independence, the ZANU-PFP coalition government appointed a group of bureaucratic officials to head the economic and finance ministries and the central bank.[31] These state bureaucrats were professionally trained and had been grafted onto the inherited Rhodesian state apparatus.[32] Some were Western-trained intellectuals who were in exile during the war. Others were key functionaries in the Rhodesian civil service or represented farming or business interests under that regime.

They assumed their positions after Zimbabwe's independence without, however, participating in ZANU's seven-year-long guerilla war. Hence, the technocratic faction of the state bureaucracy was not part of ZANU's radical populist tradition that took root in the party's rural branches during the war. The exclusion of technocratic elites from ZANU's supreme policy-making organ is thus indicative of the fact that their policy positions do not necessarily coincide with the positions articulated by popu-

[31] The leading representative of this faction is the head of the ministry of Finance, Economic Planning, and Development (FEPD), Dr. Bernard Chidzero. The FEPD included top-level civil servants who worked closely with Chidzero, such as Tom Mswaka, Tim Mzondo, and Mudzi Nziramasanga. It also included Dr. Simbarashe Makoni, minister of industry and energy development, Dr. Witness Mangwende, minister of foreign affairs, a white minister of agriculture, Denis Norman (dismissed in July 1985), and white deputy ministers John Landau for trade and commerce and Chris Anderson, minister of state for public service.

[32] Professional training alone did not determine members' identification with the technocratic state faction. For example, Dr. Herbert Ushewondunze, the ex-minister of health and recently minister of transport, was a medical doctor by training, a member of the central committee and politburo of the party, and a leading representative of the populist faction. Likewise, Dr. Sydney Sekeramayi, the minister of health, was a medical doctor, member of the central committee and the politburo, and yet he was also associated with the populist faction of the party. Technocrats tended to be located in the technical economic ministries and departments and the central bank, and they have largely been excluded from the party's supreme policy-making organ—the politburo.

list politicians. Hence, key representatives of the state apparatus, such as the minister of finance, economic planning, and development, are not members of the politburo.

The technocratic faction of the state assumes that high productive output and high export earnings from modern sector industries should be Zimbabwe's overriding economic objective. Hence, the principal preoccupation of the technocrats is with attracting and retaining foreign and local capital and skills required to maintain high levels of growth in modern sector industries. They take the position that capitalist sources of aid, trade, and investment are essential for the implementation of the country's developmental goals. Therefore substantial Western aid and favorable terms of trade is a sine qua non for redistributing land to the peasantry and achieving a more equitable distribution of income in the country.[33] By implication, adverse trade balances, low world prices for export commodities, and low levels of aid (all beyond Zimbabwe's control) are major barriers to achieving the country's developmental objectives.

Technocrats also believe that in order to "bring development to the people" public expenditure should focus upon expanding social services, education, health, and employment. However, this public expenditure for "development" should be strictly conditioned by Zimbabwe's export earnings, foreign investment, and Western aid. Therefore, without high annual growth rates (contingent

[33] Zimbabwe has one of the highest income differentials in the world. The annual income of European, Asian, and coloreds in urban areas in 1979 was $8,500, while the average income of rural farmers who were dependent on peasant agriculture was $220 a year. The income differential between these two groups was 39:1. The high-income urban elite total 90,000, whereas the peasant cultivators number approximately 750,000. The within-group income differentials are also just as great. For example, income differentials between the top and bottom in the urban economy are on an order of magnitude of 27:1 (Zimbabwe 1981a:77-78).

upon large inflows of foreign capital and aid) governmental expenditures for developmental needs must give way. This outcome was explicitly acknowledged by the minister of finance, Dr. Bernard Chidzero, when the Three-Year Transitional Development Plan (1982-1985) was released. In response to questions about the plan's ambitious projected annual growth rates, Chidzero said that given the country's high population growth rates "we are sunk" (referring to developmental plans) if Zimbabwe has an economic growth rate below 8 percent (*Africa Research Bulletin* 1982a:6,668).[34]

The actual growth rate in 1982 was closer to 2 or 3 percent, with a negative rate of growth in 1983 and little or no prospect of improvement through 1985. The decline in Zimbabwe's real growth in 1981 was the backdrop for the fiscally conservative 1982/1983 budget, which made major cuts in social welfare programs, and severely reduced governmental expenditures for developmental programs.[35]

[34] The assumption that Zimbabwe's developmental objectives were dependent upon high annual rates of growth in the modern sector was undoubtedly a major reason (apart from lack of analysis) for the optimistic projected real growth rate of 8 percent compounded each year to 1985 on which the Transitional Development Plan was based. This also helps explain the conservative population estimates in the plan, which were based upon an extrapolation of the 1969 population census projected for 1981. While there is still speculation as to whether the population estimates in the plan were lower than the actual population figures, there is little doubt that the actual annual population growth rate of between 3.5 and 4.3 percent exceeded the plan's 3.3 percentage estimate.

[35] Lower than expected export earnings, investment, and foreign aid combined to erase projected economic growth and planned developmental objectives. For example, the September 1981 London sugar price was £220 a ton, or one-half the November 1980 price of £410 a ton. Beef exports, which were valued at 30 million Zimbabwean dollars in 1979, will be negligible for the foreseeable future due to severe domestic shortages of beef. Likewise, the volume of mineral production has fallen since 1976, and the value of mineral production dropped by 10 percent in 1981 with no real prospect for higher world mineral prices in the near future (EIU 1981:101). The three-year program for Zimbabwe's "reconstruction and development" announced in March 1981 has also fallen far short of

The stated objectives of the 1982/1983 budget were to re-
dress imbalances between recurrent spending and investment, to encourage exports, discourage imports, and to
meet the skills-training needs of industry (*Standard Chartered Review* 1982:10).

The 1983/1984 budget resulted in further austerities,
and the minister of finance acknowledged the government's inability to achieve planned objectives. While the
representatives of modern sector industries were not entirely satisfied with the budget, they said that it was less severe than they had expected. The Confederation of Zimbabwe Industries, for example, called the budget "fair."[36]
The 1984/1985 budget followed the pattern of the previous

---

expectations (*Standard Chartered Review* 1981:7). Of the total external
resources required for the plan—known as the Zimbabwe Conference on
Reconstruction and Development (ZIMCORD)—only $400 million of the
nearly $2 billion ZIMCORD pledge had actually been disbursed. In addi-
tion, ZIMCORD's major donor country, the United States, cut its aid to
Zimbabwe by almost 50 percent in 1984 in response to Mugabe's criticism of the United States for trying to turn the Korean airliner incident
into a "superpower versus superpower confrontation" (*African Business*
1984w:6). According to the Three-Year Transitional Development Plan,
developmental objectives were based on the assumption that the net inflow of private foreign investment would be 175 million Zimbabwean
dollars per annum during the 1981 to 1984 plan period. However, in fact,
during this period, an estimated total net foreign investment of less than
40 million Zimbabwean dollars was made (*African Business* 1984:31).

[36] The business community expressed its satisfaction that, given the
government's commitment to "socialist transformation" of the economy,
the 1983/1984 budget was the best that could be expected in difficult
times. The budget increased the 1982/1983 allocation for the export incentive scheme for manufactured goods (to $9.8 million) and retained in-
vestment allowances in manufacturing and mining. It also allocated a $64
million subsidy for the mining industry (*Africa Research Bulletin*
1983:6,949-6,951) Seidman has noted in this regard that Chidzero refused
to tax the investable surplus in the country, which was largely in the
hands of the transnational corporations, in the hope that that surplus
would be redirected into restructuring the economy (private communication 1984). The upshot of this, however, was that an estimated 50 percent of the after tax profits of these corporations was allowed to leave the
country.

two budgets. Faced with contracting GDP (−1 percent in 1982 and −4 percent in 1983), rising budget deficits (717 million Zimbabwean dollars in 1984), and high inflation (19.5 percent in 1984), the budget called for more austerities for urban workers and rural peasants. However, it provided substantial assistance for modern sector industries. For example, during the period February 1983 to May 1984, the government provided state aid to manufacturers and to the mining companies exceeding 75 million Zimbabwean dollars (U.S. $68 million). The government's Industrial Development Corporation also invested a further 5 million Zimbabwean dollars in private enterprises that were threatened with closure. There were major export incentives, and the government secured a U.S. $75 million loan from the World Bank to promote exports (*African Business* 1984i:69-71; *African Business* 1984:31; and *African Business* 1984u:7).

Outside of the business community, however, the reaction to the budgets was less than enthusiastic. From the point of view of the majority of rural and urban poor the budgets (in conjunction with other governmental policies such as a wage freeze in force since 1981) were disastrous. Food subsidies were eliminated and yet there was an 80 percent increase in the price of goods purchased by low-income groups since the last wage increase. The 1983/1984 budget also introduced a 2 percent tax on low-income workers who earned more than 100 Zimbabwean dollars per month and who were not previously subject to income tax. This means that an additional 500,000 workers were subject to taxes in 1984.[37]

The budgets have also drastically cut allocations for the government's major developmental programs. For exam-

[37] Ann Seidman has pointed out that while the government's economic strategy placed the burden of the country's economic crisis upon the urban workers and peasants, corporate capital did not share in that sacrifice (private communication 1984). For example, the effective corporate tax remained under 30 percent.

ple, the housing allocation for low-income families was cut by more than 67 percent in the 1983/1984 budget. The rural development program (where 60 percent of the population resides) was cut by 50 percent to only 32.1 million Zimbabwean dollars. Allocations for the crucial land resettlement program were also virtually eliminated in the 1984/1985 budget. The political significance of this budget cut is that ZANU'S 1980 election platform that brought Robert Mugabe's government to power was based upon a promise to redistribute land to peasants.

The initial resettlement program involved moving roughly 18,000 families onto 1.1 million hectares of formerly white-owned commercial farmland over a three-year period. However, by March 1982, only 8,600 families had actually been settled on 520,000 hectares of farm and grazing land. Furthermore, with the drastic reductions for land resettlement, the government's promise to redistribute land in the rural areas will go unfulfilled.[38]

The disruption of Rhodesia's original trading pattern was regarded by the technocratic faction as being a major reason for Rhodesia's declining terms of trade and its balance of payments disequilibria. During the fifteen years of UDI from 1965 to 1980, the country's terms of trade shifted downward from an index value of 100 in 1964 to only 55.9 in 1979. Zimbabwe's terms of trade improved to 76.8 in 1981 as a result of the removal of international sanctions and the partial restoration of the country's pre-UDI trading pattern (Zimbabwe 1983:15). However, this was still substantially below the 1964 figure. The decline in Zimbabwe's terms of trade is undoubtedly related to the domination of South Africa as its principal trading partner and the fact that the relationship favors South Africa. For example, in 1983, Zimbabwe's external trade with South Af-

---

[38] Riddell (1984:468) estimates that by the end of 1983, no more than 40,000 families had been resettled out of the targeted 162,000 families that required land.

rica registered a deficit of 73 million Zimbabwean dollars (EIU 1986:25).

The backdrop of the technocrats' efforts to restore Zimbabwe's original pattern of trading relationships was the decline in real growth rate and record deficits shortly after independence. In 1981, Zimbabwe experienced a record deficit on current account of balance of payments of U.S. $382 million, rising to about $500 million in 1982 (10.7 percent of GDP), and with $800 million projected for 1983. This growing deficit was largely due to lower commodity prices for Zimbabwe's primary products in world markets.

The government's negotiations with the International Monetary Fund for balance of payments financing in 1982 (after a drawing in 1981) strengthened the technocrats' ability to determine the country's economic policy. Following the standard format for "stabilization" agreements authorizing balance of payments assistance, the IMF presented a package of policy prescriptions as a condition for their funding. Foremost among the fund's policy proposals was a devaluation of the Zimbabwean dollar within the range of 30 to 35 percent and a reduction in the government's external deficit.[39] They also insisted upon cuts in current expenditures for defense, education, health, and other social services and employment for the rural and urban poor.

The IMF recommended that wage increases be kept in line with productivity, that consumer subsidies be reduced, that there be a freeze on short-term (one-year) foreign loans, and that restrictions on the repatriation of capital abroad be relaxed.[40] All of these measures had the support of the technocratic faction.

---

[39] Seidman has pointed out the fact that the devaluation actually increased the deficit by as much as one-third (private communication 1984).

[40] Seidman also notes that as a result of the initial relaxation of controls on the repatriation of capital abroad, the outflow of investment income

A major objective of the fund's stabilization program was to make Zimbabwe's export industries more competitive. Of particular significance in this regard was the country's manufacturing export industry. For example, the devaluation was expected to make Zimbabwe's exports in Southern Africa more competitive with its chief rival—South Africa.[41] Zimbabwe's large external deficits, its massive importation, and high inflation tended to "overvalue" its currency against the South African rand. In addition, South Africa devalued the rand by 20 percent against the U.S. dollar in 1981. This added further competitive pressure on Zimbabwe's regional exporters.

In recommending a devaluation of Zimbabwe's dollar, the IMF was urging a policy that it was also simultaneously recommending for other Southern African countries such as Botswana and Malawi. However, devaluation was particularly important for Zimbabwe because the terms of trade with its main trading partner, South Africa, were deteriorating and its exporters were threatened with losing markets in Southern Africa.

The growing foreign exchange shortage and increasing indebtedness placed the government in a dilemma of allocating limited foreign exchange between export industries and developmental programs. The fact that the IMF was practically the only source of funding on the scale required (upwards of 300 million Zimbabwean dollars) available to Zimbabwe gave the technocratic faction the necessary leverage to outcompete alternative positions.

---

rose from about $80 million in 1980 to $250 million in 1982 (private communication 1984).

[41] The tobacco industry favored the devaluation in order to lower its costs of production. However, the violent fluctuations in the price for tobacco and other primary commodities tended to override the price competitiveness of these products. The mining industry also welcomed the devaluation, hoping that it would earn greater revenue and thus improve the industry's cash flow situation. However, because of low international demand for minerals and resulting low prices, low or no growth was expected in the mining industry in the foreseeable future.

In December 1982, the government devalued by 20 percent. This was followed by a "managed float" that in effect increased the devaluation by an additional 10 to 15 percent. This brought Zimbabwe's dollar value within the 30 to 35 percent devaluation proposed by the IMF. An added significance of the managed float is that it was based upon the value of Zimbabwe's major trading partners' currencies (using the Reserve Bank's daily exchange rate quotations) rather than being based upon the IMF's "basket of currencies." This was designed to improve Zimbabwe's terms of trade with its partners in Southern Africa.

The day following the 20 percent devaluation, Finance Minister Chidzero announced further changes in policy. In order to reduce the "excessive demand" for imports he stated that wages were to be frozen and governmental subsidies on maize meal (the food staple) would be eliminated. The effect of this action was to increase the price of maize by as much as 50 percent. The price rise in maize meal was part of the government's efforts to phase out food subsidies altogether. The prices of bread, cooking oil, and margarine had already been raised by 12 percent (having been subsidized under the first two post-independence budgets).

Populist Opposition

There is a powerful populist political faction within the Zimbabwean state that is opposed to the technocratic faction's efforts to restore the country's pre-UDI regional trading pattern.[42] The populist faction of politicians is concen-

---

[42] The priority that was assigned to restoring Zimbabwe's pre-UDI regional trading pattern was not the only issue dividing the technocratic and populist factions of the state. Other areas of disagreement included the "reform" of the judicial system, civil service, and police, the narrowing of the wage gap in the labor force, the role of private capital in the economy (foreign private capital in particular), the Lancaster House agreement (constitutionally valid until 1990) that guarantees property

trated in the central committee and the politburo of ZANU.[43]

The base of ZANU's popular political support is the peasantry in the rural areas of the eastern provinces where ZANU's guerilla army, the Zimbabwe African National Liberation Army (ZANLA), created a grass-roots party structure during the war. Beginning in 1972, ZANLA cadres established party organs from the village unit up to the provincial level in order to create a popular base of support necessary to carry out the classic guerilla tactic of hiding among the people as "fish in the sea." As the war progressed, ZANLA forces elaborated party organization in order to incorporate the rural population and thereby expand their popular base of support in the countryside (Cliffe et al. 1980; Rich 1982; Bratton 1978).

An important legacy of ZANLA's mobilization of the peasantry during the liberation war was their indoctrination of a radical Marxist ideology. The ideology advocates a form of socialist rural economy with Yugoslavia, Romania, Bulgaria, and mainland China as models. ZANLA guerillas apparently had great success in indoctrinating the peasantry in *pungwes* (public meetings). As the outcome of the 1980 independence election revealed, ZANU's

---

rights and requires compensation for nationalization in foreign exchange, and the extent and speed of land resettlement for the majority of landless peasants. For a discussion of the political controversy between the factions, see Libby (1984).

[43] Leading representatives of this faction were Edgar Tekere, the exsecretary-general of ZANU, provincial chairman of Manicaland province, and member of the central committee; Enos Nkala, ex-finance minister, minister of national supplies, member of the central committee, and chairman of the economic committee of the politburo; and Herbert Ushewokunze, minister of transport, member of the central committee, and member of the politburo. While no single politician nor indeed group of them represent the populist faction within the Zimbabwean state, the public statements and argumentation used by these three party leaders constitutes the basis for my characterization of the economic policy positions of the faction.

ideology proved to be a major source of popular appeal in the rural areas of the eastern provinces. The party's radical ideology was also attractive to Shona youth, intellectuals, and the urban middle class.[44] It made the party and its national leadership appear to epitomize militant nationalism and also made it seem to many to be the only one capable of implementing radical social, economic, and political change. Rich points out, for example, that in the Midlands, where rival guerilla armies operated, ZANU's ideology played an important role in its election victory (Rich 1982:47-48).

ZANU's populist ideology has also influenced the government's economic policy documents. For example, the 1981 white paper entitled "Growth with Equity" bore the rhetoric of the populist position on economic policy. One of the fourteen listed objectives of the government is to "end imperialist exploitation" (implying foreign investment) and to "promote participation in, and ownership of, a significant portion of the economy by nationals and the state." When this objective was added to the highest listed priority of establishing a "society founded on socialist, democratic and egalitarian principles" (Zimbabwe 1981), the effect was to discourage foreign investors.

The populist faction emphasizes expansionist, redistributive, inward-looking, and noncapitalist policies. However, this mitigates against the technocratic faction's monetarist and free trade orientation that supports the restoration of Zimbabwe's pre-UDI regional trading relationships. The populist position on the country's economic policy was that the redistribution of national wealth must take precedence over the growth of export industries.

---

[44] An indication of the strong ideological orientation of the party was the resolutions that were adopted by the August 1984 ZANU party congress, which was attended by six thousand party officials. The congress adopted by acclamation a resolution that committed ZANU to follow "Marxist-Leninist principles to transform the society and its economy" (Africa Research Bulletin 1984a:7,345).

The most prominent exponent of the populist position on this issue is Enos Nkala. Nkala's presentation of Zimbabwe's 1982 budget to the Parliament was an occasion for elaborating the populist position on the issue of redistributing national wealth. In his speech Nkala argued that the budget was designed to transfer wealth from whites and middle-class blacks to the poor (mainly unskilled black workers and the unemployed) and to expand land resettlement,[45] public housing, education, and health services. He explained that the budget asked the rich to pay so that the poor would have something to look forward to in the future if not immediately. Nkala pointed out that if the program as outlined in the budget were properly carried out, it would substantially benefit the rural and urban poor. He also underscored the fact that everyone must sacrifice and that the more affluent one was, the bigger the sacrifice would have to be.

Specific budget measures included a capital gains tax on all sales of immoveable property at a flat rate of 30 percent, an increase in the general sales tax, and a cut in travel allowances by half. However, despite tax measures aimed at the affluent, budget deficits increased dramatically. For example, the abolition of primary school fees and the provision of free medical services for lower paid workers and their families increased national expenditure by 40 percent in one year alone, producing a budget deficit of nearly U.S. $400 million (*New African* 1981:59).

The country's critical foreign exchange shortage and increasing indebtedness, which precipitated IMF intervention, led to a setback for the populist faction. However, populist pressure within the ruling party remains power-

[45] Seidman has noted the fact that the government did not nationalize badly needed land for resettlement on the grounds that they did not have the resources to purchase the land from settler farmers and that it would threaten cash crop output. In Seidman's view the problem was a lack of political will to carry out the necessary "socialist" restructuring of the economy. (Private communication 1984.)

ful. At ZANU party meetings in the rural areas, for example, there are reports of growing demands for more radical socialist development programs, particularly in the area of land reform. This is a major source of popular frustration since there are estimated to be 800,000 families or more living on communal lands (formerly Tribal Trust Lands). These lands are only capable of providing low but adequate income for 325,000 families.[46]

One consequence of the inadequate carrying capacity of the communal areas is a growing number of illegal squatters on commercial land. In late 1982, it was estimated that there were ninety thousand illegal squatters in eastern Manicaland alone. This has placed pressure on the government to provide squatters with free food distribution and subsidies.

There have also been a series of protests in the villages led by ZANU party activists, including some of the twenty thousand ex-ZANU guerillas who are unemployed. ZANU activists have challenged the policies and the authority of local government administration. For example, beginning in September 1981, there were protests against district officers accused of favoritism, nepotism, and malpractice. This prompted the progovernment daily, *The Herald*, to warn that protests were a new and dangerous precedent; there was no guarantee that demonstrators would not turn against the government whenever they felt they had a case

[46] Zimbabwe's three-year-long drought had a particularly crippling effect in the communal areas. For example, it was estimated that in 1983, the value of crop sales from communal areas was down by 30 percent, with a 40 percent decline estimated for 1984. This prompted the government to institute a drought levy to finance the National Drought Insurance Fund to help alleviate some of the effects of the drought in the communal areas. A related consequence of the drought and a relaxation of population control originally instituted by the Rhodesian regime has been a large-scale urban migration and the emergence of squatter settlements in the cities. The government has been ambivalent on this issue. While publicly condemning illegal squatting, for example, they have yet to systematically evict squatters (*Africa* 1984g:34).

(*The Herald* 1981). Demonstrations among villagers have continued, and their demands for radical reform have grown in intensity.

To date the technocrats, with the backing of the IMF, have been able to ensure priority governmental support for the modern sector industries. However, this is not to say that the populist faction has not also received state support for their policy priorities. For example, despite Chidzero's persistent plea for budgetary restraint and, in particular, his opposition to external borrowing to support recurrent budget items such as health and education, the government has increased its public sector debt by 600 percent since independence. Zimbabwe's debt service ratio (interest on principal) has also increased from 2 percent of export earnings to a hefty 30 percent (*African Business* 1984:31).[47]

In the midst of worldwide recession, low growth of export industries, and shortages of foreign exchange the conflict between the technocratic and populist factions has increased. This is evident, for example, in Chidzero's threat to resign following the August 1984 party congress in response to the elevation of his arch-rival, Enos Nkala, to the dominant position of politburo chief of economic affairs.

Clashes between the factions have tended to center upon priorities of state support. The technocrats, for the most part, have favored major export industries, and the populists have supported expanded social services and subsidies for health, education, food, employment, communal, and smallholder peasant farming.

The excess capacity of Zimbabwe's manufacturing industry, which was originally designed to serve regional markets in Southern Africa, makes it a strategic sector for the technocratic faction. Its revival is expected to improve

[47] Riddell (1984:474) points out that allocations for health, education, defence, debt servicing, and labor in the 1983/1984 budget constituted 72 percent of total governmental spending. This contrasts with allocations for these items in the 1979/1980 budget of 46 percent of the total.

Zimbabwe's declining terms of trade and help stimulate the growth needed to finance (along with Western investment and aid) the country's developmental program. However, technocrats' success in securing priority treatment of export industries in a depressed economy inevitably means a diversion of imports for rural development projects. This would adversely affect programs that have the strong support of the populist faction.

The devaluation of the Zimbabwean dollar, wage freezes, and reduction in fiscal and balance of payments deficits will improve the competitive position of the country's manufacturing export industry in Southern Africa. However, it will also have the inadvertent consequence of imposing economic austerity upon the rural and urban poor who comprise an estimated 70 percent of the population. Hence, the technocratic faction's success in securing high priority support for the export industries will tend to erode the ruling party's base of political support in the rural areas and among the urban poor.

CHAPTER THREE

Urban Threat and Defensive State Strategies: Botswana, Lesotho, and Swaziland

IN THE SECOND CATEGORY of state involvement in the regional economy, economic ties provide the principal source of state finance and revenue and yet they constitute the social base of political opposition to the regimes in power. This ambivalent relationship places these states in a defensive position. They must depend upon the resources and revenues derived from their economic ties with South Africa but at the same time must devise strategies to cope with the political threat that emanates from the economic relationships.

Botswana, Lesotho, and Swaziland and Namibia (discussed in Chapter Six) fall into this category. All rely heavily upon their economic relationships with South Africa for most of their foreign exchange earnings, investments, and governmental revenue. In addition, the majority of Lesotho's labor force plus laborers from Botswana and Swaziland work in South Africa and remit substantial foreign exchange to their countries.

These regimes depend heavily upon rural peasants, civil servants, and business elites for their political support. However, modern sector growth in these countries plus most wage-earning labor tends to function as integral parts of the South African economy. For example, South African capital dominates their economies, and urban workers have tended to adopt the higher wage levels and benefits that prevail in South Africa in making labor demands in their own countries. However, their demands have been met with tough governmental controls and repression, creating fertile ground in which to mobilize political opposition to their government. In all three countries the political opposition has had success in organizing disaffected wage earners in opposing the regimes in power.

Botswana

In Botswana the development of a dominant mining industry (financed largely by South Africa) that earns substantial revenues for the government was accompanied by the emergence of a powerful urban wage-earning labor force. These workers have tended to use South Africa's higher wages and benefits as their standard for labor demands. However, the ruling Botswana Democratic party (BDP) is dominated by large-scale commercial cattle ranchers whose base of political support is a rural bourgeoisie.[1] The wage-earning labor force has pressured the government for higher wages and better working conditions, which has placed the state in a dilemma: to ignore the economic grievances of organized labor places the strategically important mining sector in jeopardy and yet to favor the relatively small urban population at the expense of the rural

[1] Cattle owners in Botswana constitute the leading section of the governing class. Large-scale cattle owners have been described as the dominant or leading section of an emergent petite bourgeoisie that also includes middle-level and senior civil servants, teachers, and operators of trading stores, as well as representatives of major ethnic groups such as the Bamangwato. The consensus of scholarly opinion is that the petite bourgeoisie does not, however, constitute a ruling class since they do not control the country's principal source of economic surplus—the mining industry. Botswana's governing class is said to be so heavily dependent upon foreign capital (primarily South African) for its mining industry that the country is subordinated to South Africa (Parson 1981:240, and Southall 1984:152). Nevertheless, despite its dependence upon South African investment and technology, Botswana has managed to retain a measure of autonomy in its foreign policy toward South Africa.

peasantry[2] tends to undermine the economic position of the rural bourgeoisie that is the political base of the state.

The Botswana Democratic Party's Base of Support

Research surveys carried out in Botswana reveal that a high proportion of Botswana's politicians and candidates for office were relatively prosperous cattle owners and farmers (Holm 1972[3]; Parson 1977; Cohen 1979). The most comprehensive survey, made shortly after the 1974 general elections, included all candidates for the National Assembly and candidates for town and district councils. The data contained in Tables 3.1 and 3.2 are based on the survey and give the distribution of cattle holding and the acreage planted by candidates for the Assembly and the councils. The data show the extreme disparity in cattle ownership between candidates for political office and the general population. A similar pattern is evident in the acreage planted by Assembly and council candidates. Sixty-three percent of Assembly candidates reported planting more than twenty acres, and 45 percent of council candidates planted over twenty acres (Holm's figures were 42 and 51 percent respectively). The survey of the economic wealth of Botswana's politicians and candidates for

[2] Parson (1983:44) has argued that the peasantry has been transformed into a national working class in Botswana. This class has been termed the "peasantariat" to denote their involvement both in migratory wage labor and peasant family homesteads in the rural sector. There is no question that the majority of Botswana's rural peasant population depends upon wage labor remittances from family members who are engaged in formal or informal employment in the modern sector. However, this tells us little about the willingness of migratory peasant wage earners to support trade union action in their work place in order to advance their status as urban workers.

[3] Holm's findings are based upon 1970 interviews with twenty-one (about two-thirds) of the members of Parliament and forty-five (approximately three-quarters) of the elected and nominated councilors in the three southern districts of Ngwaketse, Katleng, and South East.

Table 3.1 Cattle Holdings of Candidates in Botswana

No. of Cattle	Assembly		Council		All Candidates[a]		All Rural Households
None	—		—		—		45%
1-25	15%	(4)	33%	(49)	32%	(53)	39
26-50	19	(5)	24	(35)	24	(40)	9
51-100	7	(2)	19	(28)	18	(30)	5
More than 100	48	(13)	13	(19)	14	(22)	2
No answer	11	(3)	11	(16)	12	(19)	

SOURCE: Cohen (1979:357).
NOTE: [a] This was Botswana's third general election, which was held to fill legislative positions in the National Assembly, in ten district councils, and in three town councils. The responses are to questionnaires that were sent to all candidates who were contesting seats in the election. There were a total of 63 parliamentary candidates contesting 32 seats and 296 council candidates contesting 176 seats. The response rate was 42.9 percent for Assembly candidates and 49.8 percent for council candidates. There were no significant differences in the pattern of wealth among the three parties contesting the elections.

Table 3.2 Acreage Planted by Candidates in Botswana

Acreage	Assembly		Council		All Candidates[a]	
None	7%	(2)	1%	(1)	2%	(3)
Less than 20	26	(7)	43	(63)	40	(70)
More than 20	63	(17)	45	(66)	48	(83)
No answer	4	(1)	11	(17)	10	(18)

SOURCE: Cohen (1979:357).
NOTE: [a] See Table 3.1 note.

political office suggests, therefore, that they are cattle owners and commercial farmers.[4]

State policies toward the rural sector have played a major role in fostering the economic prosperity of the rural
bourgeoisie. From 1962 to 1973, the government's approach to agricultural development was to concentrate its
extension services upon roughly 10 percent of the farmers
who had the necessary cattle to plough and who were receptive to modern farming techniques (these included the
more educated and successful farmers). Once registered in
the scheme, farmers received considerable support and advice from governmental extension agents (Colclough and
McCarthy 1980:129). In 1973, the government announced
a new program that included poorer farmers in a more
comprehensive extension program. However, preliminary
evaluations of the new system suggest that extension services were still strongly focused upon the more successful
and prosperous farmers. Poor farmers did not have the necessary security to satisfy the commercial credit requirements for loans, and they were also less willing to incur
debt in order to purchase the necessary inputs required for
major increases in crop yields.

The government also supported public marketing institutions that were primarily designed to serve the large successful farmers. For example, the Botswana Meat Commission (BMC), a parastatal corporation with a monopoly over
the export of Botswana's cattle and beef, caters primarily to
large cattleowners. The BMC only purchases cattle at its
front gate at two locations in Lobatse and Maun and only

---

[4] The surveys also reveal that the political elite had attained a higher
level of formal education and tend to have long tenure in political office.
For example, only 9 percent of all candidates for the National Assembly
and the councils had no formal education compared to 67 percent of the
general population. And of 32 candidates who were elected to the National Assembly in 1974, 26 of them, or 81 percent, were incumbents; of
the 176 local councilors elected in 1974, 66 of them, or 38 percent, were
incumbents in 1969 (Cohen 1979:351-352).

in accordance with prearranged quotas.[5] Moreover, it is a burden on small cattle owners to make a long trek to the abattoir to sell an occasional animal, and it is difficult for them to handle the complexities of the quota system.

Between 1971 and 1975, about 60 percent of all cattle purchased by the BMC was supplied by commercial farmers, traders, and speculators only 40 percent by traditional tribal land producers and tribal cooperatives. Hence, an estimated 350 large-scale ranchers provided 60 percent of the BMC's total stock while roughly 63,700 traditional peasant farmers supplied the rest. Since the BMC is a public nonprofit corporation that on occasion operates at a loss (it incurred a 2 million pula loss in 1984), it represents a major state subsidy for large commercial cattle owners.

Botswana's land tenure and grazing system has also contributed to an unequal distribution of cattle ownership in the country. For example, in 1975, the government adopted the Tribal Grazing Land Policy (TGLP), which was ostensibly designed to arrest the deterioration of tribal grazing land and thereby assist smallholders. In reality, however, it had the effect of exaggerating the already skewed distribution of wealth and income in the rural areas. The policy involved the allocation of portions of tribal land for long-term commercial leases (of fifty years) in order to encourage investment and sound rangeland conservation practices. However, the effect of the law has been to favor the large cattle holders who are the only ones who can afford the commercial leases in the sandveld of western Botswana. Smallholders are thereby increasingly confined to overgrazed communal areas on tribal land in the east.

---

[5] The abattoir at Lobatse is the largest single integrated operation of its kind in Africa. The Maun abattoir has not fully utilized its kill capacity and is a loss-making operation (*The Courier* 1985:26). The EMC's usual minimum quota is twelve cattle, which can be worth as much as 2,000 pula (U.S. $1.00 = 1.15pula).

Botswana's crop production and marketing system parallels the pattern of cattle ownership. It is estimated that even in a good crop year, only half of all rural households produce enough cereal for their own consumption (Colclough and McCarthy 1980:131). Before 1974, only the larger arable farmers who tend to be in the southeast corner of the country could readily sell to the South African Maize Board. The smaller farmers who are far removed from the South African border could not afford the high costs of transport and were therefore forced to sell their surplus to local trading stores at a low price. In 1974, the government established the Botswana Agricultural Marketing Board (BAMB) with several buying depots throughout the country and cooperatives acting as agents of the board. Although BAMB has been successful in providing a market for the small farmer, it does nothing to assist the roughly 50 percent of all rural households who produce no surplus at all.

The government's National Development Bank was established to encourage agricultural development in the rural areas. However, in the area of agricultural credit, small holders do not have the necessary security to satisfy NDB lending requirements. In addition, since NDB clients must have the recommendation of agricultural extension agents to qualify for loans, those households who do not have cattle, and therefore have no contact with agents, receive little assistance.

Another important source of support for large commercial cattle owners in Botswana is the government's efforts to guarantee an export market for the sale of Botswana's beef. The government has, in fact, sought to diversify its beef export market by expanding sales to Europe. However, following the outbreak of foot and mouth disease in 1977, the country's beef was shut out of the EEC market (which usually takes 70 to 80 percent of the total) until the ban was lifted in 1980. Since then, Botswana has attempted to add Germany, Greece, France, Holland and Belgium as well as South Africa, Zambia, Reunion, and Hong Kong to its export markets. It also embarked upon a massive vaccination campaign to prevent further outbreaks of foot and mouth disease. Nevertheless, the 1978 to 1980 disaster plus the seven-year drought that followed it threatened to destroy the livestock industry. This has made economic planning for the industry difficult, and it has discouraged investment. The uncertainty constitutes a major economic threat to the country's cattle-owning elite.

The cattle-owning and agricultural elite were instrumental in establishing the dominant political party in Botswana. Shortly after founding the ruling Botswana Democratic party in 1962, party branches were established in villages throughout the country.[6] Meetings were held, and village committees were elected. This marked the emergence of the so-called "new men" in district affairs,[7] a phenomenon that facilitated the penetration of BDP influence in the rural areas. The elected councilors tended to come from social groups that had prospered under the colonial

[6] A unique characteristic of traditional societies in Botswana is that they tend to cluster in large towns or "tribal" villages. Each of the eight major tribes has an administrative capital and related villages. The general census in 1971 reported that 49.8 percent of the total population was living in such villages, with only 8.4 percent of the total population living in modern towns. According to the 1981 census, the population living in towns had grown to 17 percent of the total. Modern towns are the centers of urban employment, the base of the country's trade unions, and centers of attraction for rural migration.

[7] This is not to say, however, that the "modern" elite does not also have "traditional" status. In fact, the traditional and modern statuses of the new rural elite are interconnected. Most elected councilors are supported by the BDP, and they tend to be paternal relatives of the chiefs and local headmen. In Tswana society such men are called *bakosi*. In Holm's survey (1972:86), it was estimated that not more than 20 percent of the total public has this status. However, among the local politicians who were interviewed, 47 percent of the members of Parliament and 59 percent of the councilors reported that they had kinship ties with a local chief or headmen. For a discussion of the interconnection of modern and traditional statuses among political elite in Northern Nigeria, see Whitaker (1970).

administration. For example, in terms of education they were among a small group who managed to receive formal education (mostly from missionary schools). A knowledge of the English language is, for example, a constutional requirement for election to Parliament. English is also necessary for district councilors who must deal with agencies of the central government where English is the working language. Most members of Parliament and councilors are prosperous farmers or small-scale entrepreneurs specializing in small shops, restaurants, or *shabeens* (traditional beer bars). Holm notes, for example, that many of the politicians he interviewed were wage earners who were formerly employed by Europeans for the colonial government. After independence they returned to their home areas in the rural districts with their savings and experience to take advantage of the new economic opportunities created by the transfer of power to the Tswana.

The BDP actively promoted the political status of this new class of smallholders and businessmen by transferring many of the powers of the chiefs to district councils where the petite bourgeoisie predominated as elected councilors. Shortly after taking power in 1966, the BDP government legally curtailed the powers of the chiefs. The local government (District Councils Law No. 11 of 1965) established nine district councils with powers superseding the traditional authorities[8] (Tordoff 1973:174). The Ministry of Local Government and Lands, which has legal jurisdiction over both traditional authorities and councils, transferred to the district councils the power to allocate tribal land, license commercial businesses, authorize new water boreholes, appropriate funding for the construction

[8] With the exception of Ghanzi District Council, which includes a white farming bloc and adjacent nontribal state land, the district council areas correspond to the eight main tribal divisions of Botswana. For example, the Central District Council corresponds to the Bamangwato tribal area. In addition, there are five town councils—Gaborone (the capital), Francistown, Lobatse, Selebi-Phikwe, and Jwaneng.

and operation of primary schools, collect and dispose of lost cattle, and collect local taxes. District councils also were given authority to regulate the manufacture and sale of traditional beer, construct and maintain public roads, establish markets, provide sanitary services and water supplies, draft development plans, and administrate local health clinics. Councils may make by-laws, appoint subcommittees to carry out the council's specialized functions, and raise their own funds through taxation.

Under the terms of the Chieftainship Law of 1965, the recognition, appointment, disposition, and suspension of the eight Botswana chiefs was vested in the president. The central government also determines the salaries and conditions of service of the chiefs, deputy chiefs, headmen, tribal police, and all other tribal employees. The effect of the law was to transform traditional authorities into minor civil servants.[9]

This subordination to the district councils was resented by the chiefs, at least initially. It was also a source of confusion to the majority of the rural peasantry who remained overwhelmingly loyal to their traditional leaders. For this reason it was necessary for the government to appease the traditional authorities with high salaries and emoluments as well as honorific appointments such as council president. The overall effect of the transfer of the chiefs' powers to local government was that it vested power in the hands

[9] Chiefs have retained their customary tribal powers over traditional courts, their powers to arrest those who violate traditional laws, their right to engage a tribal police, to seize stolen property, and to regulate tribal affairs. However, they have lost most of the assets and staff of their administration to the district councils as well as the traditional right to take custody of *matimela* (that is, impounded) cattle and to regiment labor in their areas; they have also been denied commissions for tax collection and have lost the crucial right to allocate land in their tribal areas. The latter power was transferred to land boards where the chiefs are merely exofficio members. The chiefs are also members of Botswana's House of Chiefs, which is strictly an advisory body to the National Assembly (Proctor 1968).

of the district councils. And in the rural areas, at least, the district councils are controlled by elected and nominated BDP politicians.[10] For example, in the 1984 local government election that coincided with the general election, the BDP retained control of all rural district councils. However, in the same election, with the exception of Selebi-Phikwe, the ruling party lost control of all town councils (Gaborone, Jwaneng, Lobatse, and Francistown).[11]

Although the councils have been given wide-ranging power, it was not until the 1970s that they acquired sufficient financial resources to fulfill their mandate. In 1973, the government found itself in the fortunate position of having a windfall in surplus funds due to an increase in Botswana's share of duties from the customs union with South Africa. Renegotiations of the agreement in 1969 increased revenue from duties from one-fifth of total domestic revenue to one-half of domestic revenue in 1970. With a general election approaching, and with unexpected surplus funds, the government launched an ambitious rural infrastructural development program in 1973 called the Accelerated Rural Development Programme (ARDP). This

[10] Under the terms of the Local Government Act, the government has the power to nominate additional members to each council and can theoretically, at least, prevent an opposition party from taking control of the councils. The act does not specify the number of elected or nominated members of any local council, but it leaves it to the discretion of the minister of local government and land to decide. This means that the ruling party can take control of any council regardless of the election outcome without reference to the National Assembly. In practice, however, the ruling BDP has never been seriously challenged by opposition parties in national elections to put their democratic principles to the test.

[11] The official opposition party, the Botswana National Front (BNF), won 3 seats in the National Assembly compared to the BDP's 29 seats (out of 34 parliamentary seats) in the 1984 general elections. However, the BNF won the majority of seats in the town councils of Gaborone, Jwaneng, and Lobatse, while the Botswana People's party took control of Francistown town council. The BDP was only able to win control of the Selebi-Phikwe town council.

resulted in a major (albeit shortlived) expansion of the activities of district councils.

The central government has continued to allocate most of its developmental funds to rural district councils. For example, a comparision of town and rural district development budget expenditures in 1976 shows that rural district councils received 4.72 million pula of a total of 5.32 million—or 89 percent of the central government's total development allocation. A similar situation prevails in relation to governmental grants for recurrent budgetary support. In 1976, town councils received only 50,000 pula of a total of 5.1 million in recurrent budget support, which is less than 1 percent of the total (Colclough and McCarthy 1980:40).

The significance of the BDP's strong financial support for the rural district councils (while relatively ignoring the town councils) lies in the fact that district councils constitute the core of the rural bourgeoisie—the BDP's base of political support.[12] Without new development projects that central governmental grants to the rural district councils make possible, the political status of councilors would be undercut. This is particularly the case in light of the chiefs' resentment of what they regard as councilors' usurpation of their powers.

The political status of councilors is largely based upon their role as "communication brokers" between the central government and their villages. Councilors transmit village

[12] The BDP government of Quett Masire, which succeeded the government of Seretse Khama after his death in 1980, has continued the ruling party's tradition of recruiting district council administrators for top political positions in the central government. For example, the late Vice-President Lenyeletse Seretse formerly administered the important central district council as council secretary, and in 1983, President Masire appointed Jabavu Butale who was a former Kgalaghadi district council secretary to a specially elected parliamentary seat to replace a member of Parliament who had resigned. In 1983, five of the eleven cabinet members of Masire's government were retired civil servants who were on government pensions (Legum 1984a: B613).

demands to the district commissioners and agencies of the central government and in turn carry back the policy decisions to their villages. In this role they have acquired influence within the government and thereby enjoy a leadership role in their villages. The ability of district councilors to effectively transmit the economic demands of the rural peasantry that cannot be met within the framework of traditional village government is central to the maintenance of the councilors' status. For example, demands relating to schooling, pastoralism, agriculture, migrant labor, and hunting are normally beyond the power of village authorities. In such matters councilors have the responsibility of putting pressure upon the central government through district authorities or through members of Parliament according to a patron-client relationship to get developmental projects and support for their villages. Since the status and influence of councilors at the village level is largely dependent upon meeting local economic demands, continued major financial funding for district councils is essential in order to maintain the BDP's rural support.

Threat to the BDP

The source of domestic political pressures on the ruling BDP emanates from the growing urban population in the towns. Table 3.3 shows the population in the towns, in the major villages, and in the rest of Botswana for the periods 1975, 1978, and 1986 (projected).

The data indicate a pronounced population growth rate in the towns, estimated to be 9.9 percent per annum during the 1975 to 1986 period. Total urban population was projected to increase threefold from 86,000 to 232,590, rising from 12.8 percent of the population to 33.4 percent. By contrast, the national population growth rate during this period was projected to increase by only 3.3 percent per annum. With the exception of two small mining towns (Or-

Table 3.3 Population of Towns and Villages in Botswana

	Resident Population Mid-1975	%	Population 1978	%	Projected Population Mid-1986	%
Towns:						
Gaborone	28,000	4.2	44,000	5.8	96,080	8.5
Francistown	23,000	3.4	28,000	3.7	39,650	3.5
Lobatse	15,000	2.2	19,000	2.5	24,290	2.1
Selebi-Phikwe	18,000	2.7	25,000	3.3	34,660	3.1
Orapa	2,000	0.3	4,000	0.5	6,150	0.5
Jwaneng	—	—	—	—	8,970	0.8
Total	86,000	12.8	120,000	15.8	209,800	18.5
Major villages[a]	86,000	12.8	116,300	15.2	167,800	14.8
Rest of Botswana	500,000	74.4	406,800	53.3	754,000	66.6

SOURCE: Fair (1981:10), and Botswana (1984:209-211).

NOTE: [a] Botswana's seven major villages are Mahalapye, Palapye, Serowe, Ramotswa, Molepolole, Kanye, and Mochudi.

apa and Jwaneng), the urban growth has occurred along the line-of-rail from Mafeking in South Africa to Zimbabwe via Botswana's eastern region. An estimated 80 percent of the total population resides in the eastern region along the line-of-rail (see Map 6).

Only one-third of the growth in the urban population, however, was attributable to natural increases, with the remaining two-thirds due to in-migration from rural areas. The combination of governmental policies such as the TGLP, which worsened the position of the small cattle owner, the seven-year drought, which lowered the country's feed and grain harvest to less than 10 percent of its requirements, and the cutback in South Africa's demand for Batswana in mineworkers contributed to the rural migration. In addition, the fact that urban wages exceed rural

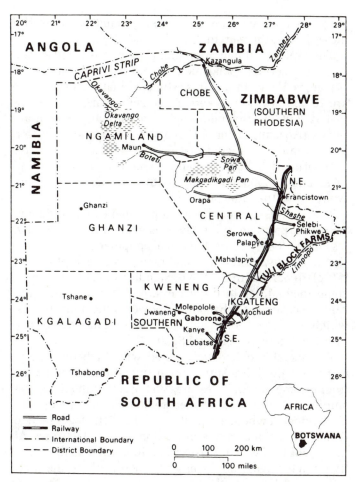

Map 6. Botswana
SOURCE: Reproduced from Christopher Colclough and Stephen Mc-Carthy, *The Political Economy of Botswana: A Study of Growth and Distribution*, Oxford University Press, 1980, frontispiece, by permission of the publisher and the Director of Surveys and Lands, Government of Botswana.

wages by a margin of four to one has acted as a powerful attraction for the marginal rural population.[13]

The rapid rural migration to the towns has been accompanied by serious social and economic problems in the urban areas. For example, it is estimated that each year there are 20,000 new job seekers in the labor market. Approximately 8,000 of them are unable to find employment annually (*African Business* 1984b:65). The finance minister, Peter Mmusi, estimated that by 1991, 110,000 graduates with primary school education would be unable to find jobs, and 29,000 graduates with secondary education would be in the same position.

The seriousness of the unemployment and underemployment problem in the towns is evident in the fact that less than 20 percent of Botswana's population of one million is employed in the formal sector. An unemployment rate of 30 percent in the towns significantly adds to the income inequalities in the urban areas. It has also significantly weakened the bargaining power of the trade unions, which are forced to accept a low minimum wage of just over half a pula per hour (U.S. $0.37).

The social problems associated with high unemployment and the burgeoning urban migration have created troublesome internal pressures on the government. For example, Botswana's continued reliance upon foreign experts (most of whom are white) and the high wages paid to them have been a source of tension among Batswana. At the Selebi-Phikwe copper-nickel mine, which is the country's single largest employer with 5,000 workers, the wage differential between the roughly 500 skilled foreign em-

---

[13] For example, the modern urban sector of the economy has had three major wage and salary adjustments in 1974, 1976, and 1982, while the rural population has had its income eroded by inflation and rising costs of imported goods (including food and agricultural supplies). Colclough and McCarthy (1980:197) point out that despite higher costs of living in the urban areas, the poorer rural population enjoys higher income benefits (in both the formal and informal sectors) when they move to town.

ployees was estimated to be 10 times greater than the wages paid to unskilled Batswana (Hodges 1977:42). In addition to racial tension arising from income inequalities in the urban areas, there is a serious housing problem. It was estimated, for example, that there was an urban housing shortage in 1984 of 20,000, which would cost the government 50 million pula (U.S. $33.6 million) over a five-year period. Moreover, this would not take into account new demand for housing during that period.

The seriousness of these urban problems for the BDP was highlighted during the 1984 general elections. The major campaign issues in the towns were rising unemployment, the shortage of housing, and the effects of the seven-year-old drought upon the agricultural and urban sectors, which had worsened economic conditions for the majority of the urban population. The oppositions' success in town council elections has reportedly stirred undercurrents of division within the ruling party.

At the end of 1980, for example, there were rumors of a serious division within the BDP. The basis of the division was that younger members of the party were concerned about the opposition's growing political support in the urban areas. One issue in particular that surfaced was the success of the opposition party's criticism. The BNF attacked the ruling BDP for presiding over a rigime that polarized the economy into an improverished rural area for the Batswana and a prosperous urban sector for foreign capital interests. One proposal within the BDP for dealing with this criticism was to have the party emphasize the "indigenization" of the urban economy so that Batswana would feel that they were running their own affairs (Cornwell 1982:164-165).

The emergence of large numbers of urban wage earners in Botswana corresponds to the transformation of the economy from being predominately pastoral and agrarian to being a mineral-led economy. The dominance of mining in Botswana's economy is clearly evident, accounting for roughly 75 percent of the country's total foreign exchange earnings and 60 percent of government revenue. In 1971, the value of Botswana's mineral production was about 10 million pula. By 1975, it had increased to 53 million pula, and by 1983, it had reached 618 million pula (U.S. $547 million), of which diamonds accounted for 538 million (*African Business* 1984a:66). Botswana's export-oriented mining industry was largely responsible for the economy's high annual growth rate. From 1973 to 1980, for example, the economy grew at an average of 23 percent of GDP, while inflation only averaged 13 percent. The rate of growth slowed during 1981 but picked up again in 1982, averaging 13 percent of GDP in real terms.

The foreign exchange and income from taxes on the mining industry have enabled Botswana to finance its ambitious developmental programs in education, health, and infrastructure. They have also enabled the country to survive the effects of a devastating and prolonged drought, largely from its own resources. For example, it is estimated that 80 percent of the population is within fifteen miles of a health center or clinic, 90 percent of all school-aged children are attending classes, and infant mortality is below 100 per 1,000 (Cornwell 1982:163). This is a remarkable achievement for a country that was classified as one of the poorest in the world at the time of independence in 1966.

The significance of Botswana's mining sector for understanding the impact of the regional economy upon the regime is that it is primarily based upon South Africa's mining industry. Not only is the majority of capital, equipment, and expertise in Botswana's mines from South Africa but South African corporations have managerial control over most of Botswana's mines. For example, De Beers, a South African corporation (which controls about 85 percent of the world's production of precious diamonds) has managerial control of the diamond mines. Anglo American Corporation, the largest mining company in South Africa, along with American Metals Corporation (Amax), a major

American mining company, have major financial interests plus managerial control over the copper-nickel mine at Selebi-Phikwe.[14]

South African involvement in Botswana's mining sector has also had a profound effect upon Botswana's urban labor force. It has given rise to a small group of urban mine workers whose expectations for wage rates and benefits are linked to those prevailing in South Africa where many of them have worked. As late as 1976 there were 40,390 Batswana migrant mine workers in South Africa. However, by 1980, this number had declined to around 19,000, where it has remained.

Migratory workers who were unable to find employment in South Africa were absorbed into Botswana's rapidly expanding urban economy. While the number of wage earners in Botswana's mining sector is relatively low (8,095 out of a formal labor force of 97,400 in 1981), the political significance of mine workers has been considerable.

The reason for this is that the crucial importance of the mining sector to the government gives the Botswana Mining Workers' Union leverage, and yet the government has sought to keep the wages of urban workers down in order to ensure a favorable investment climate in the country

[14] In 1969, the Government of Botswana went into partnership with the South African De Beers Consolidated Mines and incorporated what is known as Debswana (De Beers Botswana Mining Company) to develop the country's diamond deposits. The shares are 50/50 between De Beers and the government, but the government receives the larger share of the profits—roughly 60 to 70 percent. Amax and Anglo American Corporation are the major shareholders in Botswana RST. The latter owns 85 percent of BCL (formerly Bamangwato Concessions), which operates the Selebi-Phikwe mine. Since De Beers and the Anglo American Corporation are interrelated South African companies, Botswana's mining investment is dominated by one South African corporate group. Other than Amax, which has a 30 percent equity in BCL, there are no other foreign investments of any significance in Botswana's mining sector (Colclough and McCarthy 1980:139-168; *The Courier* 1985a: 23, *African Business* 1984c:36; *African Business* 1984f:75).

(Cobbe 1978:466-472). The government has sought to do this by pegging the wages and salaries of union workers to what is paid to civil servants in Botswana.[15]

Trade union opposition to the government has tended to focus precisely upon the wage policy.[16] Labor union leaders have organized strikes to demand pay raises and better working conditions, and they have used the higher wage rates in South Africa as their standard for wage demands in Botswana. For example, in the most serious strike in Botswana to date, three thousand black workers at the Selebi-Pikwe mine closed down operations in July 1975. The mine workers' discontent focused upon their low wages in comparison with the wages received by their counterparts in South Africa and Zambia (Hodges 1977:42).

The disparity in wages and benefits enjoyed by workers in Botswana and South Africa has been at the heart of disagreements between union leaders and the government. The mining companies have tended to give higher wages and benefits to unskilled laborers in South Africa than they have in Botswana. Table 3.4 contains data that compare minimum daily wages and benefits for unskilled work in the Botswana and South African mines. The data show that unskilled workers in South African mines received higher wages *plus benefits* than their counterparts in Botswana. This was particularly evident beginning in 1976 after Botswana's first major mine became fully operational. The differential wage structure not only created a

[15] The government has elaborated a prices-and-incomes policy that is implemented by an agency called the National Employment, Manpower, and Incomes. The central element of the incomes policy is that basic local wages and salaries of workers in the private sector should not exceed the wages paid to comparable grades of government employees.

[16] In July 1975 the Botswana Federation of Trade Unions (BFTU) was formed and was expanded to include eighteen affiliated unions. Significantly, the exdeputy general secretary of the Mineworkers' Union became the secretary general of the BFTU.

Table 3.4   Minimum Daily Wages in Pula for Unskilled Work in the Botswana and South African Mines, 1969-1976

	1969	1972	1974	1976
Botswana government[a]	0.63	0.80	2.00	2.40
Bamangwato Concessions Ltd.[b]	NA	1.08	1.54	2.00
South African Chamber of Mines employers[c]	0.34	0.72	1.60	2.50

SOURCE: Colclough and McCarthy (1980:172).
NOTES: NA = not available.
1 Botswana Pula = U.S. $1.40 in 1969, $1.30 in 1972, $1.47 in 1974, and $1.15 in 1976.
[a] No additional allowance was given.
[b] This is the copper-nickel mining company at Selebi-Phikwe, Botswana. Employees received subsidized housing and free water, electricity, and medical services.
[c] Employees received free housing, food, water, electricity, and medical services.

problem for the recruitment of experienced miners to Botswana but it has been a major source of union grievances in the country.

Between 1974 and 1976, for example, the government wages policy committee placed a ceiling on the wages and salaries paid by the mining companies, the railways, banks, state corporations, and even small commercial and manufacturing firms in Botswana. The trade unions responded to this action by organizing strikes by miners and bank employees in 1974 and 1975. The government reacted by taking a tough stance toward the strikers by using riot police, by supporting company dismissals of strikers, and by imprisoning labor leaders. While the government later allowed selected wage increases, it has generally sought to keep modern sector wages low.

The BDP's Dilemma

The importance of the mining sector to the government is evident in the central place it occupies in the country's development plans. The stated strategy of the BDP is to emphasize mining development in order to realize high, early maturing returns with which to invest in rural development. However, the high costs of infrastructure that are necessary to support the mining industry have absorbed much of the earnings that have been generated by the mines. The result is an unbalanced development program favoring the urban areas of the country. The government's development expenditure guidelines for 1976 to 1981, for example, illustrate its emphasis upon modern sector urban projects—particularly infrastructure. Allocations for mineral resources, water development, commerce and industry, and urban development and infrastructure account for about 59 percent of the total central governmental expenditure in the guidelines (USAID 1977: II,6). In the 1983/1984 development budget, of about 206 million pula for projects, the largest share (62.9 million, or 31 percent) was allocated to the Ministry of Works and Communications, with agriculture receiving only 11 million pula, or 5 percent of the budget (*African Business* 1983:24).

The government's developmental emphasis upon the urban sector has resulted in the neglect of the rural sector. However, the continued neglect of that sector may become an acute problem for the BDP. The reason for this is that the ruling BDP is not a mass-based peasant-backed party. It relies heavily upon the support of a small group of rural bourgeoisie who act as patrons to peasants and villagers so that the latter will support the BDP. The party must also be perceived to be serving the interests of the dominant Bamangwato tribe, which comprises between 30 and 40 percent of the total population. This tribe has historically played a major role in Botswana's politics.

The political status of the rural bourgeoisie is based

upon their role as "brokers" in securing developmental projects and financial support from the central government for their villages. Therefore, pronounced stagnation or decline in developmental allocations to the rural areas will in the long run tend to undermine the position of district councils and along with it support for the ruling BDP. Hence, the emergence of a powerful mineral-based regional economic interest in Botswana that is highly sensitive to the South African labor-market constitutes both the government's chief source of finance and a potential major threat to the BDP-controlled state of Botswana.

A Balanced Foreign Policy

Botswana's foreign policy has been designed to balance conflicting regional political interests primarily in order to maintain an attractive foreign investment climate in the country.[17] South African investment in Botswana's mining sector and Western aid for infrastructure are important to the government's strategy for dealing with the emergence of urban opposition to the BDP.

The political importance of foreign investment to the government was elaborated by the president at the time of

[17] The scholarly writing on Botswana's foreign policy has tended to stress the limited options open to the government due to its landlocked status, small population, and the fact that it is sandwiched between the more powerful neighboring states of South Africa and Zimbabwe. Other than noting Botswana's democratic nonracialism as an alternative model to apartheid, little attention has been given to the autonomous dimensions of the country's foreign policy. See, for example, Morgan (1979:228-248), Dale (1978:7-23), Halpern (1965), Hill (1972:55-62), and Dale (1972:110-124). Parson (1983:46-47) alludes to the existence of an alliance between South African mining capital and Botswana's governing petite bourgeoisie and acknowledges that Botswana was able to renegotiate favorable shareholding agreements with the companies. However, whatever independent political room for maneuver Botswana had in relation to the companies is largely ignored, emphasizing instead Botswana's dependency upon South Africa.

the 1975 strike in Selebi-Phikwe. President Khama explained that it was "essential" that Botswana retain and attract foreign investment. It was also necessary to import foreign skilled labor. This was only possible if foreign investors were confident of their returns on investment and foreign specialists felt that they and their property were safe. According to Khama, for every Botswana who was employed in the mining or industrial sectors there were at least five others who would like to be similarly employed but were forced to eke out a living in the rural areas or seek employment outside of Botswana.

Khama stated that the government was committed to sharing the revenue derived from these industries. In other words, the government was committed to the proposition that if they make the economic cake larger, the people will get a bigger piece. Given this logic, Khama condemned the strikes as a threat to Botswana's reputation as a "stable and safe country in which to invest" and therefore as a threat to the country as a whole. He also placed responsibility for the strike and the violence that accompanied it on a "hard core of politically motivated individuals" (*Botswana Daily News* 1975).

Much of Botswana's foreign policy can be understood in terms of an overriding concern to maintain a stable business climate in the country. For example, Botswana is not only a full member of SADCC but President Masire is the chairman of the organization, which is also based in Botswana. In fact, Botswana was a major influence behind the establishment of SADCC. However, despite the fact that SADCC's express purpose is to reduce South Africa's economic domination of regional states by expanding economic cooperation among states in SADCC, Botswana has strengthened its economic ties with South Africa. For example, the country not only continues its involvement in the South African-dominated Southern African Customs Union, which is the second largest source of government revenue (with 180 million pula), but it has strengthened its participation in SACU. In 1982, for instance, Botswana imposed an import levy of 10 percent on all goods entering the country from outside the customs union (primarily Zimbabwe and Zambia). Furthermore, it has sought to attract further South African investment into its mining sector by attempting to interest South Africans in supporting a major new mining industry involving the country's vast soda ash deposits in the northeastern Sua Pan. Studies indicate that the development of this project could raise Botswana's export earnings by about 50 percent in 1990. However, the project depends critically upon access to South African markets.

Botswana has been clever in balancing conflicting regional political interests. For example, in response to South African pressure to sign a nonaggression pact with South Africa, President Masire argued that such a treaty would seriously damage its relations with other black African states in SADCC. Masire also argued that such an agreement would invite attacks against the Botswana government by anti-South African guerillas who have never been allowed to operate in Botswana.

By playing a leadership role in SADCC, Botswana has also guaranteed continued high levels of Western aid that the BDP needs to deal with the urban threat. It was Botswana's reputation for maintaining an attractive business climate (together with its democratic institutions) that has made it a desirable recipient for Western assistance. It was also this reputation with Western countries that augured in favor of Botswana's leadership of SADCC. An indication of Botswana's success with Western donor countries is the large inflow of grants and aid from the United States, Canada, West Germany, Norway, Sweden, the World Health Organization, the EEC, World Bank, and others. These grants and loans constituted an estimated 40 percent of the government's projected developmental expenditure in 1984/1985.

LESOTHO

The state of Lesotho is dominated by a political-administrative class that forms the social base of political support for the ruling party.[18] The formation of this class was achieved initially by transforming the traditional chieftaincy into state functionaries under centralized control. Their principal function was to allocate developmental and welfare projects and services to their rural followers who comprised 90 percent of the population. Subsequently, the leadership of the ruling Basutoland National party expanded its social base of political support by encouraging the growth of a centralized bureaucracy. They embarked upon ambitious developmental projects supported largely by foreign aid donors (along with customs revenues and labor remittances from South Africa). This foreign aid and capital was used to foster the growth of a cadre of professionals, independent traders, commercial managers, trade unionists, and civil servants to support the regime.

[18] Weisfelder adopts the concept of organizational bourgeoisie developed by Markovitz (1977) to designate Lesotho's ruling class. According to Weisfelder (1981:231-232), the absence of a sizable private sector in Lesotho led to the concentration of power in the hands of top echelon politicians, civil servants, police, chiefs, professionals, progressive farmers (beneficiaries of developmental projects), independent traders, commercial managers, and officials of voluntary organizations such as trade unions and sports clubs. Following Markovitz, Weisfelder argues that the organizational bourgeoisie controls "pivotal points" of the state structure. They constitute an overlapping network of class interests insofar as many of the independent trading firms and other businesses are owned by cabinet ministers and managers of state corporations. Their high income and class prerogatives, which derive from state patronage, set them apart from the rural poor, the urban unemployed, and the "marginal employees" (that is, blue-collar workers, domestic servants, clerks, primary teachers, and junior police officers who are denied access to state patronage and are therefore forced to live on meager wages). Hirschmann (1979:183) describes this privileged class stratum in the same way that Weisfelder does but designates it as a political-administrative class. I have used the latter term in the present discussion.

The strategy of creating a state-supported political class to form the base of the ruling BNP's political support was largely a response to the 1970 election challenge from the rival Basutoland Congress party. The BCP's social base of political support, by contrast, is a large group of migrant laborers who work in South Africa and a growing urban poor class. Hence, the principal threat to the BNP-controlled state of Lesotho is an opposition party and its liberation army that is supported primarily by a South African-oriented migrant labor force and the urban poor.

The Basutoland National Party's Base of Support

The ability of chief Leabua Jonathan's Basutoland National party to win the preindependence election of 1965 was largely due to their success in mobilizing the lower echelons of the chieftaincy system. Jonathan himself is a "Son of Moshoeshoe" (SOM)—a descendent of a minor house of Moshoeshoe, Molapo, and is therefore a cousin of King Moshoeshoe II. However, the initial base of his party's political support did not lie with the SOM but rather with a large number of lesser chiefs and headmen whose economic and social status depended entirely upon state patronage.

The BNP party constitution supports the hereditary chieftainship and is dedicated to restoring the historic relationship between the chiefs and the people. However, this did not mean that the party supported the role of the king as the ruling monarch of Lesotho. The BNP insisted that the king should assume the role of a constitutional monarch in the tradition of the British monarchy.[19] On this

[19] The timing of the BNP's declared position on the king's constitutional role for independent Lesotho suggests that its position was strongly influenced by the political fortunes of the party. For example, prior to the 1965 elections, which the rival BCP was expected to win, the BNP supported an expanded political role for the king in which he would acquire the "reserved powers" held by the British colonial government. However,

crucial point the party directly collided with the king and the majority of senior chiefs who subsequently formed their own political party to protect their interests—the MaremaTlou Freedom party (MFP).

The evidence suggests that King Moshoeshoe II did seek the position of the real head of state rather than the titular head. This was evident, for example, in 1966 when he argued for a constitution for independent Lesotho that transferred the "reserved powers" held by the British government such as foreign affairs, defence, police powers, and the public service to him in arrangements similar to the Swedish, Norwegian, Belgian, or Greek monarchies (Proctor 1969:69-70). In taking this position, however, the king was not simply arguing for the revival of the chieftancy system. In fact, he publicly committed himself to progressive changes in political institutions through "comprehensive programming and planning" by the central government.

However, Moshoeshoe II was unable to mobilize a national, independent base of political support for a constitutional government he could dominate. This was due to the cleavages existing between the SOM and lesser chiefs and the fact that under the terms of the 1959 Basutoland Constitution, the king's authority over lesser chiefs was transferred to the principal and ward chiefs in the College of Chiefs. This meant that the king's only support was among the SOM who had alienated themselves from the lesser chiefs and who therefore also lacked national political support.

By contrast, after the BNP won the 1965 elections, Chief Jonathan openly supported the chieftaincy system but argued for a nominal role for the king and, by implication, his family—the SOM. Examination of the preindepend-

---

after the elections, which they won, they shifted ground on this issue and argued for a narrow largely ceremonial role for the king. I am indebted to James Cobbe for pointing this out to me.

ence elections of 1965 that installed Jonathan's BNP in power reveals the importance of the lower echelons of the chieftaincy as its base of support. Map 7 shows the election returns for the 1965 election. With 41.6 percent of the total votes, the BNP won 31 seats, the Basutoland Congress party received 39.7 percent and got 25 seats in the National Assembly, and with 16.5 percent of the votes, the MFP was awarded 4 seats.

There was a specific geographical character to each party's voting constituencies. The BNP dominated the mountain areas where the lesser chiefs and their followers were strongly attached to traditional values of the chieftaincy. The Roman Catholic Church (which unofficially supported the BNP) also had a strong following in these areas.[20] By contrast, the BCP dominated the urban areas of the country, which are located in the lowlands. It won twelve of the thirteen constituencies in the urban areas of the country, including Butha-Buthe, Leribe, and Maseru—the capital city. The MFP was only able to win in Thaba Bosiu and Matsieng, areas of strong traditional support for the king.

Map 8 shows the areas of the country where migrant laborers to South Africa originate. The laborers are most heavily recruited from the lowlands and foothills where the most densely populated urban areas are located. Map 9 shows the topographical regions of Lesotho. A comparison of Map 7 with Map 9 reveals that the BNP's electoral support in the 1965 election came primarily from the moun-

[20] Because of the Catholic Church's tolerance of traditional institutions and its willingness to work with the chiefs, it gained a strong following among chiefs and their followers. The church also pioneered mission work in the eastern mountain areas of the country and came to enjoy dominant support in the mountains generally. However, Weisfelder (1981:242-243) argues that the church no longer enjoys the influence it once did among BNP supporters. This is reportedly due to the BNP's transition from a predominately rural-based party dominated by chiefs to a secular cosmopolitan party in which the interests of chiefs and commoners have been merged into a unified governing class.

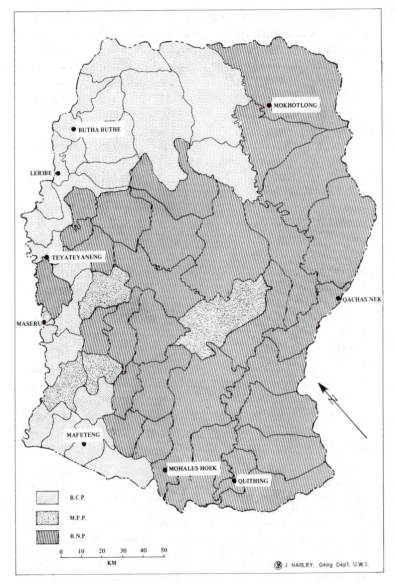

Map 7. The Election of 1965: Lesotho

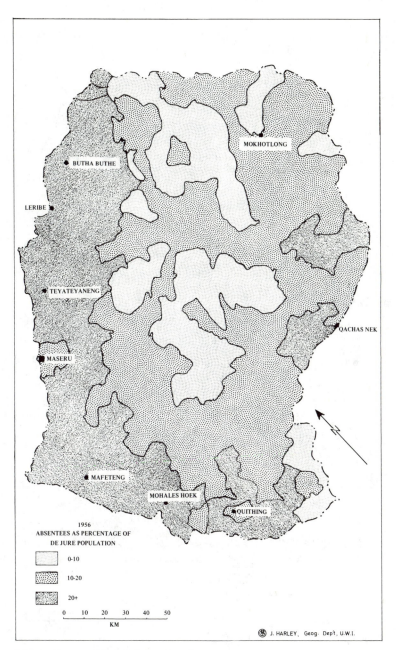

MOKHOTLONG

BUTHA BUTHE

LERIBE

TEYATEYANENG

QACHAS NEK

MASERU

MAFETENG

MOHALES HOEK

QUITHING

1956
ABSENTEES AS PERCENTAGE OF
DE JURE POPULATION

	0-10
	10-20
	20+

0   10   20   30   40   50
KM

Ⓗ J. HARLEY, Geog. Dep?, U.W.I.

Map 8. Absentee Migrant Labor: Lesotho

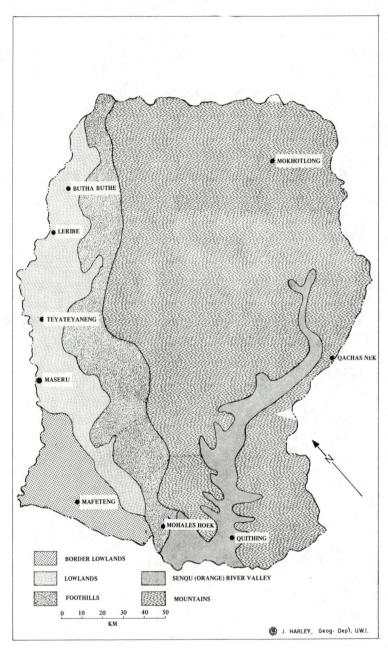

BUTHA BUTHE

LERIBE

MOKHOTLONG

TEYATEYANENG

MASERU

QACHAS NEK

N

MAFETENG

MOHALES HOEK

QUITHING

BORDER LOWLANDS

LOWLANDS

SENQU (ORANGE) RIVER VALLEY

FOOTHILLS

MOUNTAINS

0 10 20 30 40 50
KM

J. HARLEY, Geog· Dep't, U.W.I.

Map 9. Topographical Regions: Lesotho

tainous regions that have the lowest absentee migrant labor population (see Map 8). The party's electoral strength was in the mountains and the Senqu River Valley. The BCP's strength was in the lowlands, border lowlands, foothills, and urban areas, which have the highest absentee migrant labor force.[21]

The difference in the social composition of the BNP and the BCP was also evident in the background of National Assemblymen who were elected in 1965. Table 3.5 outlines the differences in the social background of fifty-four BNP and BCP assemblymen (out of sixty). The BNP group included eleven Sons of Moshoeshoe from the junior lineages (Molapo, Masupha, Majara) rather than from the royal lineage (Letsie). In addition, the BNP delegation was primarily rural (twenty-eight members) and Roman Catholic (twenty-seven members). Thirteen members were farmers by occupation and another thirteen were teachers—primarily in Catholic schools. This shows the strong orientation of the BNP toward lesser chiefs and headmen in mountainous areas where their traditional following was strong and where the influence of the Catholic Church was also strong.

By contrast, the social composition of the BCP delega-

[21] The border lowlands are in the southwestern portion of Lesotho and comprise about 6 percent of the surface area of the country, at an altitude of between, 1,500 and 1,800 meters and comprising 11 percent of the total land surface. The foothills lie at an average altitude of 2,000 meters and contain about 15 percent of the total land surface area. The Senqu River Valley is a wedge-shaped zone stretching into the southern mountain region of the country, encompassing about 9 percent of the total land surface. The mountain region comprises about 58 to 60 percent of Lesotho and is suitable only for the summer grazing of cattle and sheep.

Population density is highest in the lowlands, with more than half of the population residing in about 11 percent of the total surface area of the country that contains the highest percentage of arable acreage (38.2 percent). The mountain zone includes about 60 percent of the total land area, but it only has 19 percent of the total arable acreage and supports about 30 percent of the total population.

Table 3.5   Social Background of BNP and BCP Members of the
National Assembly, 1965

	BNP (31)	BCP (23)
Descent		
Commoners	20	21
Sons of Moshoeshoe	11	—
Non-Koena	—	2
Demography		
Mountains (rural)	28	19
Lowlands (urban)	3	4
Church Affiliation		
Roman Catholic	27	3
Lesotho Evangelical Church (LEC)	4	15
Anglican	—	2
Unknown	—	3
Occupation		
Farmers	13	9
Teachers	13	6
Traders	3	3
Politicians	—	2
Other	2	3

SOURCE: Breytenbach (1975:98-99).

tion in the National Assembly consisted primarily of commoners and members of non-Koena tribes who resided in
the lowlands, foothills, and the river valley. They tended
to be affiliated with the Lesotho Evangelical Church, a
protestant church that is strongly based in these areas.
Their occupations were more evenly divided among farmers, teachers, traders, and businessmen. Another major difference in the electoral support for these parties was the
fact that the areas of the BCP's strongest support were also

areas of the highest recruitment of South African labor. In the 1965 elections the absentee migrant workers were allowed to submit absentee ballots; however, few did. By contrast, it was widely reported that the wives of absent migrant workers (who were allowed to cast their votes for the first time) voted strongly for the BNP for fear of losing to the BCP. The women were apparently concerned that the pan-Africanist and socialist ideology of the BCP would threaten the migrant labor flow from Lesotho and thereby jeopardize their husbands' employment in South Africa.

Threat to the BNP

The migrant mining labor force in South Africa constitutes the principal base of political opposition to the BNP-controlled state of Lesotho. Migrant labor is Lesotho's major source of national income as well as household income. For example, while there are estimated to be approximately 187,000 farm households in Lesotho, contributing 45 percent of GDP (the rural sector contributes 60 percent of GDP), 51 percent of these households do not have the male head of household present for most of the year.

In 1975, an estimated 175,000 to 200,000 Basotho working in South Africa remitted to Lesotho roughly 78 million rands of their total earnings of 200.4 million rands (USAID 1977a: II, 10). In 1983, the number of Basotho migrants working in South Africa was estimated to be 130,000, with 106,000 of this number working in the mines (Kalter 1984:67). Remittances were over 154 million rands in that year.

An indication of the dominance of labor migration in the economy of Lesotho is the fact that remittances equalled the value of the country's total GDP in 1975, and the total earnings of migrant laborers were 2.6 times the estimated value of the GDP. In 1983, remittances from Basotho working in South Africa (primarily miners) equalled one-half of the country's GNP (Wallis and Henderson 1983:191).

The importance of the migrant labor force to Lesotho's economy is underscored by the absence of alternative domestic employment opportunities. It was estimated, for example, that in 1975, only 21,000 persons or 4.6 percent of the work force of 460,000 were employed in the domestic economy. Furthermore, the domestic economy was only able to create a few thousand new jobs each year during the 1970 to 1976 period, reflecting a basic stagnation of the economy. Between 1980 and 1984 only five thousand new jobs were created in Lesotho for eighty thousand new job seekers (Kalter 1984:69).

The social origins of the large migrant labor force is a growing landless urban poor class in Lesotho. For example, in 1970, it was estimated that only about two thousand families in Lesotho were landless. However, by 1980, the number of landless families had grown to thirty-five thousand, which represents a percentage increase of from 13 percent of the total population to over 20 percent (Kalter 1984:70). The highest proportion of migrant mining laborers as a percentage of the population originates in the lowland areas. These are precisely the areas of the opposition BCP's greatest strength. The BCP was, in fact, founded and led by migrants with experience in the African National Congress of South Africa or who were active in BCP politics in South Africa. The party has always drawn its strength from the urban migrant element of the population. For example, it has had success in mobilizing its urban following through the Lesotho Federation of Labor and the Protestant Lesotho African National Teachers Association as the base of strike action supported by the BCP. Since the migrant mine workers constitute the bulk of the male population (involving approximately two-thirds of the migrant male labor force), they are a particularly important source of support for the BCP. The opposition party's pan-Africanist rhetoric along with public attacks against apartheid are designed to appeal to the miners who have suffered some of the more violent aspects of apartheid while working in South Africa.[22] It has been estimated, for example, that about 160 Basotho miners have been killed in South African mines during disturbances stemming from labor disputes.

The potential political explosiveness in Lesotho of assaults on Basotho miners in South Africa was clearly apparent during the Carltonville shootings in 1973. Five Basotho were killed during police suppression of a labor dispute involving pay wages. The government of Lesotho declared a national day of mourning, and thousands of Basotho converged on the capital out of respect for the slain miners.

In addition to this issue, miners resent the government's compulsory transferrence of deductions from their pay to government-controlled banks in Lesotho. They have in fact violently protested their government's compulsory deferred pay scheme. According to a secret South African report, the scheme was said to be the principal cause of seven riots in South African mines from 1974, when the scheme was inaugurated, to 1975 (SAIRR 1978:215).

After the 1970 elections, which the BNP lost to the BCP (despite the fact that migrant laborers could not submit absentee ballots), the BNP began to elaborate a political strategy to broaden the party's base of political support. When it became apparent that the BNP had lost the elections (reportedly by a margin of 35 parliamentary seats to 23), the

---

[22] The antiapartheid image of the BCP has been somewhat tarnished recently by political factionalism within the party and growing suspicions that BCP insurgents are receiving tacit South African support in infiltrating Lesotho from the nearby homelands of Bophuthatswana and Qwaqwa. The BCP hierarchy has split between internal and external wings of the party. The leader of the internal wing is Gerald Ramoreboli, who was appointed minister of justice in Lesotho. The leader of the external wing is Ntsu Mokhehle. The general-secretary of the BCP, Koenyama Chakela, defected from Mokhehle's leadership and returned to Lesotho under amnesty in 1980. However, Chakela was assassinated, and Mokhehle's Lesotho Liberation Army took credit for it. The LLA was also reported to be divided into factions. See Wellings (1985a) and Cobbe and Bardill (1985:127-163).

prime minister invalidated the results and declared a state of emergency. The significance of the election outcome was that it showed the BNP that relying upon the allegiance of the chieftaincy and its traditional adherents was an insufficient strategy for maintaining its power. Furthermore, the election returns showed that the BNP did not even retain its support in certain supposedly safe constituencies in the northern mountain regions, such as Malibamatso and Kau, and in the southeastern mountain regions (Weisfelder 1972a:126).

The BNP's poor showing in certain traditional strongholds was undoubtedly partly due to the fact that the people in these constituencies felt that their economic interests were being neglected, while the western lowlands were being favored with agricultural projects, roads, and improved communication facilites. On the other hand, the BNP won back two formerly BCP constituencies in the Leribe district near the Peka area where two new agricultural projects were located: a UNDP pilot project near Ficksburg bridge and the Khomokhoana Project bordering the Hlotse River.

The lesson of the 1970 election debacle to the BNP leadership was clear. They recognized that they were vulnerable to the BCP's appeals to the marginal urban population (low-income wage earners and the umemployed) and to the migrant laborers in South Africa to champion their interests. On this point the BNP recognized that it had no real leverage with the South African government. BCP followers saw the government as a willing collaborator with the South African regime primarily at their expense. Therefore, instead of competing with the BCP for the political support of migrant laborers and marginal workers, the BNP embarked upon a strategy of fostering a national political-administrative class. The privileged access of members of this class to the state for patronage depended upon their allegiance to the BNP. The logic behind this strategy was that if the economic viability of the modern sector could be achieved, the BNP would at least have the political support of a national class. Their support was necessary to offset the urban-migrant support for the rival BCP.

A New Strategy

In the aftermath of the 1970 elections, the government announced its First Five-Year Development Plan. The plan was designed to coincide with the prime minister's declared "five-year holiday" from politics, ostensibly because the people wanted economic development. However, this did not mean that the BNP's new strategy would exclude the chiefs. To the contrary, the prime minister reaffirmed that the chieftaincy system would be preserved and developed. Nevertheless, the role of the chiefs in the new strategy was substantially changed to ensure centralized control over them in a new role. They were to be dispensers of developmental project benefits and welfare to their people on behalf of the BNP. The effect of this was to transform the chiefs' traditional role of allocating land to their followers. In the new strategy their revised function was to dispense state patronage in their areas on the basis of their followers' demonstrated loyalty to the BNP. The chiefs' importance in this regard is evident in the fact that the state bureaucracy is virtually invisible in the countryside where chiefs are in most respects the only representative of the Lesotho state (Weisfelder 1981:233).

The government's official plan was to encourage "urban dispersal" by decentralizing administrative and commercial infrastructure in selected "growth centers" outside of the urban areas of the country. According to the plan, there was to be at least one growth center in each ward. At each center there was to be a cluster of offices for administrative services, with the principal or ward chief's office at the center. Other offices would include a health clinic, water department, a school, a commercial store, and a police post. For example, the small villages in the districts of Mohale's

Hoek and Quthing are growth centers within the scheme area of the Senqu River Agricultural Extension Project.

An example of state patronage in rural areas is the Technical Operations Unit (TOU). The largest agricultural program in the country, it is designed to support small farmers' production of food grains. For a small fee the government cultivates the farmers land. Most of the beneficiaries of the TOU program are supporters of the BNP (Cobbe 1983:310). Likewise, the Land Act of 1979 vests the important power to allocate land for farming and other purposes in committees likely to be dominated by BNP supporters.

A closely related element of the government's strategy for broadening the regime's base of political support is the growth of a cadre of urban elites who are dependent upon the state for employment, contracts, grants, or loans. While good detailed data do not exist on the size and composition of this urban social formation, there is agreement that the growth in this political-administrative petite bourgeoisie class has been substantial. For instance, there has been considerable growth in the central bureaucracy (accompanied by purges of BCP supporters from the civil service). This has given rise to a sizable group of civil servants and employees of state corporations. In addition, the state has supported the establishment of independent commercial business, transport, and construction firms plus small-scale manufacturers who are BNP supporters. One indication of the growth of this class stratum is that employment in the modern sector increased from approximately 14,000 at independence to 40,000 in 1980. Almost all of the growth was concentrated in the urban areas—especially in the capital city, Maseru.

The substantial expansion in public investments, improved urban services, and the size of the bureaucracy have been financed in large part by foreign aid. The government has been highly effective in appealing for aid from Western donor countries on the basis of preventing the "strangulation" of Lesotho's economy by South Africa. For example, for the five-year period from 1966 to 1970, Lesotho's total official developmental assistance was U.S. $62.8 million, whereas foreign assistance for the period 1975 through 1980 totalled US $199.6 million. This represents a 300 percent increase in ten years (Woodward 1982). Lesotho's total loans, grants, food aid, and technical assistance grew from U.S. $48.6 million in 1977 to U.S. $220 million in 1982, making the country one of the world's largest per capita aid recipients. Foreign aid contributes an estimated 60 percent of Lesotho's total developmental financing (Kalter 1984:70).

The BNP has not only been successful in attracting large inflows of foreign aid but, more importantly, the government has diversified its list of donors. In 1966, for instance, the only aid donors Lesotho had were the United Kingdom, the World Bank, and U.N. agencies. However, in 1985, that list had expanded to include Western European countries, the United States, Nordic countries, several OPEC sources, and communist countries (the Soviet Union, the Chinese People's Republic, North Korea, Romania, and Yugoslavia).

Role of Foreign Assistance

The significance of the BNP's political strategy to increase foreign aid to Lesotho is its importance in sustaining the developmental projects and patronage necessary to retain the support of the political-administrative class whose political support for the regime is essential to offset inroads by the rival BCP.

Foreign assistance has become a critical if not overriding, factor in maintaining the BNP in power. This is evident in the fact that foreign assistance along with migrants' remittances and customs union receipts are the only major sources of economic growth in Lesotho's economy.[23] With the recession in the South African economy and the severe black unemployment problem in South Africa, remittances and customs union receipts are unlikely to increase. This means that foreign assistance assumes a crucial role in terms of providing social services and economic opportunities for the political-administrative class.

A combination of drought and mismangement, for example, has virtually undermined rural development projects such as the TOU/Food Self-Sufficiency Program. This has resulted in a decline in the agricultural sector. Lesotho's small industrial sector is practically stagnant. Domestic revenues are also at a standstill, while the population is growing at an annual rate of 2.4 percent. Unemployment is growing, and significantly the South African recession and growing black unemployment have put the squeeze on Basotho seeking employment in South Africa. Cobbe (1983:299) estimates, for example, that legal Basotho migrants in sectors other than mining declined from over 38,000 in 1973 to just under 21,000 in 1981. In addition, Lesotho's main source of migrant labor, mining, is subject to the same competitive pressure from South African blacks eager to work in the mines. Hence, this sector is not expected to absorb the growing numbers of umemployed Basotho.

The economic recession in South Africa, the effects of the drought upon Lesotho's agricultural sector,[24] and declining domestic revenues are major factors behind the

[23] In addition to the substantial remittances that Basotho migrant workers return to Lesotho, the government of Lesotho is dependent upon an estimated 70 percent of its revenues from the common revenue fund of the Southern African Customs Union, which South Africa dominates (Wallis and Henderson 1983:191).

[24] The Southern African Development Coordination Conference has estimated, for example, that the financial cost and losses of the 1982/1983 drought to Lesotho were in excess of $123 million. SADCC's proposed agricultural aid program for Lesotho was over $78 million (SADCC 1984: i, iii).

BNP's push to secure new large inflows of aid. This is undoubtedly the reason Chief Jonathan attempted to secure assistance from communist countries. While this effort may not net the BNP government major new sources of aid, it is certain to catch the attention of Western aid donors and may induce larger aid flows to enable the government to compensate for declines in the economy and especially declines in domestic revenues.

The principal threat to the BNP remains the BCP and its ability to mobilize its supporters among the migrant laborers and the marginal urban workers and the unemployed. Ironically, any reversal in Lesotho's economic dependence (especially the access of its migrant laborers to South African mines) will tend to strengthen the BCP opposition and thereby threaten the BNP regime.

In order to cope with this threat Jonathan's government walked a political tightrope. On the one hand, the government's efforts to secure communist and noncommunist support on the basis of the apartheid regime's threatened strangulation of Lesotho's economy netted the BNP substantial inflows of donor assistance. It also had the beneficial result of depriving the BCP of the support of the OAU and the antiapartheid movement. Jonathan's success in this regard was evident in the fact that it placed the BCP in a defensive position. Since 1979, the BCP's military wing, the Lesotho Liberation Army, has concentrated its operations in mountainous areas against chiefs and district government agents and recently against urban elites and Western aid donors. However, this inadvertently produced a blacklash by prompting many Basotho to ask what plans or strategy the BCP had to improve the economic conditions of the people.[25]

---

[25] For an elaboration on the theme of the BCP's irrelevance to Lesotho's current political problems by students of Roma University (Lesotho) who formerly supported the BCP and who have strong antiapartheid views, see (CASSAS 1979).

The BCP has also been criticized for being dependent upon the South Africans for turning a blind eye to the LLA's operations, which are launched from South African territory. In addition they have been censured for depending upon South Africa to guarantee economic opportunities for the party's principal supporters—migrant laborers.

On the other hand, the government's ties with Soviet bloc countries with embassies in Lesotho (anathema to South Africa and comparable to an ANC presence) threatened to provoke South African retaliation. In addition to armed attacks against the BNP—either directly, such as the December 1982 bombings of suspected ANC leaders in Maseru, or indirectly, by supporting the LLA—the South Africans have a battery of economic levers they can use against the country. Nevertheless, Jonathan apparently calculated that his defiance of RSA, which was designed to secure large inflows of foreign aid, would not provoke drastic punishing reaction from South Africa. He reasoned that a break in South Africa's economic ties with Lesotho would involve unacceptable costs to the South African government as well.

Above all, the South Africans wish to avoid economic chaos and political turmoil on their border with Lesotho, which threatens to spill over into South Africa itself where there are more Basotho than there are in Lesotho. Any drastic economic retaliation by South Africa such as a prolonged economic blockade or closing its borders to migrant workers will inevitably produce economic and political disorder. This could easily spread to South Africa's vital mining-industrial heartland in the Transvaal.

Therefore, the BNP's political strategy for sustaining a national political-administrative class is predicated upon Lesotho's economic dependence upon South Africa and its political independence in securing foreign aid and assistance from Western and communist sources. The January 1986 coup by General Justin Lekhanya that ousted

Chief Jonathan is testimony to the difficulty of balancing these conflicting objectives.[26]

Swaziland

The Swazi state is controlled by a powerful chieftaincy[27] The state also relies upon a modern foreign-owned sector

[26] Lesotho's three-thousand-strong paramilitary force reportedly moved against Jonathan after a twenty-day economic blockade of Lesotho by South Africa. The country was running short of gasoline, medicines, and supplies due to the blockade. The paramilitary apparently felt that Jonathan's government had gone too far in the direction of asserting Lesotho's political independence from South Africa. In order to ease the tension between Maseru and Pretoria, Lekhanya pressed Jonathan to make some political concessions to South Africa such as removing fugitive ANC members. Jonathan refused these demands and vowed he would seek support from Soviet bloc countries if Western governments did not come to Lesotho's assistance in breaking the blockade (*New York Times* 1986).

[27] Fransman (1978) and Daniel (1982) argue that "traditional rulers" who lacked a "material base" in the capitalist sector of the economy assumed political power in Swaziland at independence. Daniel argues that the "Swazi ruling class" acquired a material base in the capitalist sector after independence by entering into an alliance with foreign capital through a state institution the *Tibiyo Taka Ngwane Fund* as a vehicle for domestic capital accumulation under the control of the chieftaincy. By contrast, Levin (1984) argues that the "king has spearheaded an emergent bourgeoisie," which dominates the state apparatus. However, I would argue that while the chieftaincy has indeed acquired a "material base" in the capitalist sector of the economy, that has not transformed the Swazi aristocracy and chiefs into an indigenous petite bourgeoisie or comprador class in the Marxist sense of a class that appropriates surplus through wage labor and market rents and reinvests that surplus to expand capitalist relations of production and industrialization. The Swazi nation is comprised of a number of major clans or families, the largest and most important of which is the king's royal lineage—the Dlamini clan. They constitute an estimated 18 percent of the total population of Swaziland. By virtue of their family ties the members of this clan and members of other important clans are given preferential access to state patronage and positions within the modern sector. In contrast, many Swazi nationals who were not born into one of the major clans or who are out of favor with the traditional hierarchy are denied state patronage.

that is based primarily upon linkages with the South African economy for budget revenue, foreign exchange, production, and employment. Like Botswana and Lesotho, the most serious threat to the Swazi regime emanates from its South African-oriented urban wage-earning sector.

Unlike the traditional peasant sector in which an estimated 90 percent of the population resides, the industrial urban areas have been experiencing rapid growth. The peasant sector (the state's base of political support) is economically stagnant, and its communal land is overcrowded. The urban sector has eroded the peasant sector by attracting the young working-aged population off the traditional agricultural land. Urban trade unions have also directly challenged the authority of the state. The ruling Swazi elite have sought to counter this threat by embarking upon an ambitious program of commercializing the peasantry. The strategy is designed to foster a class of semicommercial peasant farmers and thereby raise their living standards. The objective is to revitalize the rural base of the Swazi state.

The Chieftaincy

The chieftaincy in Swaziland is unique in the history of British colonial Africa. It has largely remained intact due to the reluctance of the British government to take financial responsibility for Swaziland's economic development. Although there was constant friction between Swazi traditional authorities and the British over land and mineral rights, the chieftaincy was allowed to govern the Swazi people according to its traditional laws and customs. Colonial administrations were primarily concerned with the affairs of the white community and thus left the affairs of the Swazi people to their chiefs. Despite being placed under British colonial administration, being forced to adopt a British-imposed constitution, and being required to hold democratic elections in 1964 and 1967, the traditional chieftaincy remained the effective government of the Swazi people.

The Imbokodvo National Movement (INM) that the Swazi rulers used as an election front to win preindependence elections and acquire control of the government in 1968 was completely subordinate to the chieftaincy system. For example, the Imbokodvo was never officially declared a party. All of its candiates were selected according to Swazi tradition, and its sweeping electoral successes were largely due to support from the institutional resources of the chieftaincy. From the standpoint of the traditional Swazi authorities, there is no confusion or ambiguity in the existence of modern institutions of government under the political control of the chieftaincy. Positions in the Western administrative hierarchy complement rather than replace the traditional offices. Persons possessing the qualities appropriate for each position are selected. Taken as a whole, the political elite hold overlapping positions in the governmental, and traditional, hierarchies. Every member of the Imbokodvo was automatically a member of the Swazi National Council, and almost every Swazi who is elected or appointed to legislative bodies has an important position in the traditional hierarchy.

The traditional structure is a highly centralized monarchy headed by a king—the Ngwenyama—who performs executive, legislative, and judicial functions, holds land in trust for the Swazi nation and allocates its usage, performs sacred rituals, and is the symbol of national unity.[28] This is not to say, however, that he monopolizes all power. His authority is, in fact, balanced by the Ndlovukazi (the queen mother), and it is shared by two traditional institutions— the Liqoqo (inner or family council) and the Libandla (General Council or Council of the Nation). The Liqoqo functions in much the same way as a cabinet in a parlia-

[28] For a description of the traditional Swazi chieftaincy, see Kuper (1947 and 1963), Matsebula (1976), and Bonner (1983).

mentary or presidential system of government. It is a small group of between ten to twenty senior princes (that is, descendants of the king's royal Dlamini line), important representatives of the queen mother's Nxumalo clan, senior chiefs from outside the Dlamini, and Nxumalo clans and a few commoners of outstanding importance in the country. The Liqoqo meets informally, and certain of its members are consulted frequently by the king. However, while the king is supposed to be guided by its advice, he is not bound to follow its recommendations. The Libandla, by contrast, is regarded as having binding authority on actions taken by the king on behalf of the Swazi nation.[29] It is comprised of the Liqoqo members, all of the chiefs, their counselors, and all adult men in the country. Although it normally meets only once a year, in principle its approval is required for all important new laws and decisions.

In 1950, efforts were made to bring traditional Swazi authorities into alignment with the colonial administration. The Swazi National Council was created to provide advice to the British high commissioner for Basutoland, Bechuanaland, and Swaziland on matters affecting the Swazi. In practice, however, the Swazi National Council is simply a formalized version of the Liqoqo, with a secretary, the treasurer of the Swazi National Treasury, and six other members representing the districts of Swaziland. All members are appointed by the king. Below the national institutions are 172 chiefs (and their counselors), each of whom has his own local Liqoqo and Libandla.

Central-local ties within the chieftaincy are important for understanding the state's base of support. The chieftaincy derives its strength from its control of all Swazi Nation Land. The allocation of land, the settlement of land disputes, and related questions are under the authority of

[29] In practice, however, the Libandla has tended to fall into disuse as the authority of the chieftaincy became highly centralized with decision making being dominated by the king and the Liqoqo (Halpern 1965:368).

the king's appointed (that is, recognized) chiefs. Hence, the most important function of the chiefs is the allocation of land to the people who are obliged under the system to give a portion of their produce to their chief. Commoners may participate in discussions with the king and their chiefs through regional forums called Tinkhundla. Participation is limited, however. Those who overstep their ascribed social status are subject to attack for *umbango*, or illicit disputation for power.

Chiefs allocate homestead and arable crop land to individual Swazi households. Only Swazis may use Swazi Nation Land. As a prerequisite for obtaining land, each individual must swear allegiance to the king and his chief.

In October 1978, the king inaugurated a new constitution that was described as being more in keeping with Swazi traditions. It replaced the country's independence constitution (embodying a Westminster type Parliament), which was repealed by Sobhuza in 1973. A significant aspect of the new constitution was the devolution of formal constitutional powers of local government to chieftaincies that are located primarily in the traditional sector.

Under the new constitution, the country is divided into forty chieftaincies or Tinkhundla. They were the constituencies for the National Assembly and Senate. Adults in each Inkhundla vote to elect two members of an electoral college who must be chiefs or their representatives. Election is by open public acclamation, and all nominees are vetted by the king in advance. The electoral college of eighty elected members then elects forty representatives to the National Assembly and ten to the Senate. The king himself appoints a further ten members each to the National Assembly and to the Senate and nominates the ministers and deputy ministers from the parliament. The king also retains the right to dismiss ministers and their deputies and has the power to veto any measure that passes the National Assembly.

While it is obvious that the chieftaincy system is entrenched in power by the constitution (without any possibility of a legal opposition), the real significance of it lies in the enhanced status of important chiefs in the traditional sector. Their increased political status represents an effort to revitalize the political power of the chieftaincy.

Land Tenure System

In order to appreciate the strategic importance of the traditional sector to the Swazi state and the threat that economic linkages with South Africa pose to it, it is necessary to examine the role of land ownership in the country. There are essentially two types of land tenure in Swaziland: Individual tenure farms (ITF; freehold) and Swazi Nation Land (SNL; communal land). Map 10 shows the chaotic pattern of land tenure in Swaziland at the time of independence in 1968. The major private farms are scattered throughout the country. Table 3.6 gives the size of SNL and ITF in terms of usage and hectares.

The origins of this peculiar pattern of land tenure lies in the late nineteenth century when Transvaal farmers obtained land and mineral concessions in Swaziland from Swazi paramount chiefs. For example, in 1907, about 60 percent of all land in Swaziland was owned by foreigners. The British colonial administration intervened in that year by instituting a land partition policy that primarily served the economic interests of less than six hundred white settlers. According to Crush (1980a: 85), the political objectives of the colonial state (the British government) and the interests of the white settlers in Swaziland were complementary "at virtually all points."

The land partition that the British instituted in 1908 apportioned two-thirds of the land surface of Swaziland to the crown and white settlers while leaving only one-third of the land for the Swazi. Crush points out that the parti-

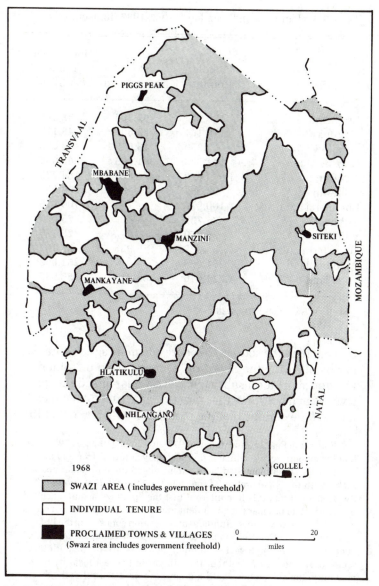

Map 10. Swazi Nation Land and Individual Tenure Land
SOURCE: Reproduced from T.J.D. Fair, G. Murdoch, and H. M. Jones, *Development in Swaziland*, figure 4, p. 26. © Witwatersrand University Press, Johannesburg, 1969.

Table 3.6   Land Use in Swaziland, 1981/1982 (in hectares)

Land Use	Whole Country	Swazi Nation Land	Individual Tenure Farmland
Crop land	135,974	97,260	52,341
Crops	118,181	83,633	48,115
Fallow	17,853	13,627	4,226
Grazing land	1,144,879	861,895	282,984
Natural veld	1,046,620	861,895	184,725
Improved	98,259	—	98,259
Commercial forests	100,916	—	100,916
Pines	75,737	—	75,737
Others	25,179	—	25,179
Other farmland	33,027	5,925	27,102
All other land	251,863	—	251,863
Total land	1,721,615	965,080	756,535

Source: Swaziland (1984:20).

tion enabled the settlers to secure adequate agricultural labor by allowing the Swazi only enough land on which to provide short-term subsistence. This guaranteed inexpensive wage labor for settler farmers.[30] Crush (1980:85) estimates, for example, that the partition left 42 percent of the

---

[30] Following Palmer and Parsons (1977-20), Crush (1979:57, 59) argues that the modern sector, which is dominated by South African and British capital, has "interpenetrated" and subordinated the traditional peasant sector with the collaboration of the state (first the colonial and then the Swazi state). From this it is inferred that the "political acquiesence" of the Swazi state has made it dependent upon South Africa. However, this approach fails to consider a fundamental question concerning the linkage between political and economic relationships. It ignores the political "dependence" of the Swazi state upon the peasantry in the traditional sector of the economy. Without the support of the vast majority of the peasantry, the chieftaincy could not have captured control of the Swazi state in the first place. Equally, the loss of the chiefs' political support

Swazi population on the settler estates, thereby constituting a potential labor reserve for the white settlers. However, the partition did not interfere with the right of traditional authorities to allocate their land to subordinates according to Swazi custom. This ensured that the traditional authority of the cheiftaincy would remain intact.

The British later decreed that the land that was orginally transferred to the settlers become freehold land until 1972, after which the king would assume jurisdiction. In practice, however, the settlers were allowed to retain their ownership rights with a 99-year lease, after which the land was to revert to Swazi Nation status.

Since 1907 some of the private farms and estates have been purchased on behalf of the Swazi nation. However, the basic division between freehold and Swazi Nation Land has remained. For example, individual tenure farmland constituted 42 percent of the country's total land area in 1982, while Swazi Nation Land was 56 percent of the total. The majority of ITF estates are five hundred hectares or less in size, but twenty-four separate holdings account for 63.5 percent of the total ITF land. ITF in conjunction with agro-based industries account for roughly 43 percent of GDP and three-quarters of the country's total exports.

By contrast, there were an estimated 56,115 Swazi farm households comprising 82 percent of a population of 634,000 in 1982. They engage primarily in subsistence agriculture. The average size of these farms (which are communally owned) is three hectares. Table 3.7 shows the differences in crop production in SNL and ITF areas. Maize, for example, is the major food staple for the Swazi, and it contributes about 80 percent of the total crop production on traditional land. However, despite the government's stated objective of achieving self-sufficiency in maize production by 1983, food imports (primarily maize) have in-

---

within the traditional sector is the most serious threat to the traditional Swazi state.

Table 3.7   Major Crop Production on Swazi Nation Land and
Individual Tenure Farmland by Volume of Production, 1981/
1982 (in metric tons)

Crop	Swazi Nation Land	Individual Tenure Farmland	Country (Total)
Maize	52,267	—	52,267
Groundnuts (nuts)	481	—	481
Cotton	8,445	5,810	14,255
Jugo beans	712	—	712
Sorghum	720	—	720
Beans	404	—	404
Sweet potatoes	1,192	—	1,192
Tobacco	83	117	200
Sugar cane	—	3,249,659	3,249,659
Pineapples	—	35,150	35,1050

SOURCES: Swaziland (1984:20, 22).

NOTE: Drought seriously affected rain-fed crops such as maize during 1981 and 1982. However, Swaziland received good rains in 1983 and 1984.

creased by an annual average rate of 35 percent during the 1978 to 1981 period (*Africa South of the Sahara* 1984:854).

Since 1970, the output SNL farms has grown at an average of 3 percent a year. However, the Swazi population has been growing at a high annual rate of 3.4 percent. Since the vast majority of the population lives on SNL, per capita agricultural output has actually declined in the traditional sector.

By contrast, the output of production on freehold title land increased in value, volume, and acreage under cultivation. This was largely due to the expansion of sugar production. For example, the value of sugar exports increased from 53.2 million emalageni in 1977 to 109 million in

1982, making sugar production the dominant industry in the country.

Mining, forestry, and manufacturing are also important industries, and they are situated on freehold land and in the urban areas of the country. While mining and quarrying have declined since the late 1970s, they contributed an estimated 3 percent to total GDP in 1982 and constituted 6 percent of total exports in 1981. Anglo American Corporation's Ngwenya iron ore mine closed in 1978, and the Havelock asbestos mine is threatened with closure by 1986. The greatest future potential for growth in this industry lies with the exploitation of Swaziland's large reserves of bituminious and coking coal especially for the conversion of coal to oil along the lines of the SASOL project in South Africa. The only colliery currently in operation is Mpaka, which is owned by the Anglo American Corporation.

Commercial forestry plantations in Swaziland occupy an estimated 100,000 hectares of land and forestry and contributed 2 percent to GDP in 1982. The exportation of wood pulp and wood products constituted about 17 percent of the total value of Swaziland's exports in 1982. The country's largest timber company is Peak Timbers, which is owned by Anglo American Corporation of South Africa. Manufacturing in Swaziland is largely confined to agricultural and wood processing. Manufacturing production contributed an estimated 23 percent of the country's GDP in 1982 and grew at an annual rate of 7.4 percent during the period 1977 to 1982.

Threat to the State

The major threat to the Swazi state is the erosion of support for the chieftaincy. If the traditional areas continue to stagnate economically, the peasantry will be deprived of economic opportunities, roads, communication, marketing facilities, and social services. This could become a serious political problem for the chiefs. An expanding and prosperous modern sector has, in effect, become the standard by which the Swazi peasantry judges the regime's ability to serve their needs.

The rapid economic growth in ITF areas and urban centers since 1960 was the result of the opening of two new railway lines, the inauguration of a 500,000 rand hydroelectric scheme, the mnjoli dam, a new coal mine, the Lozitha state house, and irrigation in the lowveld. This was accompanied by the establishment of the important sugar industry (including three sugar mills) and the creation of company towns. However, most of these developments occurred in relatively few geographic locations. Four main areas—Piggs Peak-Havelock, the Mbabane-Usutu-Manzini matrix, Big Bend and Nsoko, and Tshaneni-Mhlume—are estimated to employ 80 percent of all wage earners in the country. They cover only 15 percent of the total land area and contain 24 percent of the total population.

The main characteristic of the modern sector is its small base, intimate linkage with the agricultural sector and its ties with the South African economy.[31] It was estimated that 70 percent of Swaziland's total private investment in the modern sector from 1945 to 1968 came from South Africa (Leistner and Smit 1969:89). Since 1968, South Africa's economic interests in Swaziland have grown in importance. In fact, with the exception of banking and agriculture, South African capital dominates the modern sector of Swaziland's economy.[32] There are only a half dozen important firms engaged in the processing of agricultural produce for export, and these industries rely upon

---

[31] For a description of South Africa's economic linkages with Swaziland, see Winter (1978), Crush (1979), and Daniel (1982).

[32] Daniel (1982:100-101) notes that South African capital threatens to displace British capital in the agricultural sector. For example, if Anglo American concludes its purchase of the Usuthu forest, then Anglo will control more than 90 percent of the country's second largest earner of foreign exchange in the agricultural sector—wood pulp and wood products.

South Africa for their marketing services, transportation, supplies of machinery, oil, and technical expertise. The Southern African Custom Union agreement of 1910 (as amended) also generates tax receipts that amounted to 62 percent of Swaziland's total revenue in 1983.

The major plantations and manufacturing industries in the modern sector have also had a significant impact upon the traditional sector. De Vletter (1982:23 and 1984:854) estimates, for example, that four-fifths of all traditional homesteads have one or more members involved in wage employment away from their homesteads. It is also estimated that the earnings from wage employment or remittances from migrants constitute about three-fourths of cash income and 45 percent of the total income of homesteads (in cash and kind). Hence, traditional rural homesteads are heavily dependent upon wage earnings in the modern sector for their livelihood.

Table 3.8 shows that most wage employment is in the private sector. This reflects the historical fact that the modern sector in Swaziland was established and controlled by foreign investors—British and South African. Privately owned enterprises employ an estimated 71 percent of all Swazis in wage employment.[33] Since 1960, modern sector employment has experienced a substantial overall increase each year. For example, in 1971 wage employment was 47,000, in 1977 it increased to 69,306, and in 1982 it was 77,253, with the private sector accounting for almost three-fourths of the total. Agriculture and forestry employed the greatest number, with 24,557 or 32 percent of the total. Manufacturing accounted for 15 percent of total wage employment in 1982.

A significant aspect of the expanding modern sector in

[33] De Vletter (1982:119) had documented the fact that most Swazi labor migration is from the rural homesteads in the SNL to the farms, plantations, or urban areas in Swaziland. However, an estimated 13,590 Swazi laborers were officially reported to have been recruited for work in the mines in South Africa in 1982 (Swaziland 1984:69).

Table 3.8   Employment in the Public and Private Sectors of
Swaziland by Industry, 1982

Sector	Private	Public	Total
Agriculture and forestry	22,446	2,111	24,557
Mining and quarrying	2,492	—	2,492
Manufacturing	11,708	—	11,708
Electricity and water	—	1,091	1,091
Construction	4,644	2,782	7,426
Distribution	6,923	9	6,932
Transport and storage	1,709	2,478	4,187
Finance	1,682	551	2,233
Social Services[a]	3,171	13,456	16,627
Total	54,775	22,478	77,253

SOURCE: Swaziland (1984:66).
NOTE: [a] Includes Ministry of Agriculture headquarters and Veterinary
Service staff.

terms of its impact upon the traditional sector is the disparity in the wage earnings of workers in the modern sector compared with earnings in the traditional sector. In
1975, for example, an unskilled worker earned 442 emalageni and a semiskilled worker 875 emalageni per year. By
comparion, the subsistence farm per capita income was 92
emalageni per annum. Per capita income in the traditional
sector was therefore one-fourth of the 1975 national per
capita figure. It has since been in serious decline, while at
least some of the modern sector wage earners have kept
pace with cost of living increases due to inflation.[34]

[34] Per capita income in the traditional sector was 84 rands (U.S. $125)
in 1966 and 92 emalangeni (U.S. $137) in 1975. Dr. M. S. Matsebula, a
Swazi economist, has argued that the average standard of living for the
Swazi as a whole has been falling, with the most alarming drop in Swazi
Nation Land. He stressed the fact that the standard of living in SNL has
been in serious decline since 1974 (Times of Swaziland 1981). The effects
of the 1981 and 1982 drought plus the damage caused by cyclone Do-

Table 3.9 Population and Income Distribution in Swaziland, 1977

Sector	Population	Personal Income
Urban areas (including company towns)	15%	43%
Rural areas	82	34
ITF	20	16
SNL	62	18[a]
Total Swazi	97	77
Other population groups	3	23[b]

SOURCE: ILO (1977:138).
NOTES: [a] This figure is probably inflated due to the linkage between modern sector employment and income from subsistence farming. Income earned in the modern sector is frequently remitted to the farm household.
[b] This includes the large highly paid expatriate work force.

The disparity between income in the urban areas and rural areas is even greater than it is within the rural areas. Table 3.9 shows the relative income figures between the rural and urban areas of the country. These data provide a clear picture of income distribution by sector. Fifteen percent of the urban population received 43 percent of total personal income, while 20 percent of the population on ITF received 16 percent of personal income. By contrast, 62 percent of the population on Swazi Nation Land received only 18 percent of the personal income. While overall income may have declined since 1975, income in the traditional rural areas has declined by as much as or more than the decline in income levels in the modern urban sector (de Vletter 1982:116-122).[35]

monia in 1984 have unquestionably added to the overall deterioration in the economy (*New African* 1984d:42).

[35] Cohen (1984:3) argues that calculations of the disparity between ru-

The growing economic disparity between the modern and traditional sectors has been identified by the traditional authorities as a major threat to the state. Just prior to independence, for example, the head of the Imbokodvo, Prince Makhosini, made a final appeal to the British government on behalf of the king. He warned of a "time bomb" that the British had planted in Swaziland and said that the Swaziland government did not intend to sit idly by and watch it explode (Kuper 1978:196-197). Makhosini was referring to the fact that 47 percent of the country's total land area was still controlled by whites—many of whom are absentee owners. This situation has remained largely unchanged. For example, in 1982, there were eight hundred farms on ITFs. About one-fourth of the total area of Swaziland was under the control of thirty-five private farms. Moreover, only twenty-four farms accounted for 63 percent of the area under cultivation, and only 5.7 percent of the ITF land area of approximately 800,000 hectares was under cultivation at any given time. This means that large areas of land on the ITFs are not effectively occupied or were used exclusively for winter grazing of South African livestock.

The prince pointed out that in the midst of growing affluence in the modern sector, Swazi in the traditional sector are crowded with insufficient land to grow food for themselves.[36] It has been estimated, for example, that the importation of foods and foodstuffs constituted 9.6 per-

---

ral and urban income have tended to exaggerate the actual difference. He estimates that the per capita rural homestead income is within the range of 425 to 475 emalangeni, whereas the per capita income in one part of the capital city, Mbabane, was 820 emalangeni, and it ranged between 411 emalangeni for low-income families and 710 emalangeni for middle income families in the country's other major urban area, Manzini.

[36] Total cultivated area on Swazi Nation Land is 67 percent higher than it is on ITF land. The only potential for expanded cultivation on Swazi Nation Land is in the lowveld, where crop production is restricted by insufficient rainfall. In the middle and highveld, arable land is almost fully utilized (ILO 1977:88).

cent of the country's imports in 1971 and 8.5 percent in 1974. Food imports have increased in terms of volume and value, rising by an estimated 17.8 percent a year from 1971 to 1974 and by 35 percent a year from 1978 to 1981 (ILO 1977:71, and *Africa South of the Sahara* 1984:854).

This has placed the Swazi rulers in a serious dilemma. The shortage of arable land available to the Swazi is depressing the economic conditions in the traditional sector. This has tended to undermine the authority of the chiefs and their counselors and thus erode the entire chieftaincy system.[37] However, the regime depends upon the modern sector for revenue, investment, and foreign exchange.[38] Thus it cannot act against it by incorporating commercial and freehold land into Swazi Nation Land without weakening the financial basis of the state.

An indication of the extreme sensitivity of the land issue to the chieftaincy was the queen regent's dismissal of Prime Minister Mabandla Dlamini in March 1983, acting

[37] Population pressure on limited land area has resulted in increasing conflict between chiefs, sometimes causing the destruction of property, gardens, and huts. The reason for the conflict is that the prestige of a chief rests largely upon the size of his following. Since each chief is obliged to allocate land to each family sufficient for their needs, as the population in a chief's area increases, he is forced to search for idle land outside of his jurisdiction to satisfy the demand for land. This situation inevitably leads to conflicts between chiefs and to illegal squatting on unused ITL (Kuper 1978:111).

[38] In addition to receipts from SACU, the sugar levy, and company taxes, the traditional authorities have transferred economic surplus from the modern sector to the traditional sector. The medium of transfer is the Tibiyo Taka Ngwane Fund (renamed the Tisuka Taka Ngwane in 1975), which enters into joint ventures with private sector capital. Originally set up to manage mineral royalties that were held "in trust" for the Swazi nation by the king, it has become involved in practically every industry in the modern sector from asbestos mining, sugar production, the national airline, hotels, banking, and insurance to breweries and construction. The fund is not accountable to Parliament but is under the exclusive control of the ruling Liqoqo—the Supreme Council of State. Its 1981 balance sheet was 41 million emalangeni (U.S. $47 million) in assets (Daniel 1982:103-105, and *African Business* 1984t:6).

on behalf of the powerful Supreme Council of State (SCS). In addition to the royal family's concern over Mabandla's investigation of official corruption, powerful members of the Liqoqo were outraged over the prime minister's opposition to pursuing an agreement with South Africa in 1981 to annex certain South African territories (large parts of KaNgwane and Ingwavuma) to Swaziland. The Swazi have historically claimed these territories as Swazi national land. Mabandla's successor was the deputy prime minister, Prince Bhekimpi Dlamini, who was a strong supporter of the land takeover.

A problem that is closely related to the land issue is the exodus of the productive labor force from the traditional sector to the urban areas in search of wage employment. This has tended to add to the size of the urban labor force and has produced a class of unemployed urban squatters that has tended to undermine the traditional social order in the urban areas. For example, in February 1982, the minister of finance, J.F.L. Simelane, presented an economic review for the 1978 to 1981 period accompanying the 1982 budget.

Job creation in the modern sector was identified as a serious problem. According to the review, the creation of jobs in the modern sector was too low to meet the demand.[39] Just under three thousand workers per year have found employment in the modern sector, which left an estimated five thousand to be absorbed by agriculture and the traditional sector (*Africa Research Bulletin* 1982:6,553). Just before his death in August 1982, the king referred to the urban unemployment problem as one that was "bound to reach crisis proportions" (*Times of Swaziland* 1982).

[39] An estimated seven thousand seek employment primarily in the urban areas at the end of each school year. Of this, fewer than three thousand will be successful. It is estimated that thirty thousand were unable to find employment during the period from 1975 to 1982 (ILO 1977:33-36, and *Africa Insight* 1984:7).

The obvious solution to the land shortage problem appears to be the reacquisition of idle individual tenure farmland from non-Swazis. However, the government fears that such action would discourage private investors and foreign businessmen and thereby undermine the private sector. Since Swaziland's economy is heavily dependent upon the private sector, its decline would deprive the government of crucial revenues and foreign exchange. Hence, the government has tended to follow an ambivalent policy on the land issue.

On the one hand, the government has enacted legislation designed to buy back unused ITF, while on the other hand, it has not actually carried out the enactments. For example, in an effort to win support for the INM in a general election scheduled for 1972, the government sponsored the Land Speculation Control Bill of 1971 in Parliament. The bill was ostensibly designed to prevent the sale of ITF to noncitizens without the approval of a land control board. The stated objective of the legislation was to control land speculation that would have placed the ITFs beyond the means of the Swazi to purchase. This legislation was followed by the introduction in 1974 of a penalty tax on cultivable freehold land that was kept out of cultivation. The United Kingdom Overseas Development Ministry also gave the Swaziland government a grant of $3.6 million to buy back unused ITF on behalf of the Swazi nation. However, only one-third of this sum was used, and ITF remained largely in the hands of foreigners.

Ironically, it is in the relatively prosperous modern sector (which includes the ITF land) that the government has experienced political opposition. Even before independence the urban labor force openly confronted the colonial government and ignored appeals from the traditional authorities to settle their labor disputes.[40] The most notewor-

[40] Mbabane and Manzini are the only two urban centers in the country, with populations of about 39,000 and 14,000 respectively. However,

thy example of the workers' refusal to accept the authority of the chieftaincy was the Havelock mine workers' strike of 1963. Union leaders called for an increase in the minimum wage, an end to racial discrimination, more food, and, significantly, the dismissal of royal *tindvuna* (or "Ndabazabantu")[41] who were accused of corruption. In the ensuing strike, workers ignored the king's personal appeal to return to work (Potholm 1972:90). In October 1977, riots also broke out as a result of the government's suppression of strike action called by the now-banned three-thousand-member Swaziland National Association of Teachers, who were protesting their low salaries. And in June 1982, four hundred workers at the Luphohlo project in the Ezulwini Valley went on strike to protest the dismissal of their representative. When ordered to return to work, the strike leaders challenged the authority of the state to force them to resume work and condemned the threats that were veiled in appeals for loyalty to the king and nation (*Times of Swaziland* 1982a).

It is clear to the traditional authorities that laborers in urban and industrial centers (where most of the estimated 7.2 percent of the non-Swazi population is) are neither loyal nor accountable to their chiefs. Workers obviously feel that

there are several other smaller townships with populations ranging from 500 to 4,000. Several of them were built by the mining, agricultural, and forestry companies to house their workers and families and are administered directly by the companies. Other townships, such as Siteki, Pigg's Peak, Mankayane, Lavumisa, Nhlangano, Hlatikulu, and Matsapha, are under the administrative jurisdiction of government appointed district commissioners. An estimated 47,000 or 15 percent of the African wage labor force resides in designated urban areas in the country (Kuper 1978:260; Swaziland 1983:11: and *Africa South of the Sahara* 1984:858).

[41] Ndabazabantu is the name for the king's representative in an area (that is, village or compound) who is supposed to work with a Libandla consisting of Libandla workers' representatives whom they elect. He is the eyes, ears, and spokesman of the workers when dealing with the management on behalf of the workers. All requests for the holding of workers' meetings are supposed to go to the Ndabazabantu first.

their interests can only be adequately represented by trade unions and political parties—both of which have been outlawed.[42]

The events leading to the suspension of the constitution in 1973 suggest that the action was directly related to the growing political strength of industrial workers. For example, from 1964 to 1967, the leading nationalist party, the Ngwane National Liberatory Congress (NNLC), substantially increased its electoral strength. In the first national election of 1964, the NNLC received only 11,464 votes (9.1 percent of the total). However, in 1967, it received 48,744 votes (or 20.2 percent of the total). In the 1972 election, the party (which divided into two factions—one led by Ambrose Zwane and the other by K. M. Samketi) again won about 20 percent of the total vote cast but for the first time defeated the Imbokodvo's candidates in a constituency and elected three candidates to Parliament. It is significant to note in this regard that one of the Imbokodvo members who lost his seat in this election was Prince Mfanasibili Dlamini and that he was defeated by a future prime minister, Prince Mabandla Dlamini representing the NNLC.

The NNLC's popularity has always been among the industrial workers and the urban population. Hence, it is not surprising that the first constituency won by the party was Mphumalanga, where the unions have a strong following among sugar cane workers and where the nontraditional missionary influence is strong.

However, the most serious challenge to the traditional Swazi state to date came from within the regime. The power struggle within the royal family following the king's death in 1982 had its origins in a direct challenge to the traditional monarchy and the chieftaincy system itself. Iron-

---

[42] The only union that has been allowed to operate is the small Bank Workers' Union, which is recognized by the employers and has not challenged the authority of the state.

ically, it began before the king's death and was a result of his own appointment of a "modernist" in the person of Prince Mabandla Dlamini to the position of prime minister after the death of a "traditionalist" prime minister, Prince Maphevu Dlamini.

Prior to Mabandla's appointment he was a manager of a large sugar estate. His only previous experience in politics was to oppose the Imbokodvo, representing the opposition NNLC. In addition to Mabandla's reputation for honesty and managerial competence, it appears that the king took a calculated risk in appointing him to the prime ministry. The assignment must, in part at least, have been designed to appease industrial urban worker dissatisfaction with the traditional Swazi state. By appointing someone who would be seen as representing their interests and someone who at one time had openly opposed the king's party the king hoped to defuse a threat to the regime.[43]

The idea backfired, however, when, instead of being guided by his royal advisers and senior chiefs, Mabandla set out to assert the constitutional primacy of the government over traditional authorities. He sought to do this by attempting to remove a powerful "traditionalist" (Senator Polycarp Dlamini) from the cabinet and by arresting the two most powerful members of the Liqoqo, Prince Mfana-sibili and Chief Maseko, on charges of sedition. The action failed, however, and Mabandla was removed from office instead.[44]

[43] It was consistent with King Sobhuza's style of political leadership to forgive former political opponents and to coopt them into his government. For example, Sobhuza pardoned his daughter, Princess Betfusile, Prince Dumisa, Arthur Khoza, Sishayi Nxumalo, George Msibi, as well as Prince Mabandla.

[44] Mabandla's strategy miscarried when the remaining members of the Liqoqo acted in self-defense and pressured the queen regent, Dzeliwe (acting on behalf of the designated successor to King Sobhuza who was a minor) to dismiss the prime minister. In his place, Dzeliwe appointed the more conservative traditionalist Prince Bhekimpi Dlamini, one of the architects of the Swazi army, to the prime ministry. In August 1983, the Su-

Had Mabandla been successful in establishing the supremacy of the modern executive apparatus of the state (cabinet and civil service) over the chieftaincy, however, it would undoubtedly have set Swaziland on a more conflictive political course in its relations with South Africa. This is evident, for example, in Mabandla's opposition to South Africa's proposed annexation of South African land,[45] which was undoubtedly due to the high political costs of the agreement to his government. The stigma associated with such a land deal was that it would appear to the OAU and SADCC (Swaziland belongs to both) as support for South Africa's policy of "denationalizing" blacks. However, the greater cost to Mbandla would have been the loss of urban support within Swaziland for his "modernist" reform policies because of his obligation to collaborate closely with South African security forces. The implied agreement was that in return for the land concession the Swazi government would cooperate with the South Africans in removing the ANC presence in Swaziland. However, not only was there opposition to South African security "assistance" within Swaziland's paramilitary police but the South African ANC had support within the urban areas of the country. In addition, since many ANC members were ethnically Swazi from South Africa, it was

---

preme Council of State dismissed the queen regent, who herself had tried to dismiss the entire Supreme Council. The SCS proceeded to appoint a new queen regent, Ntombi La Thwala, and thereby confirm their dominance of the state apparatus. This was formalized in the November 1983 elections for a new Parliament. However, the widespread fear in the urban areas that Bhekimpi might compromise Swaziland's sovereignty by collaborating too closely with South Africa was a real constraint upon the traditional rulers.

[45] The proposed incorporation of Ingwavuma (in Kwazulu) and Ka-Ngwane (in KaNgwane—the so-called Swazi national state in South Africa) would have increased the surface area of Swaziland from 17,357 square kilometers to more than 25,000 square kilometers. This would have tripled the population of Swaziland and, importantly, it would have given the landlocked country an outlet to the sea at Kosi Bay.

feared that the Swazi police and army in collaboration with the South African security forces would use this as a pretext to eliminate enemies of the Swazi state.

The Swazi government signed a nonaggression pact with South Africa in 1982. However, they only announced the pact in 1984. The timing of the announcement was probably connected with the growing urban opposition to the new Swazi government led by the traditionalist Prince Bhekimpi. The Swazi rulers undoubtedly felt that it was necessary to put their opponents on notice that they might request security assistance from South Africa to put down any urban rebellion.

Strategy for Dealing with the Threat

In order to control the political pressures emanating from the modern sector and to reconsolidate the rural basis of the state, the government has embarked upon a program of commercializing the peasantry in the traditional sector. In this undertaking, however, the government rejected proposals to grant freehold title to peasants on SNL. To follow such a course clearly would undermine the power of the chiefs. In the rural areas, conditions of work are associated with rights to land that is regulated by the chiefs according to family and community obligations and commoners' loyalty to the Ngwenyama. If the existing land tenure significantly altered, it would undermine the social base of the traditional Swazi state.

In addition, since the government depends upon the modern sector for revenue and foreign exchange, it cannot act against the private sector without weakening the economic base of the state. Therefore, the only real option open to the government is to concentrate upon developing thousands of lucrative family farms in the traditional sector to enable Swazi peasants to achieve a standard of living comparable with that of wage earners in the urban sector (Maina and Strieker 1971:4).

The government's efforts to help subsistence farmers make the transition to semicommercial farming is through the introduction of large-scale area-based integrated agricultural projects called the Rural Development Areas Programme (RDAP), which are located on Swazi Nation Land (see Map 11). The RDAPs are the focal point of the government's developmental strategy (Swaziland 1974:32). Although they originated in 1965, the government only placed major emphasis upon them after 1970.

By 1985, an estimated 43 million emalangeni, funded largely by Britain, the World Bank, and the European Economic Community, will have been spent on the program. At the end of the second phase of the project (1977 to 1983) it covered roughly one-half of total SNL and included about one-half of the total rural population. The principal economic objectives of the program are to achieve self-sufficiency in staple foods (such as maize) and to increase the production of cash crops (primarily cotton and tobacco) in the traditional sector.

The RDAP is designed to help fulfill these objectives by providing necessary infrastructural support such as roads, irrigation, livestock development, agricultural extension, marketing, grazing, fencing, employment, and other social services to encourage increased productivity on SNL. However, to date, at least, the RDAPs have failed to realize their economic objectives. While there are some isolated successes such as the Vuvulane Irrigation System, and while SNL producers now account for 90 percent of cotton production and 80 percent of tobacco output, the total production of SNL cash crops is low, with few homesteads producing them (only 15 percent of SNL homesteads produce cotton). Instead of achieving food self-sufficiency, peasants have become more dependent upon food imports.

The significance of the RDAP developmental strategy for understanding Swaziland's political economy turns on the key role of the chiefs in the program's implementation. Lo-

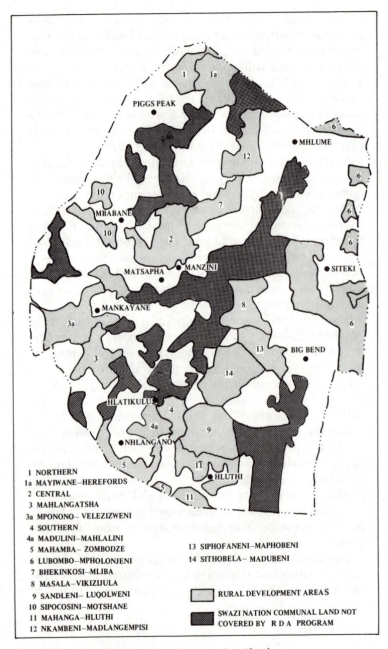

1 NORTHERN
1a MAYIWANE–HEREFORDS
2 CENTRAL
3 MAHLANGATSHA
3a MPONONO– VELEZIZWENI
4 SOUTHERN
4a MADULINI–MAHLALINI
5 MAHAMBA– ZOMBODZE
6 LUBOMBO–MPHOLONJENI
7 BHEKINKOSI–MLIBA
8 MASALA–VIKIZIJULA
9 SANDLENI– LUQOLWENI
10 SIPOCOSINI–MOTSHANE
11 MAHANGA–HLUTHI
12 NKAMBENI–MADLANGEMPISI

13 SIPHOFANENI–MAPHOBENI
14 SITHOBELA– MADUBENI

RURAL DEVELOPMENT AREAS

SWAZI NATION COMMUNAL LAND NOT
COVERED BY R D A PROGRAM

Map 11. Rural Development Areas Program: Swaziland
SOURCE: Third National Development Plan, Mbabane, Swaziland.

cal chiefs and Tinkhundla are the local units of government under the terms of the 1978 constitution. The Tinkhundla have direct jurisdiction over modern governmental
offices that operate in their locale. They have all-embrac-
ing authority to draft development plans for their area (in
consultation with the central Rural Development Board)
and have the authority to supervise and coordinate all governmental agencies involved in implementing the plan.
This means, in effect, that the RDAPs are under the control
of chiefs at the traditional regional level. The political status of major chiefs has thus been increased. They now have
the power to approve the establishment of RDAPs in their
areas and to authorize the distribution of RDAP service
and benefits to their followers.

The government's efforts to create a prosperous rural
bourgeoisie under the auspices of the chieftaincy is related
to the underlying objective of revitalizing peasant support
for the traditional Swazi state, which is being eroded by
the modern sector and is unable to absorb more than a few
hundred new job seekers each year.

The implications of Swaziland's political economy for
an understanding of potential threats to the traditional
state are clear. Since the state is primarily based upon the
peasant sector, major changes in Swaziland's economic
ties with South Africa would not in itself constitute a significant threat to the regime. By contrast, since the modern
sector is based primarily upon links with the South African economy, disruption of that economic relationship
would have a direct and adverse impact upon the urban
sector. If it were to decline seriously, it would ultimately
force the industrial urban workers to either migrate to
other countries in search of employment or it would force
them to rely more heavily upon the traditional sector.
Either event would tend to strengthen the social base of the
traditional state.

By contrast, nationalist organizations such as the NNLC
and the Swaziland Liberation Movement depend heavily

upon the modern urban sector for their political support. Hence, Swaziland's continued economic dependence upon South Africa is necessary to sustain the modern sector, which is the base of political support for the opposition movements. While the traditional state would likely survive a disruption of its economic ties with South Africa, it is unlikely that its nationalist opponents would remain a potent political threat to the traditional rulers if ties with South Africa were cut. Therefore, contrary to conventional wisdom, instead of the Swazi state being an "economic hostage" of South Africa (Halpern 1965:92-107), it is the nationalist opposition that is most heavily dependent upon those economic ties.

CHAPTER FOUR

Bolstering State Power through Regional Inputs: Malawi, Mozambique, and Zambia,

THE THIRD CATEGORY of state involvement in the regional economy is one in which regimes have, for the most part, effectively used their economic ties with other countries in the region to strengthen their domestic base of power. States that fall into this category are Malawi, Mozambique, Zambia, and Zaire (discussed in Chapter 5). In these countries, regimes have strategically manipulated regional economic ties to build and defend their national political power.

They have, for example, maintained their economic ties with South Africa, despite joining SADCC, openly attacking South Africa in international fora, and even supporting movements dedicated to the overthrow of South Africa. An indication of this strategic manipulation of economic ties with states in the region is Zambia and Mozambique's decision to break off economic relations with Rhodesia during the 1970s despite great economic costs to them. This action was taken in conjunction with final efforts to remove the illegal Rhodesian regime from power. Importantly, neither action involved major domestic political costs to the regimes in power.

The Zambians reversed their decision to break off ties with Rhodesia, however, after domestic political costs began to mount. Mozambique did not because the economic costs did not lead to undermining the regime's domestic political support. In its relations with South Africa, by contrast, Mozambique has made every effort to maintain and expand economic ties because they have tended to bolster the regime's domestic political power despite the armed insurgency within Mozambique that, ironically, has been supported by South Africa.

MALAWI

In Malawi, the life president, Dr. Hastings Kamuzu Banda, effectively used investment, trade, aid, and labor remittances primarily from South Africa to build a personal base of political power to support his rule. He sought to achieve this by following a twofold political strategy. First, he used economic inputs from South Africa to transform political supporters into commercial agricultural estate owners whose prosperity and economic security depended upon their personal loyalty to the president. Second, he adopted a "divide and rule" strategy of forming "ethnic" patron-client relationships with chiefs and their traditional following against ethnic groups that had supported leaders of the Malawi Congress party (MCP) who challenged Banda's leadership.

Under Banda's rule Malawi followed a "neutral" foreign policy toward Rhodesia, South Africa, and Portuguese Mozambique primarily to ensure that his agricultural estate and "divide and rule" strategies succeeded. For example, Banda sought to take advantage of cooperative economic relations with these countries to foster the accelerated growth of the estate sector. When the Frente de Libertçao de Moçambique (Frelimo) came to power in Mozambique in 1975, Banda maintained Malawi's neutral foreign policy by seeking a rapproachement with the new and "hostile" government of Mozambique and by joining SADCC while maintaining diplomatic ties and economic relations with South Africa.

Colonial Legacy

In order to understand the domestic political importance of Banda's neutral foreign policy toward Rhodesia,
South Africa, and Mozambique, it is necessary to appreciate the colonial economic ties that Banda's government inherited at independence in 1964.[1] Historically, Malawi has
played the role of a labor reservoir primarily for Zimbabwe
and South Africa. Boeder (1984) notes, for example, that
Rhodesia and South Africa competed for Nyasaland (Malawi) labor to develop the mines and farms in Rhodesia
and the diamond and gold mines in South Africa.

Boeder (1984:22) estimates that according to the 1966
population estimates (the first census), the number of Malawians living and working outside of the country was
266,000. The actual figure was probably twice that number. The 1971 figure was 487,932 living abroad, which was
about 10 percent of Malawi's total population of 4,670,000.
An estimated 375,000 Malawians had applied for Rhodesian passports in 1973, there were 179,932 Malawians living and working in South Africa, 43,000 Malawians working in Zambia, and 8,000 in Tanzania during the period
between 1963 and 1967 (Boeder 1984:22,24).

The significance of the roughly half million migrant labor force to the Malawian government was the large inflows of migrant labor remittances. Boeder notes, for example, that between 1965 and 1967 labor remittances
averaged 4 million kwacha in foreign exchange annually.
This made labor remittances the third largest foreign exchange earner (after tea and tobacco). Remittances grew to

[1] The tendency in the literature is to focus upon the personality and
ideas of Dr. Banda in attempting to explain Malawi's foreign policy. See
for example, Humphrey (1973), McMaster (1974), Thomas (1975), and
Williams (1978). While Banda has unquestionably dominated the country's foreign policy, his government was nevertheless forced to formulate
foreign policy within the context of regional economic relationships inherited at independence.

7 million kwacha in 1969, 12 million (U.S. $15 million) in 1972, and peaked at 32 million kwacha in 1975. Labor remittances were second only to tobacco as the country's largest earner of foreign exchange.

Until the mid-1960s, Rhodesia and South Africa competed for Malawian labor. However, after the Rhodesian Unilateral Declaration of Independence in 1965, South Africa became the dominant market for Malawi's migrant labor. Malawi's shift away from Rhodesia toward South Africa as her principle market for migratory labor was largely due to Rhodesia's restrictive policy toward foreign African workers.[2] This policy placed Malawi in a precarious position. It had the effect of threatening the large Malawian migratory labor force with sudden explusion from Rhodesia, thereby posing a threat to sizeable labor remittances. As a consequence the annual flow of Malawians to Rhodesia declined from 21,838 shortly after UDI in 1965 to only a few thousand (Boeder 1984:21).

Boeder (1984:20) explains Malawi's decision to establish diplomatic relations with South Africa and to conclude the so-called "trade with the devil" and labor agreements with the country in terms of Malawi's economic relationship with South Africa. Apart from the jarring psychological impact of being the only black African country to have diplomatic relations with South Africa, the agreements were simply a formal recognition of the country's importance to Malawi's economy. Hence, Boeder explains Malawi's policy of "dialogue" with South Africa in terms

[2] Boeder (1984:21-22) notes in this regard that the Rhodesian government adopted the Closed Labour Areas Order of 1966, which prohibited new arrivals from looking for work in the major urban areas. In 1967, Rhodesia took "administrative action" to replace "alien Africans" with local Africans. In 1972, the government amended the Africans Registration and Identification Act which empowered the regime to refuse to register or reregister foreign Africans for employment purposes without explanation or legal appeal.

of an exchange of Malawi's "political neutrality" toward South Africa for important economic benefits.

The Malawi Congress Party's Base of Support

In order to appreciate the political significance of Malawi's economic ties with South Africa it is necessary to understand the nature of the political threat to Banda's leadership of the Malawi Congress party in 1964. The unique history and organization of the MCP played an important part in Banda's strategy for coping with the threat to his rule. Vail and White (1984) point out, for example, that the Congress party had a weak organization. It was little more than a coalition of regionally oriented economic interests with a common grievance in breaking the political ties binding Malawi to the Central African Federation (Northern Rhodesia, Nyasaland, and Southern Rhodesia). They argue that the MCP managed to forge a loose coalition of political support from the three regions of Malawi (northern, central, and southern) based primarily upon specific economic grievances toward the federation.

The principal grievance in the north against the federation was that it threatened to block the Africanization of Malawi's civil service. Northerners had the advantage of educational opportunities due to the strong mission school system in the region. Therefore they clearly stood to gain the most from an accelerated Africanization of the country's state bureaucracy. Hence, northerners perceived the federal civil service as the chief barrier to their economic advancement.

In the central region the principal economic grievance was the unfair pricing and buying policies of the government's tobacco marketing board. Vail and White (1984:81) point out, for example, that since the tobacco boom of the 1920s, Chewa-speakers in the region openly opposed the Native Tobacco Board's discriminatory pricing policies. Hence, a major political grievance in the central region against the federation was based on the desire to secure the economic advantages that European planters and Asian merchants enjoyed.

In the southern region the primary economic grievance directed at the federation was the shortage of land. There was a strong desire to take possession of unused estate land and to produce cash crops. Malawians in the south also wished to participate in the migratory wage-earning labor force.

Apart from these regionally specific economic grievances directed at breaking the federation, the MCP had little in the way of a program of action, ideology, or party principles.[3] Hence, the MCP was a party without a political agenda and without a strong organizational base. Its primary raison d'être was simply a commitment to rid the country of domination by the federation. There was little or no consideration given to what was to follow. Apart from prominent personalities who had regional followings, the party had little direct contact with the majority of the population (Vail and White 1984:2).

In this situation, Dr. Banda, the leader of the ruling MCP, was challenged shortly after independence in 1964. Among the six cabinet ministers who opposed him were the founders and principal organizers of the party.[4] In op-

[3] The closest thing to a party platform or principles was Banda's famous "Gwelo Dream," which he reportedly had while imprisoned by the colonial authorities. The vision was that of a lakeshore highway, a university, and a new capital for the country.

[4] The ministers who opposed Banda in the so-called cabinet crisis of 1964 were Yatuta Chisiza, Kanyama Chiume, Orton Chirwa, Augustine Bwanausi, Henry Chipembere, and Willie Chokani. Only two ministers, John Msonthi and John Tembo, supported Banda in the dispute. Of the ministers who opposed Banda, only three of them have survived. Orton Chirwa was imprisoned in Malawi in 1981 and given a life sentence for treason, Kanyama Chiume is leading the Dar es Salaam-based Congress for the Second Republic, and Willie Chokani retired from politics and is living in exile.

posing Banda, the ministers raised three specific points of criticism and had two general grievances. The specific criticisms of Banda were his foreign policy alignment with Southern Rhodesia and Mozambique, the institution of the fee of a "tickey" (threepence fee) for hospital out-patients, and his acceptance of the Skinner Report, which recommended continued low wages and conditions of service for Malawians in the civil service. The first general grievance was with Banda's autocratic style of policy making in which he failed to consult his cabinet. The second charged that Banda practiced nepotism and favoritism in making key political appointments. For example, the ministers criticized Banda's appointment of John Tembo to the cabinet on the grounds that Tembo was the uncle of Cecilia Kadzamira who was Banda's private secretary, personal nurse, and the official government hostess. The ministers also accused Banda of favoritism for appointing Aleke Banda (no relation of Dr. Banda) as secretary general of the MCP (Short 1974:197-230).

The significance of the alienation of senior party officials from Banda was that it isolated the president within the MCP. After surviving the immediate crisis, however, Banda purged and transformed the party, the state apparatus, and the private sector.[5] The president set out to cre-

[5] The so-called "cabinet crisis" occurred in October 1964, and by December of 1964 about fifty people were under police restriction and large numbers of people, especially from the ministers' constituencies, were suspended from party membership. A number of chiefs from the ministers' areas were also deposed, and district councils were dissolved. Banda received the endorsement of the Parliament to reinstitute the powers of preventive detention that the colonial authorities had used against the MCP during the independence struggle. He also received parliamentary approval for the Young Pioneers Act, which made the party's youth movement (a paramilitary force) independent of both the police and army—answerable only to Banda. Critics have accused the Young Pioneers of being Banda's personal bodyguard and the enforcer of party

ate a network of national patronage that formed the basis of his personal political power.

Banda was absent from the country for almost forty years prior to returning to Malawi in 1958 to lead the MCP. He had returned at the request of party leaders who were now in rebellion against him. This made it incumbent upon Banda to establish an independent base of political power on which he could rely to rule Malawi. He was aided in this task by the absence of a well-organized national party apparatus.

Banda's Political Strategy

Malawi's economic relationship with South Africa played a crucial role in enabling President Banda to foster the creation of a prosperous estate sector that he used as political patronage. After the Malawi-South African trade agreement was signed in 1967, trade, investment, and aid from South Africa increased significantly.[6] For example, the trade agreement granted Malawi the duty-free importation of five hundred thousand pounds annually of its tobacco, tea, oils, and other manufactured goods into South Africa.[7] In addition, agricultural and animal products that

---

rules and discipline. For a discussion of Banda's consolidation of control over the party and the state apparatus see Williams (1978:196-269).

[6] Malawi also signed a labor agreement with South Africa in 1965. The agreement gave Banda's government control of supplying Malawian labor to the Witwatersrand Native Labour Association (Wenela), which recruited foreign labor for the gold mines in South Africa. In addition to earning a commission for each laborer that was delivered to Wenela depots in the country and granting an unlimited recruitment for Malawian labor, it gave Banda political control of migratory labor opportunities for Malawians wishing to work in South Africa. An indication of the importance of this agreement to Banda's government is that the number of Malawian workers who were recruited by Wenela increased from 29,180 in 1964 to 129,207 in December 1972 (Boeder 1984:20).

[7] Agriculture is Malawi's most important economic sector estimated to support about 90 percent of the population and to contribute 46 percent of GDP and about 90 percent of the country's total export earnings. In

were exported to South Africa were given most-favored nation duties. Boeder (1984:21) notes in this regard that since tobacco and tea were Malawi's most important exports, the trade agreement with South Africa tended to link the prosperity of Malawi's leading export industries to the South African economy.

In addition to this highly favorable trading agreement with South Africa, Malawi received major developmental loans from the country. South Africa made a thirty-three-million-dollar loan to Malawi for one of Banda's major projects—a new capital constructed in Lilongwe in the central region. A South African consortium also financed a twenty-million-dollar railway line between Malawi and Mozambique. And during the period from 1964 to 1972, South Africa was Malawi's third most important aid donor behind the United Kingdom and the World Bank.[8] In addition to relying upon South Africa as the cheapest supplier of imported goods (which increased from only 3 percent of Malawi's total imports in 1964 to 40 percent in 1983), South African transnational corporations became actively involved in promoting trade and investment in Malawi. For example, South African transnationals such as Lever Brothers, Lyons Bond, the Booker Group, and Leyland established affiliated companies in Malawi and made substantial investments there (Makgetla and Seidman 1980:126-127, 160-161).

Malawi's strengthened economic relationship with South Africa also played a crucial role in providing the in-

---

1979, for example, tobacco accounted for 57.9 percent of total export earnings, and tea contributed 19.6 percent of total earnings. Five export crops (tobacco, tea, groundnuts, cotton, and sugar) accounted for 91.8 percent of the country's total export earnings in 1979 (Malawi 1980: Table 4.4).

[8] For the period 1964 to 1972, Malawi's top three foreign aid donors and their contributions were the United Kingdom with £66,366,424, the World Bank with £11,702,769, and South Africa with £10,624,414 (Boeder 1984:24).

itial economic surplus necessary to finance Banda's agricultural estate and "divide and rule" strategies. For example, Malawi has run persistently large current account deficits since independence. These deficits have been offset by the annual British budgetary grant-in-aid of £3 million (terminated in 1973), long-term government borrowing, private capital investment, foreign capital inflows, and remittances from Malawians working in South Africa.[9] The importance of governmental borrowing and private capital inflows and remittances from South Africa until 1974 is evident in the relatively low proportion of domestic financing as a percentage of total investment financing in Malawi. As late as 1972, for example, only about 40 percent of Malawi's investment was derived from domestic sources (Williams 1978:272). Therefore, without the benefits that Malawi derived from its advantageous economic relationship with South Africa Banda would not have had the large-scale capital necessary to carry out his strategies.

DOMESTIC

Banda extracted economic surplus for the purpose of financing his political strategies through two commercial banks, his holding company—Press Holdings[10]—and the parastatal Agricultural Development and Marketing Cor-

[9] Kydd (1984:18) points out in this regard that Malawi's largest aid donor up until 1972, the United Kingdom, imposed firm control over the use of its assistance by setting a framework for Malawi's revenue and expenditure policies. This is in marked contrast to South Africa's willingness to provide assistance for Banda's prestige projects such as the new capital.

[10] Under the terms of the International Monetary Fund's conditions for structural adjustment loans granted in 1981 and 1983, the Press group was "restructured" under the supervision of the Malawian government. The stated objective of the restructuring was to place Press on more viable commercial footing. One major result of this change was that by virtue of the government assuming control of the Press group, it has been transformed into a parastatal institution comparable to ADMARC. For a discussion of the change in the status of Press, see Kydd (1984:61).

poration (ADMARC). Kydd (1984:22-4) notes, for example, the Press Holdings, along with ADMARC and the Malawi Development Corporation (MDC—a state corporation), were able to dominate the country's banking system by forming a controlling block of shareholders in the commercial banks. Since Press was the largest shareholder and since it was almost entirely owned by President Banda, it provided the leadership for these institutions. This gave Press access to commercial bank credit that enabled Banda to undertake major investments in agricultural estates as well as to secure a monopoly over the private sector. Even the major transnational corporations were obliged to enter into joint ventures with the Press group on terms that were highly favorable to Press.

It is instructive to mention the vast scope and magnitude of the Press group. Press has large investments in estate agriculture and 50 percent equity in Limbe Leaf, which controls the purchase of Malawi's tobacco at auctions and processes and exports the product. It also has investments in rubber and sugar estates, cattle ranches, ethanol production, owns the country's largest retail chain, transport company, and bakery chain, has investments in the largest civil engineering firm, and has interests in a large clothing manufacturing company, to mention only a few.

Press was also the recipient of large loans from ADMARC and the MDC, and it has borrowed on the Eurocurrency market with the benefit of government guarantees. Hence, through the medium of a virtually wholly owned private investment corporation and parastatal institution, Banda was able to accumulate large capital reserves that enabled him to finance his political strategies.

Banda sought to carry out his agricultural estate strategy of creating a personal base of power by first gaining parliamentary approval of the Malawi Land Bill in 1965, which gave the president absolute power over the use and ownership of all land in the country. The land act created three classes of land: public, private, and customary. Banda was most interested in the private land called estates because of their strategic importance in his political strategy. Most of the new estates under Banda's control were on land leased under the 1965 act. In 1974, the commercial banks were directed to provide loans for tobacco estate development. In 1980, an estimated 50 percent of total advances by commercial banks went to agriculture, almost all of which went to tobacco estates (Kydd 1984:37).

An indication of Banda's success in fostering the accelerated growth of the estates sector is evident in the growth in estate production compared to nonestate or smallholder production.[11] Table 4.1 shows the comparative growth rates of tobacco production (the country's chief cash crop) in the two sectors.[12]

---

[11] The peasant or "smallholder" farms are on "customary land," which is controlled by traditional authorities such as chiefs, headmen, "traditional courts," and district commissioners according to local custom. In contrast, leasehold and freehold land is farmed by estates and can be owned by individuals or companies and transferred by sale (Kydd 1984:46-47). Smallholder farms (1.6 hectares or less) represent 63 percent of all farms. They cultivate about 35 percent of the total acreage but only receive approximately 28 percent of total farm cash income. By contrast, the larger farms, which include the estates (that is, about four hundred major commercial farms averaging 380 hectares in the mid-1970s), constitute 19 percent of all farms. They cultivate 42 percent of total acreage and receive 51 percent of total farm cash income and 30 percent of total cash receipts (USAID 1977b:IV,4). In 1983, smallholder cash crops contributed 37 percent of total export earnings, while the estates accounted for over 60 percent of total agricultural exports. Kydd (1984:47) indicates, however, that the number of estates and their average acreage is not known nor is the total occupied area. The best estimate of the size of the estate sector is roughly 14 percent of the total cultivated land (Kydd 1984:47).

[12] The production estimates for the peasant sector were based upon annual growth rates of ADMARC's purchase of peasant production of tobacco. Since the smallholders, unlike the estate owners, were forced to sell their tobacco and other cash crop production at below market prices to ADMARC, Banda was able to extract economic surplus from peasant producers and transferred it to the estate sector and to other investments through Press Holdings. Christiansen (1984:46) estimates that between

Table 4.1 Annual Growth Rates for Estate and Peasant Production of Tobacco in Malawi

Period	Estate Production	Peasant Production
1960-1969	20.5%	−0.5%
1970-1981	37.6	12.4

SOURCE: Kydd (1984:86).

NOTE: The mean values in millions of kwacha of estate production for the period 1960-1969 was 2.1 million, and for the period 1970-1981 it rose to 29.2 million. The mean value of peasant production during these periods was 4.3 million and 16.9 million respectively.

In 1964, smallholders' exports exceeded estates' exports by about 19 percent of total export earnings. However, by 1976, the relationship had been reversed, and estate farms contributed 25 percent more than smallholders to total export earnings (USAID 1977b:IV, 4). Kydd (1984:85) has presented more recent evidence in support of the tendency of estate production to increase relative to smallholder output. During the 1970 to 1981 period, for example, estate production was calculated to have increased in terms of mean value of output at an annual growth rate of 29.2 percent for tobacco, 22.8 percent for tea, and 22.2 percent for sugar. By contrast, smallholder peasant production for the same period was 16.9 percent for tobacco, 9.9 percent for groundnuts, 8.9 percent for cotton, 4.8 percent for rice, and 4.2 percent for maize. Therefore, in contrast with smallholder production, which showed relatively weak growth in cash crop output, estate production grew rapidly.

The major reason for the increase in estate sector output was the president's use of the state to transform MCP elites into estate owners. This trend was especially noticeable in

1972 and 1981, Press Holdings was the single largest recipient of ADMARC's loans. He points out that about 27.9 million kwacha was transferred by ADMARC to the president in this way.

the mid-1970s after Dr. Banda secured his leadership position and was able to manipulate state intervention in the economy through Press Holdings and ADMARC to support the expansion of the estate sector. Banda had long expressed his commitment to encouraging Malawians to break the European monopoly on commercial farming— particularly in the production of the superior grades of tobacco. However, the timing of the program coincided with the political objective of securing political support for his regime.[13]

Most of the new estates were acquired by senior politicians, civil servants, and police and military officers who had demonstrated their personal loyalty to the president. Williams (1978:213) points out that Banda created his own system of informal political control with communication channels and sources of information that were outside of the regular party bureaucracy.

Banda's reliance upon political organizations such as the paramilitary Young Pioneers and the Youth League,[14] Women's League, traditional chiefs, and other societal elites was also part of the strategy. These elites (all of

---

[13] Kydd (1984:34-39) describes Banda's efforts to expand the estate sector in terms of three periods encompassing twelve years of highly profitable tobacco growing seasons. The first period was from 1968 to 1973 and is called the "presidential fiefdom," the second period from 1973 to 1977 is termed the "broadening of the political base of the estates," and the third period was from 1977 to 1980 and is referred to as the "crisis of viability."

[14] The Young Pioneers and the Youth League are regarded as Banda's personal political weapon of terror and intimidation. There are numerous reports of their involvement in beatings, torture, and killings of those suspected of disloyalty to the president. The Young Pioneers are, in fact, above the law and report only to Banda in carrying out their duties. Banda's use of the traditional courts (whose jurisdiction is above Malawi's High Court) to carry out his personal justice, and the ever-present threat of detention without trial, intimidates and cows elites into subservience. No one, including the highest party official or minister in Banda's government, is immune from this threat (Alifeyo Chilivumbo, private communication 1985).

whom were also members of the MCP) were personally be-
holden to Banda for loans, jobs, status, and benefits from
state programs. Banda even elevated this class privilege to
a political duty. For example, the president exhorted every
minister to have an estate. He has also constructed at his
own expense modern fully furnished houses for senior
members of the Women's League. In most of the twenty-
four districts of Malawi, for example, the chairwomen, sec-
retaries, and treasurers of MCP committees were rewarded
with houses. Banda also built houses for important chiefs
in the country—seven in Mzimba alone.

At the time of the cabinet crisis of 1964, public support
for the rebellious ministers surfaced primarily in their constituencies. Several of the ministers had considerable personal support—particularly Chipembere. Their constituencies tended to be among the more educated population
in the northern region and in the densely populated southern region.

Three of the ministers in opposition—Chiume, Chirwa,
and Chisiza, plus many top-level civil servants who sym-
pathized with them—were from the northern region. Chipembere, Chokani, and Bwanausi were from the southern
region. Of the two ministers who supported Banda, Msonthi, like Banda, was a Chewa from the central region, and
John Tembo was a Ngoni, also from the central region. In
the southern region areas of Blantyre, Zomba, and Fort
Johnston, supporters of the exministers violently clashed
with Banda's paramilitary Young Pioneers, eventually requiring troops to suppress the rebellion. While there were
no major disturbances in the northern region, many of the
civil servants who clashed with the Young Pioneers in the
southern region were, in fact, northerners.

What was significant, however, to Banda about the display of public opposition (apart from the threat) were the
areas that remained loyal to him. In the light of the political threat by northerners and southerners to Banda's rule,
he began to elaborate a populist ethnic political strategy. It

was initially designed to reward the largely rural elite in the central region (where he had taken refuge during the cabinet crisis) in order to establish a base of political support there.

From Banda's point of view the fact that he had received strong support from the central region during the cabinet crisis coincided with the fortuitous circumstances that the central region had a large population (about 37 percent of the total in 1966) and was the homeland of the Chewa, which was his ethnic identity. Hence, Banda set out to extend his personal base of political power to traditional leaders as well as to estate owners in the central region.

Banda elaborated an ethnic "divide and rule" strategy by identifying Malawian nationalism with the Chewa culture, which was based in the central region. This was accompanied by a systematic discrimination against major ethnic groups in the north and south who were suspected of sympathizing with the ministers who had opposed him. Banda also formed political alliances with the traditional rivals and enemies of the northern and southern groups he targeted for punishment.

Vail and White (1984:81-90) have described the effects of Banda's strategy upon important groups in the three regions. They note, for example, that numerous governmental departments and parastatals including the new capitol at Lilongwe were moved from the southern to the central region. Most agricultural loans were made to and most estates were located in the central region. This enabled Banda to claim with some justification that he had redressed the grievances of Chewa in the central region against the federation's barriers to Africans who wished to enter commercial farming and business. In addition, Thomas (1975:49) has noted the significant increase in the government's developmental budget allocation to the central region: the percentage increased from 11 percent in 1967 to 40 percent of the total in 1972. At the same time the percentage of the total development budget allocated to the Southern region declined from 77 percent of the total in 1967 to only 42 percent in 1972. The percentage allocated to the northern region increased nominally from 12 percent of the total development budget to 18 percent.

By contrast, the economic grievances of northerners and southerners against the federation were largely ignored and, in fact, became more severe. For example, not only has northerners' demand for accelerated Africanization of the state bureaucracy not benefited them but they have been systematically removed from government service. In addition to wholesale purges of non-Chewa civil servants from government departments and ministries, Banda imposed a mandatory retirement age of fifty in order to remove non-Chewa officers who tended to dominate government service at independence.

Likewise, in the south none of their economic grievances against the federation have been addressed. For example, there is still severe land shortage and overcrowding. In addition, ADMARC sets its prices at below market values, and southerners' opportunities for migratory work in South Africa is restricted. Preference is given to Chewa who are concentrated in the central region. This has left the southern region in much the same state that it was in before independence.

However, Banda's ethnic "divide and rule" policy did not mean that non-Chewa political elites did not prosper under his regime. In fact, the president formed political alliances with the traditional rivals of the northern and southern groups suspected of disloyalty to him. For example, Banda allied with the Lomwe in the south who tend to dominate the army. In addition, the three most powerful political elites working directly with Banda—the former Reserve Bank of Malawi governor, John Tembo; his niece Cecilia Kadzamira, the official government hostess, nurse and companion of Banda; and John Ngwiri, the secretary to the president and cabinet, head of civil service, and the presidential liaison with the police, special branch, and security forces—were all Ngonis.

FOREIGN

The loosening of Malawi's economic ties with South Africa after 1974 can be understood as an adjustment of Malawi's neutral foreign policy to the changed external political situation. The success of Banda's strategy to secure his domestic base of political support facilitated this relaxing of economic ties.

The occasion for reducing Malawi's economic dependence upon South Africa came in April 1974 after a Wenela DC-4 crashed upon takeoff at the Francistown airport in Botswana killing seventy-four Malawian labor recruits en route to mines in South Africa. Banda immediately suspended all Wenela flights pending the results of an investigation of the accident. On June 30, 1974, the government announced that South African recruitment of mining labor in Malawi would cease. Within eighteen months of the decision the number of Malawians working in South Africa mines declined from about 130,000 to only 12,000. In addition to the loss of labor remittances, the government was faced with the problem of reabsorbing a large surplus labor force.

The significance of this action in terms of Malawi's foreign policy was that it occurred at the time of the April 1974 coup in Portugal, which led to the installation of a "hostile" Frelimo government of Mozambique bordering Malawi.

In fact, the September 1974 annual meeting of the MCP that called for the termination of the recruitment of Malawians to work on South African mines virtually coincided with the formation of a transitional government of Mozambique under Frelimo's control.

The significance of the change of governments in Mozambique was that it threatened Malawi's vital access to

Mozambique's rail, road, and port facilities.[15] Malawi was heavily dependent upon Mozambique's transport and ports (primarily Nacala and Beira) for the shipment of its major export commodities and for the import of its fuel, fertilizers, and manufactured goods.

In order to guarantee Malawi's access to Mozambique's transport and port facilities, Malawi remained "neutral" during the liberation war in Mozambique and forged close external relations with the colonial government under the Salazar and Caetano regimes. This extended to cooperation with the notorious Portuguese secret police, the Polícia Internacional de Defesa do Estado (PIDE), which Frelimo accused of torturing and killing civilians and captured Frelimo insurgents.

Frelimo accused Banda's government of cooperating with PIDE by turning over suspected Frelimo guerillas who had taken refuge in Malawi. Banda was also attacked for allowing Portuguese security forces to operate in Malawi against Frelimo during the liberation war. The political tension between Malawi and Mozambique continued after its independence in 1975. This was evident in the stream of accusations by Frelimo officials that Banda allowed MNR insurgents to operate from bases in Malawi. Another indication of Frelimo's suspicion of the Malawian

[15] Since Malawi is a landlocked country, reliable and inexpensive transit of its exports and imports is essential for economic viability. An indication of just how crucial transport routes are is the additional cost associated with finding alternative routes due to both the breakdown of Mozambique's railway system (operating at about 30 percent of capacity) and the sabotage of Malawi's transport system by the MNR. The disruptions of the most convenient trade routes (via road or rail to Mozambique's ports of Nacala and Beira) have involved costly rerouting through Zimbabwe and South Africa. By one estimate, the disruption of the Nacala railway alone during the 1979 to 1983 period cost Malawi at least $140 million in foreign exchange (*Africa Confidential* 1984). As a result of the breakdown of Mozambique's railway system, in June 1984, an estimated 80 to 90 percent of Malawi's total external traffic went through South Africa (*African Business* 1984p:74).

government was its frequent references to "deserters" from Frelimo and "collaborators with Portuguese colonialism" who were given positions in the Malawian army and police after 1975. The implication of Frelimo's suspicions of the Malawian government was clear. Frelimo feared that Banda's regime was prepared to cooperate with South Africa as they had done with the Portuguese in attempting to destroy the party.

Malawi's suspension of migratory mine labor to South Africa was a recognition that it was necessary to establish a rapproachement with Frelimo to guarantee Malawi's access to Mozambique's rail, road, and port facilities.[16] It represented in part a symbolic display to Frelimo and the other Frontline States of Africa (especially Zambia and Tanzania) that Malawi shared the foreign policy goals of its African neighbors. Malawi's success in identifying its foreign policy objectives with the FLS (without, however, breaking its diplomatic relations with South Africa) was evident in the country's acceptance as a member of SADCC when it was established in March 1980.[17]

The timing of the decision to suspend South African recruitment of mineworkers in Malawi was propitious from another point of view as well. In 1974, Banda's agricultural estate strategy was paying off. In that year, for example,

---

[16] Banda sought to reassure Frelimo of his government's cooperative intentions by signing accords with Mozambique during President Machel's visit to Malawi in 1984. The accords set up a joint permanent commission and a railway cooperation agreement. Banda even offered to contribute Malawian troops in a joint effort to combat MNR sabotage against Mozambique's transport lines and facilities.

[17] By joining SADCC, Malawi improved its diplomatic relations with Zambia and Tanzania (which were strained due to the presence of the dissident cabinet ministers in these countries) and strengthened economic ties with them. Tanzania has agreed to cooperate with Malawi in constructing a road that would give Malawi direct access to the port of Dar es Saleem, and Zambia has agreed to the construction of another rail link (Mchinji-Chipata) as alternatives to the Mozambique access route to the sea (*Africa* 1984e:31 and Legum 1984:B654).

Table 4.2 Domestic Financing as a Proportion of Total Investment Financing in Malawi

Year	Percentage	Year	Percentage
1965	NA	1976	57
1966	NA	1977	68
1967	6	1978	52
1968	− 2	1979	32
1969	18	1980	28
1970	28	1981	44
1971	NA	1982	56
1972	NA	1983	57
1973	57		
1974	70		
1975	56		

SOURCES: *National Accounts Reports, 1964-1970* and *1973-1978, Economic Report 1984*, and Reserve Bank of Malawi, *Financial and Economic Review* (various years), as reported in Kydd (1984:81).
NOTE: NA = not available.

Malawi's domestic financing as a proportion of total investment financing increased to 70 percent (up from 6 percent in 1967—see Table 4.2), and, importantly, the large agricultural estates created a major new domestic source of employment. Christiansen and Kydd (1983:325) point out, for example, that the rapid growth of both large-scale agricultural estates in Malawi and the peasant sector successfully absorbed Malawi's migratory labor force after it was disengaged from South Africa in 1974 without incurring unemployment in the country.

Hence, from Banda's point of view, the Wenela air crash was an ideal opportunity to signal a shift in Malawi's regional foreign policy away from its heavy dependence upon economic ties with South Africa toward a more balanced policy regarding Mozambique and its FLS allies. The economic success of Banda's estate strategy minimized the political costs to his regime of loosening economic ties with South Africa, enabling Malawi to defuse a potentially threatening political problem that suddenly emerged on its border in Mozambique in 1974.[18]

After Banda

Banda's personal rule of Malawi for over twenty years has not only practically eliminated any likely successor to him but it has resulted in a failure to organize a legitimate system of political succession.[19] This would suggest two possible scenarios in the event that Banda (who is in his late eighties) dies while in office.

One scenario is that of a Tembo-Kadzamira-Ngwiri palace coup. Immediately after Banda's death they would seek to fill the power vacuum by inheriting the regime's vast network of legal control, including the traditional courts, land, economic, and financial resources created by

[18] Due largely to a boom in agricultural exports from the large estates, Malawi experienced a growth rate in real terms averaging 5.5 percent during the years 1967 to 1979 (*African Business* 1984o:25). Despite a decline in the country's terms of trade by about 30 percent during the 1977 to 1979 period (*African Business* 1981:24), the economy recovered in 1982 with an overall growth rate of 6.2 percent and with the estate sector showing a massive 21.4 percent increase in output (*Africa South of the Sahara* 1984:557). Malawi was also self-sufficient in food. In fact, it has exported large quantities of grain to drought-stricken countries in the region. For example, in 1984 alone Malawi exported 40,000 tons of maize to Zambia and 60,000 tons to Zimbabwe (*African Business* 1984d:51).

[19] According to the MCP constitution, if the president dies in office, the secretary-general of the party calls an emergency meeting of the National Executive Committee (NEC) within three days. The NEC will elect two members (who are also in the cabinet) to serve along with the secretary-general of the party on a presidential commission. The commission is empowered to convene an annual convention as soon as possible at which time a new president of Malawi will be elected. However, Banda has eliminated anyone occupying these key positions who had an independent base of political power or who was suspected of having presidential ambitions. Hence, those holding the positions are not regarded as having sufficient political acumen or political support to succeed Banda.

the president. They would use this blend of control and incentives to satisfy the most significant power groups in the country and would resort to repression to crush open displays of opposition or dissent. However, their lack of an independent base of power, Kadzamira's lack of political acumen, and Tembo's unpopularity would make such a scenario difficult. Even if such a coup were initially successful, it is unlikely that the police and army would support another personal dynasty under the leadership of people who are highly unpopular with the majority of the population.

A second possible outcome would be a resurrected MCP with interregional coalition support comparable with the party's support during the 1950s and 1960s. In this scenario the ultimate successors to Banda's rule would revive the party's coalition of regional political support by restoring a balance in its representation of the southern and northern interests that Banda destroyed.[20]

An important implication of such a scenario for Malawi's foreign policy is that it would be less important to maintain the country's "neutral" foreign policy toward South Africa. Banda's emphasis upon high growth in the estate sector (which primarily benefited Chewa in the central region)[21] would undoubtedly be offset by a high priority for alleviating the land shortage, crowding, and poverty

[20] Vail and White (1984:90-91) allude to this scenario by arguing that "as Banda fails the old Congress party coalition is being re-established." In this regard they point to what they see as an emerging coalition of intellectuals, small businessmen, villagers, and chiefs joining in common cause against monopoly interests, exploitative pricing policies, and corruption associated with Banda and his entourage.

[21] Kydd (1984:62) notes in this regard that under pressure from Malawi's major aid donor—the World Bank—a new technocratic administration of the estate sector was instituted after 1980 emphasizing efficiency. Kydd argues that the political implication of this development is that the new system of control was at the expense of the political elites who benefited from Banda's patronage.

of the south and the lack of employment opportunities in the north.

This would not mean, however, that trade, investment, and aid from South Africa would be less important to Banda's successors. The new leaders would undoubtedly break diplomatic ties with South Africa and attempt to strengthen their economic relationship with Zimbabwe and Zambia within the context of SADCC. Nevertheless, the economic relationship between Malawi and South Africa would remain important. What would change is that South African economic ties would cease to be used primarily for the purpose of proping up a personal base of political power on which Banda relied to rule Malawi.

Mozambique

During Mozambique's history as a Portuguese colonial possession, its economy was oriented toward servicing the South African economy. It developed as an entrepôt for regional trade and transshipment. In addition to rail, road, harbor, port storage, and processing facilities, the colonial government of Mozambique profited from remittances in foreign exchange from their migrant mine workers in South Africa.

After independence in 1975, the new government of Mozambique under the control of the ruling party, the Frente de Libertaçao de Moçambique, also benefited from the governmental revenues and remittances the country derived from its regional service sector. In fact, with the decline in agricultural production and industrial output, the service sector has become even more important to Frelimo than it was to the Portuguese colonial government.

Despite Frelimo's declared intention of forging a regional economic bloc among neighboring political allies (primarily Tanzania and Zambia) for the purpose of breaking down economic ties that benefit South Africa, Mozambique has done everything possible to expand its economic ties with the country. For example, Mozambique has tried to double its quota of Mozambicans allowed to work in South African mines despite its membership in the Southern Africa Labour Commission (*African Business* 1985:21). SALC is a regional organization comprised of countries supplying migrant labor to South Africa. Its express purpose is to break their dependence upon the South African migrant labor system. Likewise, about one-third of SADCC's transportation projects, which total an estimated $800 million, are slated for upgrading and expanding Mozambique's ports and railway system, which primarily serves South African traffic.

This had led to skeptical or cynical reactions to Frelimo's declared "internationalist duty" to help liberate Southern African countries. However, in order to understand Mozambique's foreign policy it is necessary to place it into the context of Frelimo's overriding commitment to "liberate" Mozambique itself. Mozambique's foreign policy has always occupied a secondary importance to securing the party's political control of the country. From this perspective Frelimo's internationalist duty has been shaped and defined by threats to the ruling party's political control of Mozambique.

The country's regional service sector has constituted a major source of economic support for the achievement of Frelimo's domestic political goals. It has not constrained Frelimo's freedom of political action as is usually assumed, and indeed the party has even sought to use its economic ties with South Africa as political leverage over that government.

The Regional Service Sector

Mozambique's modern industrial center is concentrated in the coastal urban areas of Maputo, Beira, Quelimane, Nampula, and Pemba and comprises 13.2 percent of the total population of 12.1 million (85 percent of the urban population is in one city—Maputo). Urbanization in Mozambique is largely attributable to the country's long coastline, which blocked the access of Southern African countries to the sea. Mozambique provides rail and road transport services, port and storage facilities for South Africa,[22] Swaziland, Zimbabwe, and Malawi directly, and it serves Zambia, Zaire, and Botswana indirectly via South Africa and Zimbabwe. The country's railway system plus the international ports of Maputo, Beira, and Nacala were expressly built by the Portuguese regime to serve the regional economy rather than to develop Mozambique's economy. For example, the railway link between the two large port cities of Maputo and Beira passes through Zimbabwe (see Map 12).

In 1975, 45 percent of Maputo's total traffic was from South Africa, 28 percent was from Swaziland, 12 percent from Rhodesia, and 4 percent was from Mozambique (Clayton 1976:1,115). Only about 10 percent of Mozambique's two major port cities, Maputo and Beira, were concerned with the country's own trade. In 1977, South African traffic alone accounted for 70 percent of Maputo's harbor activities (*Africa* 1977:43).

[22] South Africa's use of the port of Maputo (Lourenço Marques before independence) was based upon an agreement with the Portuguese colonial government to guarantee migrant labor for the mines in South Africa. The Mozambique Convention of 1928 (as amended) provided that South Africa would agree to supply at least 47.5 percent of all export traffic from the Transvaal for transit through Maputo in return for which Mozambique would supply an annual quota of workers (typically between 65,000 to 100,000). Since independence the number of Mozambican migrant workers in South African mines has declined from about 100,000 to just under 40,000 (due largely to the world recession and the preferences of the mining companies), and South Africa's export traffic through Maputo has declined from about 6 million tons in 1975 to roughly 2 million tons in 1982. Both governments have agreed to expand upon their preexisting agreement to increase service sector transactions in the future. For example, in 1979, South Africa agreed to double its volume of export traffic through Maputo during the next seven years to 12 million tons (Azevedo 1981:573).

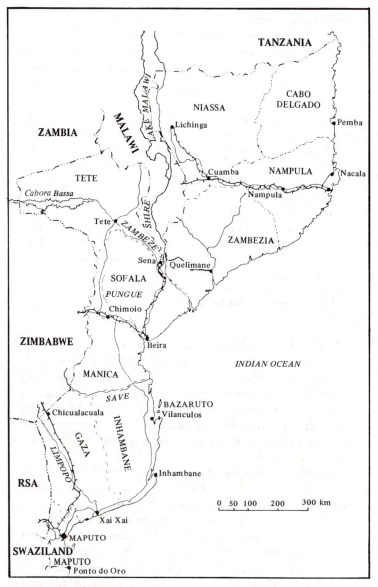

Map 12. Mozambique

Table 4.3: Mozambique's Port Traffic, 1973-1982
(in millions of tons, loaded and unloaded)

	1973	1975	1977	1979	1981	1982
Port						
Maputo[a]	14.2	10.9	8.0	8.1	6.4	6.3
Beira	3.0	3.0	1.7	1.7	1.7	1.6
Nacala	0.7	0.5	0.7	0.8	0.8	0.8
Total	18.0	14.7	10.4	10.6	8.9	8.7
Transit for						
South Africa	6.2	4.4	3.9	3.9	3.0	2.1
Zimbabwe	3.3	2.2	—[b]	—[b]	0.9	1.2
Swaziland	3.0	2.8	0.6	0.7	0.7	0.7
Malawi	0.7	0.6	0.9	1.0	0.9	0.7

SOURCES: Hanlon (1984:286), and EIU (1985:38).
NOTES: [a] Includes Matola.
[b] Period of sanctions against Rhodesia.

Table 4.3 shows Mozambique's port traffic from 1973 to 1982 and indicates countries that transited their trade through her harbors. Total port traffic has more than halved during this period, and the ports are underused and in general disrepair. However, while South African port traffic declined to only one-third of its preindependence level in 1973, it remains the most important user of Mozambique's ports.

A modern urban sector grew up around Mozambique's regional service sector to handle the trade and to provide services and consumer goods for the high income white settler urban population. It was estimated, for example, that approximately thirty-five thousand people were directly employed in the service sector with six times that number indirectly employed by them (Clayton 1976:1,115). Modern commercial farming is concentrated near the towns and cities. Non-African settlers and multinational agribusiness corporations produced food for the urban population and for agricultural export commodities. The country's industrial sector is also concentrated in the service sector.[23]

Table 4.4 provides an indication of the overwhelming importance of the regional service sector to Mozambique's economy. The data in the table indicate that the government's receipts from railways and ports in 1977 was U.S. $93 million or 60 percent of Mozambique's combined primary export earnings of U.S. $154 million. If the charges for transit and port usage are added to workers' remittances (derived largely from Mozambicans working in South Africa),[24] along with other invisibles, the earnings for the service sector rise to U.S. $193 million, which was about 55 percent of the government's total receipts of U.S. $352 million in 1977. Railway and port charges increased to U.S. $205 million in 1978, which was equal to the country's combined primary export earnings (Arnold 1979:19). The government estimates that between 1975 and 1983, however, the decline in railway-port traffic alone reduced income by U.S. $248 million (Mozambique 1984:38). Nevertheless, invisibles earned the country U.S. $216 mil-

---

[23] Two types of industries developed in Mozambique. The first included the processing of agricultural produce such as cashew nuts, cotton, sisal, sugar, and tea, and the other supplied the urban population with consumer goods and productive inputs for the domestic market such as milling, cement production, oil-refining, and brewing. Both industries were owned and controlled by Portuguese and other foreign capital interests (Fitzpatrick 1981:79).

[24] In 1975, prior to independence, when the world price of gold was high and the number of Mozambicans in the mines in South Africa was at a high point about 100,000, the proceeds acruing to the government from the sale of gold was about U.S. $150 million. The preindependence agreement between the Portuguese and South African government allowed 60 percent of Mozambican workers' remittances to be transferred to Mozambique in gold valued at the official price, which was sold on the open market at a substantial profit. This practice was ended by RSA in 1978. The United Nations has estimated that the loss to the Mozambican government resulting from the termination of the agreement amounts to U.S. $110 million annually in foreign exchange earnings.

Table 4.4 Balance of Payments Estimates for Mozambique, 1977 (in millions of U.S. dollars)

Receipts		Payments	
CURRENT		CURRENT	
Exports		Imports	
Sugar	$18	Food	$74
Cotton	10	Medicine and surgical	
Cashew nuts	33	equipment	13
Shrimp	16	Equipment and spare parts:	
Tea	13	railways and airlines	15
Coal	9	Agriculture	58
Others	55	public works	13
		Others	8
		Consumer goods	79
		Raw materials	
		(including oil)	223
		Other (fertilizers, tires,	
		etc.)	6
Subtotal	154	Subtotal	489
Invisibles		Invisibles	87
Railways and			
ports	93		
Workers'			
remittances	60		
Others	40		
	193		
CAPITAL	5	CAPITAL	55
Total receipts[a]	352	Total payments	631
		Projected deficit[a]	288

SOURCE: Table compiled by the Commonwealth Secretariat (1978:62) from U.N. sources and reprinted with permission.

NOTE: [a] Excluding foreign exchange receipts from the sale of gold received as payment for mine workers' salaries.

lion in foreign exchange in 1982 (Legum 1984:B681). Although reliable published figures on the current rail and port charges as a proportion of governmental receipts are not available,[25] this revenue appears to continue to provide the single largest source of governmental income—particularly in foreign exchange.

The country's regional service sector has seriously deteriorated since independence due to the mass exodus of Portuguese nationals at the time of independence (200,000 out of 280,000 left) plus Frelimo's decision to close its border to Rhodesian traffic in voluntary compliance with United Nations' sanctions against Rhodesia's UDI. The fear and uncertainty of living under a Frelimo government had the effect of precipitating the exodus of those who constituted the main body of skilled personnel in the country. The departure of the Portuguese, the flight of capital that accompanied them, and the sabotage of factories, plants, and farms contributed to economic decline and massive urban unemployment.

The strategic importance of the earnings derived from Mozambique's service sector is that it is the principal

[25] Mozambique only joined the World Bank and the International Monetary Fund and signed the European Economic Community's Lome Convention in 1985. Hence, the conventional sources of reporting on the country's economy were not available. However, independent sources of information on the importance of the service sector to Frelimo suggest a continuing dominant role of earnings from rail and port charges in the national economy. Mozambique had decided to double the use of the Maputo-Komatipoort line with South Africa, and South Africa has agreed to increase the use of the Witwatersrand and Komatipoort line (Azevedo 1981:573). Another indication of the importance of the service sector to the Frelimo government is their decision to capture as much rail and port traffic from Southern Africa as possible. To that end, Frelimo has undertaken a series of new transport projects such as railway track replacement, electrification, and a major new coal pier in Maputo. With the assistance of the South Africa Railway and Harbours administration, the Maputo port authority has also been streamlining and upgrading the efficiency of the port facilities (*Financial Mail* 1977:157; *Africa* 1980a: 67; Isaacman and Isaacman, 1980:7).

source of financing for the modern sector. The country had chronic trade deficits under Portuguese colonial administration, which reached a maximum of 5.9 billion escudos in 1973 just before independence. The reason for the structural imbalance in colonial Mozambique's trade was that Portugal was the principal recipient of the country's primary exports, which were purchased at below world prices.[26] From 1961 to 1973, Mozambique imported more than it exported to Portugal in terms of value. For example, in 1969 Mozambique exported 72 percent of the value of its imports from Portugal, in 1970 it exported 67 percent of the value of its imports, in 1971 the figure was 68 percent, in 1972 it was 86 percent, and in 1973 the figure was 90 percent.[27] Mozambique's earnings from its regional service sector played a major role in offsetting this perennial trade deficit. The earnings from handling the freight from South Africa alone brought in up to 30 percent of the country's total foreign exchange earnings. When added to the service fees from Zimbabwe and other regional countries plus the repatriated earnings from Mozambican labor in South Africa and Zimbabwe, the current invisibles surplus came close to paying for the country's trading deficits.

Since independence there have been two important changes in Mozambique's trading relationships. The first change is that South Africa replaced Portugal as Mozambique's chief supplier of industrial imports. Table 4.5 shows that as independence approached in 1973 (a transitional government comprising Frelimo and the Portuguese government was established in 1974), South Africa became Mozambique's main trading partner. In 1979, South Africa continued in this role, second only to Iraq, which supplied the country's crude oil. The United States, Spain,

[26] Prior to independence an estimated 91.2 percent of the value of Mozambique's imports were manufactured goods, while 73.6 percent of the value of all exports were agricultural products (USAID 1977c:II, 12).

[27] Computed from data presented in *Mozambique: Economic Survey* (1976) as reported in Azevedo (1981:569).

Table 4.5 Mozambique's Principal Trading Partners, 1965-1979 (in millions of pounds)

Countries	1965		1973		1979	
	Imports	Exports	Imports	Exports	Imports	Exports
Portugal	75.6 (35%)	50.4 (37%)	85.8 (19%)	76.0 (36%)	29.7 (5%)	40.3 (15%)
South Africa	22.4 (10%)	16.8 (11%)	90.7 (20%)	19.6 (10%)	89.0 (14%)	12.7 (5%)
U.S.A.	11.2 (4%)	5.6 (5%)	22.1 (5%)	29.4 (14%)	23.3 (4%)	65.7 (24%)
U.K.	22.4 (10%)	5.6 (5%)	34.3 (8%)	12.3 (6%)	33.9 (5%)	17.0 (6%)
West Germany	16.8 (8%)	5.6 (4%)	58.8 (13%)	7.4 (3%)	29.7 (5%)	6.4 (2%)
Switzerland	NA	—	NA	—	42.4 (7%)	—
Japan	—	0 (0%)	—	2.0 (2%)	—	17.0 (6%)
France	5.6 (3%)	2.8 (1%)	36.8 (8%)	4.9 (2%)	25.4 (4%)	8.5 (3%)
Netherlands	—	2.8 (1%)	—	4.9 (2%)	—	23.3 (8%)
Madagascar	—	—	—	—	—	6.4 (2%)
Iraq	11.2 (5%)	—	17.2 (4%)	—	110.2 (18%)[a]	—
East Germany	—	—	—	—	59.4 (10%)	23.3 (8%)
Romania	—	—	—	—	17.0 (3%)	—

SOURCE: Hanlon (1984:283).

NOTES: NA = not available.

1 pound = U.S. $2.8 in 1965, $2.45 in 1973, and $2.13 in 1979.

Trade data by country have not been published since 1979; detailed lists of imports have not been published since 1980.

[a] Iraq became Mozambique's principal supplier of crude oil in 1979.

East Germany, Japan, and Portugal respectively are Mozambique's major export markets (primarily cashews, prawns, tea, cotton, and coal—EIU 1985:41-42).

The second major change in Mozambique's trading relationships after independence was a dramatic increase in the country's balance of payments deficit. The country's payments deficit on current account increased from about U.S. $30 million in 1975, to U.S. $280 million in 1977, to U.S. $220 million in 1979, and to U.S. $409 million in 1984. The same deficit is projected for 1985.

Hence, after independence not only was South Africa substitued for Portugal as the country's chief supplier of imported goods but the decline in modern sector output plus Frelimo's ambitious developmental programs created large trading deficits with its chief supplier. This means that South Africa has become Mozambique's main creditor country as well as the principal source of foreign exchange earnings needed to pay for its imports.[28]

Frelimo's Socialist Goals

RURAL SOCIALIST STRATEGY

It was in the northernmost provinces of Cabo Delgado, Niassa, and Tete that the first guerilla operations against the Portuguese began in 1964, although by the end of the war in 1974 they were operating in five out of the country's nine provinces (a tenth province was added after independence). Frelimo's base of operations during the ten-year-long guerilla war was in the so-called "liberated

---

[28] The substitution of South Africa for Portugal as Mozambique's principal supplier country was encouraged by generous offers of credit from South Africa in addition to the country being Mozambique's lowest cost supplier. For example, in 1979, South Africa made an offer of U.S. $140 million in credit to Mozambique for the purchase of "general goods," including 100,000 tons of corn (Azevedo 1981:576).

zones" of the northern districts, which comprised about 25 percent of the country and was characterized by a peasant economy. In these areas Frelimo sought to establish an embryonic "socialist" state replete with collectivized agriculture, crop-growing schemes, village political committees, people's shops, judicial systems, and educational and health programs. Building upon the experiences in the liberated zones, Frelimo continued to emphasize the importance of the revolutionary virtues of associating closely with the peasantry and the principle of self-reliance. For example, the party took over the roughly one thousand "fortified villages" involving a million people that the Portuguese regime had created to cut off contact with Frelimo and converted them into communal villages. Other communal villages were established in the aftermath of the Limpopo and Zambezi valley floods in 1977 and 1978, and still more were created in response to the resurgence of MNR guerilla activity in Manica and Sofala.

During the war of liberation, Frelimo's party committees were concentrated in the northern provinces among the peasant population. The emphasis was upon each combat unit's self-sufficiency working in concert with the local population. Frelimo's success was, in fact, largely attributable to the creation of liberated zones where the peasantry was integrated into the political and military movement. Key elements of this movement were the collectivization of labor, Frelimo's commitment to protect the peasants from Portuguese retaliation, and the improvement of their material conditions (Isaacman and Isaacman 1982:292-295). From this experience a revolutionary spirit based upon rural socialist goals emerged within the Frelimo leadership. Henriksen (1978:454-455) has characterized this revolutionary ethos as comparable to "the Yenan spirit" with its emphasis upon sacrifice, self-denial, commitment to unending struggle, glorification of the peasantry, and the decadence of the city.

The centerpiece of Frelimo's rural social program for Mozambique was the collectivization of agriculture into communal villages and cooperative farms.[29] Agricultural cooperatives were intended to provide an integrated production base for the communal villages. Hence, villagization was designed to increase food and cash crop production and to make available common facilities for farming as well as provide social services such as education and health comparable with Ujamaa villages in Tanzania. Henriksen (1978:452) points out that a major objective of the villagization program in Mozambique was to reverse rural migration to the cities. In Frelimo's world view cities breed corrupt and foreign social values. Until 1977, Frelimo gave primary emphasis in its developmental policies to the reorganization of the rural population into communal villages.

At the time of Portugal's transfer of political power to Frelimo, roughly three-fourths of the country (including the central, southern, and coastal regions and the cities) had no direct experience with the new Frelimo government nor with its fifteen-thousand-strong guerilla army. The majority of the population (peasants and urban working class included) were ill-informed about the party. Furthermore, after an initial surge of popular feeling at the

[29] However, as Munslow (1984:207) and Kofi (1981:851-870) point out, very few of the villages (only those within Frelimo's own political structures) were actually functioning along communal-socialist lines. A minority of the roughly 1,350 communal villages involving about 1.8 million inhabitants (10 to 15 percent of the rural population) operated on the basis of collectivized work. Therefore, production in the rural areas was dominated by peasant family production. While peasant village production was largely ignored by Frelimo from independence in 1975 until 1982, the party's commitment to establish peasant cooperatives remained unchanged. What did change, however, was Frelimo's recognition that as the country's principal producer of food and cash crops, the small-scale peasant farmer required state support. They also recognized that the transformation of private peasant family production into peasant cooperatives would only occur gradually over time.

Table 4.6   Employment in Selected Sectors of Mozambique's
Economy during 1973 and 1976

| | No. of Persons Employed | |
Sector	1973	1976
Civil construction and public works	28,000	14,000
Ports, railways, and cargo handling	36,000	23,000
Selected industries:	56,660	35,900
Construction materials	20,600	9,000
Metal transforming and light		
manufacturing	6,060	4,400
Export industries	30,000	22,500
Total	120,660	72,900
Reduction in employment	47,760 or 40 percent	

SOURCE: Table compiled by the Commonwealth Secretariat (1978:65)
from U.N. sources and reprinted with permission.

overthrow of colonial rule and the new benefits of massive
free health and education services, disillusionment and resistance to the party's socialist goals set in.

The urban and migratory labor force suffered severe
hardships in the aftermath of the massive Portuguese exodus such as shortages of food and other consumer goods.
Table 4.6 shows the decline in urban employment between
1973 and 1976 in the sectors for which data were available.
There was estimated to be a decline of between 12,000 and
14,000 out of a total work force of 36,000 who were directly
involved in handling Mozambique's transit traffic. A conservative estimate is that at least 47,760 or 40 percent of the
total urban labor force has been thrown out of employment
since Frelimo came to power in 1975.

Associated with the dramatic increase in urban unemployment is the reduction in migratory contract labor demand in South Africa and Zimbabwe due partly to adverse economic conditions in those countries. In the case of South Africa, for example, Mozambican workers on the mines in the Transvaal declined from about 118,000 in 1975 to 45,472 in 1984.[30] Since these workers were recruited from the central and southern areas of the country, their loss of work has added considerably to the unemployment problem in the cities.

Concomitant with the increase in unemployment in the service sector was a major decline in Mozambique's industrial production. While reliable current industrial statistics are not available,[31] the Commonwealth Secretariat (1978:64) estimated that production in the manufacturing sector declined sharply in 1976. For example, crude oil consumption by the refinery in Maputo for 1976 was less than one-half of the consumption in 1973, fertilizer production in 1976 was about one-third the output in 1973, and eleven large firms in the metal transforming and light manufacturing sector had annual sales in 1976 of only U.S. $8.5 million compared to sales of U.S. $20 million in 1973. The report notes that the estimated 3,800 industrial establishments in 1973 with total investments of U.S. $600 million and employing over 100,000 persons experienced sharp declines in sales, production, and employment after their urban domestic market collapsed.

There was also resistance to Frelimo's villagization policy outside of the northern provinces. For example, in Zambesia province in central Mozambique Frelimo never received extensive popular support either during the war

[30] The actual number of Mozambicans who were working in South Africa in 1975 was estimated to be as high as 180,000 (Henriksen 1978:450). In addition, there was estimated to be approximately 100,000 annual migrants from Mozambique to Southern Rhodesia (Meyns 1981:46).

[31] An indication of the difficulty in obtaining reliable current information on the Mozambican economy is the fact that the government did not publish a full budget for 1983 and 1984 (*African Business* 1984l:17).

or since independence. The province's economy is dominated by large company plantations that have been heavily dependent upon state support since the era of the Estado Novo. Both the companies and the African population that supplied the labor for the plantations were heavily dependent upon the state for their prosperity and economic security (Vail and White 1980:372-381).[32] The self-help socialist doctrine of Frelimo was alien to the people of Zambesia province who had come to rely upon company plantations and a colonial bureaucratic state to organize and direct almost every facet of their lives. Likewise, a study of an agricultural cooperative named Edouardo Mondlane in Gaza province in southern Mozambique did not accord with Frelimo's villagization policy of providing the production base for the nearby communal village of approximately one thousand families. Instead, the cooperative was controlled by a small group of capitalist farmers within the communal village who were the same farmers who prospered under the 1968 Portuguese colonial program of developing "progressive capitalist" farmers (Harris 1980:338-352).

One important reason for the social stratification in the agricultural cooperative between a small group of prosperous capitalist farmers who were producing cash crops for market and the majority of communal villagers who either were not involved in the cooperative or provided wage labor for the rich farmers was the impact of migratory labor in the southern part of Mozambique. Practically every rural family in southern Mozambique as well as in the central regions bordering Zimbabwe supplied labor to the mines and farms in South Africa and Zimbabwe. Hence a

[32] Vail and White (1980:375-376) point out that thirty years of forced labor plus the impact of the cotton concession system upon the women tended to undermine the traditional pattern of food production in village life in the area. This had the result of creating serious food shortages in the peasant subsistence sector and thereby increased the African population's dependence upon the plantations for their economic survival.

proletarian attitude prevails among the men in areas where wage labor is preferred to farming. Furthermore, the income from wages came to play an indispensible role in financing family-based agriculture in these areas (Henriken 1978:250, and Harris 1980:344).

The decline in industrial production and in the service sector significantly reduced the opportunities for wage employment. The serious decline in cash crop production on the large plantations also substantially reduced wage employment in the rural areas, adding to popular resistance to Frelimo's socialist policies.[33]

INDUSTRIAL SOCIALIST STRATEGY

After the Lancaster House Agreement in 1979, which guaranteed Zimbabwe's independence under a black majority government, the Rhodesian military and the MNR ceased to be a major threat to Frelimo. With the threat removed (at least temporarily), the party set out to achieve national reconstruction goals. One major objective of these goals was to overcome popular resistance to Frelimo among urban, industrial, and migratory workers and peasants who depended upon the plantations for wage labor. Frelimo modified the party's emphasis upon villagization

---

[33] There has been a significant decline in Mozambique's production of cash crops, many of which are grown on large plantations. For example, the output of cashew nuts declined from 216,000 tons in 1973 to 76,000 tons in 1977, sugar declined from 383,000 tons in 1973 to an estimated 166,000 tons in 1978, and tea production declined from 18,700 tons in 1973 to 14,000 tons in 1978 (EIU 1979:23).

Mozambique's only other major cash crop for export—cotton—also underwent a significant decline in production during this period. For example, cotton (lint) declined from 46,000 metric tons in 1974 to 20,000 tons in 1981. Food production also declined seriously during this period. Cereals declined from 801,000 metric tons in 1974 to 478 tons in 1980, rice declined from 120,000 metric tons in 1974 to 70 tons in 1980, and maize declined from 450,000 metric tons in 1974 to 250 tons in 1980. Mozambique's index number of food production declined to 92 in 1981 with 1967 to 1971 as the base year of 100 (United Nations 1983:486, 489, 646).

in order to stress the reconstruction of the modern sector of the economy.[34]

While this change in policy was formally decided at the Third Party Congress in February 1977, it was not actually implemented until 1979. In a document entitled "Economic and Social Directives" at the Third Congress, Frelimo's new orientation was elaborated. It set out the party's objective of reestablishing the country's overall level of production in 1973 (the last year of Portuguese rule) by 1980. In August of 1977, the director of state farms in the Ministry of Agriculture outlined the new national reconstruction policy in relation to the rural sector. The policy gave primary emphasis to the plantations and exsettler commercial farms and operations in the state agrarian sector at the highest level of technology. On the all-important question of state support for communal villages and agricultural cooperatives, the director declared that the state had "no direct influence" on the family sector (Meyns 1981:62).

In taking this position, Frelimo was reversing its historic commitment to rural villagization in favor of the cash crop and export sector. A crucial underpinning of this new strategy was that industrial inputs and food (for the urban areas) were required to implement the policy. In this re-

[34] Frelimo's socialist "villagization" program in the central provinces of Manica and Sofala and the southern provinces of Inhambane and Gaza was highly unpopular. The anti-Frelimo insurgent organization, the Resistência Nacional Moçambicana concentrated its attacks against the "communal villages" in the remote areas of these provinces for this reason. The MNR made no inroads, however, in Frelimo's traditional strongholds in the northern provinces of Niassa, Nampula, and Cabo Delgado. The MNR forces were estimated to be between 6,000 and 16,000 in 1982, and they were reported to be active in all of Mozambique's ten provinces. The activities of the MNR have been concentrated on disrupting Mozambique's economy. However, the MNR has not mounted a program of winning popular support from Frelimo's opponents, nor has it established "liberated zones" free of Frelimo control.

gard Frelimo's foreign policy toward the Soviet bloc countries was expected to play an instrumental role in achieving the party's national reconstruction objectives.

Frelimo's new plan for the political and economic development of the country for the next five years (until
1982) was based upon an expanding urban industrial sector with a secondary agricultural sector serving the urban
areas. In order to carry out this state-directed urban industrial model of national reconstruction, the party relied
upon Soviet bloc support. For example, the Frelimo government signed a twenty-year Treaty of Friendship and
Cooperation in March 1977, which was designed to
strengthen economic, technical, defence, and cultural ties
between Mozambique and the Soviet Union. Other Soviet
bloc countries also had important roles to play in Frelimo's
new strategy of national reconstruction. For example, East
Germany, which had succeeded in resurrecting its industrial power from the devastation of World War II, became a
model of development for the party.

However, despite Soviet bloc assistance and military
arms supplies, Frelimo's strategy of relying upon the socialist bloc to achieve its national reconstruction goals produced disappointing results. This was partly due to the
party's unrealistically high expectations for Soviet bloc assistance. For example, while Mozambique's friendship
treaty with the Soviet Union was only the third one between the USSR and an African state, the Soviets apparently rebuffed Machel's efforts to strengthen ties by refus-
ing to conclude party-to-party agreements between the
Soviet Communist party (CPSU) and Frelimo. Such agreements or failure to conclude them are clear indications of
the extent of the Soviet Union's commitment to support
other "Marxist-Leninist vanguard parties of workers and
peasants." Frelimo's efforts to gain full membership in the
Soviet-dominated Council for Mutual Economic Assistance (CMEA), or Comecon, were also rebuffed.

In addition, Mozambique's agreements with communist

countries did not yield the expected economic or military assistance. There was criticism within Frelimo about inadequate levels of developmental assistance from Eastern bloc countries and about the negative terms of trade with them. The trade figures for 1982 showed, for example, that Mozambique's exports to Eastern bloc countries amounted to only $29 million compared to imports valued at $180 million. This was hardly favorable from Mozambique's point of view.

The party was also dissatisfied with what they regarded as inadequate arms supplies from Soviet bloc countries. Criticism was directed at outmoded military equipment supplied by the USSR. Frelimo was also unhappy with the Soviet Union's apparent unwillingness to do more than provide a symbolic presence of naval forces at Maputo harbor at a time when the South African-backed MNR insurgents were mounting a serious challenge to Frelimo's control of large areas of the country.

REVERSION TO RURAL SOCIALISM

By 1982, the failure of the urban industrial model of national reconstruction was evident in the continuing decline of the industrial sector, the serious decline in the cash and food crops, and in the effects of the drought upon the agricultural sector. SADCC (1984:i) estimated, for example, that the 1982/1983 drought induced losses and costs of $154 million plus the loss of 100,000 lives due to the famine. Even more ominous for Frelimo's tenure of power was the resurgence of the MNR guerillas who with South African backing were apparently operating in all ten Mozambican provinces by 1984.

The rapidly deteriorating economic and security situation in Mozambique plus the failure of the Soviet bloc countries to provide the necessary military and logistical support to combat the MNR-South African offensive jolted Frelimo into reassessing their strategy of national reconstruction. At the Fourth Party Congress of April 1983, Frelimo repudiated their centralized industrial and commercial farming strategy for achieving national reconstruction and revived the party's earlier emphasis upon collectivization and mobilization of the peasantry.

Faced with imminent threats to Frelimo's internal political control of the country, the leadership resorted to the peasant mobilization strategy they successfully used to defeat the Portuguese colonial army and to help remove the Rhodesian regime. Isaacman (1985) points out, for example, that "empowering the peasantry" was the central theme of President Machel's thirteen-hour speech to the Fourth Party Congress. The previous emphasis upon Eastern European style state farms and heavy industry in the urban areas was rejected. In its place, Frelimo reinstated the earlier emphasis upon peasant mobilization. And, in fact, with this change the Central Committee doubled in size from 65 to 130 members, with most of the new members coming from among former freedom fighters in the rural areas who had been overlooked by the party hierarchy after the Third Party Congress in 1977.

The significance of this shift back to the original party strategy was that Frelimo was again faced with a major threat to its political control of the country. The party neglected the countryside in favor of the industrial urban areas and large-scale state farms and plantations. However, this failed to consolidate Frelimo's control of the country and to reconstruct the economy. It also made it possible for the South African-backed MNR to organize and mobilize a serious military threat to the party. Therefore, Frelimo's reversion to its successful original strategy of peasant mobilization at the grassroots was directed at combating a threat to its political control of the country.

Frelimo's "Internationalist Duty"

In order to understand why Frelimo broke off its economic ties with Rhodesia in 1976 during the independence struggle while the party did not break its ties with South Africa, it is necessary to understand Frelimo's priorities. Article four of the party's constitution identifies the major foreign policy objectives (Henderson 1978:276). Two major objectives are to consolidate national independence and to carry out the party's internationalist duty. Of the two, Frelimo has emphasized that its internationalist duty of supporting national liberation movements would always be subordinate to its primary goal of "liberating" Mozambique itself. In other words, the primacy of securing and defending the party's internal political control of the country is the central guideline for its foreign policy. Therefore, Frelimo's policy toward Rhodesia in 1976 and its policy toward South Africa in 1984 must be understood in terms of how they affected the party's ability to secure political control of the country.

Central to Frelimo's internationalist duty is its commitment to support the liberation movements in Rhodesia, Namibia, and South Africa and its policy of strengthening ties with its "natural allies"—socialist countries. However, while that commitment remains constant in Frelimo's foreign policy, the emphasis given to it has changed since Mozambique's independence in June 1975. For example, in September 1975, less than three months after Mozambique became independent, Frelimo granted military staging bases to the Zimbabwe People's Army (ZIPA). This decision was tantamount to declaring a state of war against Rhodesia. However, Frelimo had already been fighting an undeclared war with Rhodesia in support of military operations of the Zimbabwe African National Liberation Army (the military wing of Robert Mugabe's Zimbabwe African National Union) ever since they launched their guerilla war against the Rhodesian regime in 1972. From that date Frelimo's guerilla army, the Mozambique People's Liberation Force (FPLM), fought on many occasions side by side with ZANLA to repel Rhodesian and Portuguese attacks in Mozambique. Therefore, Frelimo's decision to grant ZIPA military staging bases in Mozambique simply gave formal recognition to an existing de facto state of war between Frelimo and Rhodesia.

Likewise, Frelimo's decision of March 1976 to close its border with Rhodesia and thereby impose United Nations' sanctions against Rhodesia's UDI was viewed by the party as a tactical decision in support of its undeclared war with Rhodesia. In explaining the decision to close the border, for example, President Machel described the action in tactical military terms. He said, "we did it at this precise moment because the freedom fighters and people of Zimbabwe are organized to fight against the Smith regime, so the conditions were ripe for the application of sanctions" (Isaacman 1985).

During this period, Frelimo had not yet addressed the issue of national reconstruction. It was still largely a peasant-backed party with a strong rural socialist commitment. The party was primarily oriented towards defending the country's security from Rhodesian and MNR attacks. Isaacman (1985) estimated, for example, that between 1976 and 1979, there were more than 350 Rhodesian and MNR attacks against Mozambique resulting in widespread destruction of infrastructure, agriculture, and factories and loss of life. Clearly Frelimo's internationalist duty during this period was linked directly to the liberation of Mozambique itself.

Frelimo's internationalist duty in relation to South Africa, however, is entirely different from the Rhodesian situation. Not only have South African liberation movements failed to mount a serious military challenge to South Africa but Mozambique is not engaged in warfare with South Africa. Most importantly, breaking economic ties with South Africa (comparable to closing the border with Rhodesia in 1976) would seriously undermine the party's ability to combat the MNR. It would also add to Mozambique's grave economic crisis. In other words, a declaration of war and economic retaliation for South African attacks against

Mozambique would not contribute to Frelimo's ability to secure political control of the country.

This does not mean, however, that Frelimo does not have a political strategy for dealing with the South African threat to its security. To the contrary, the party has been ingenuous in elaborating a foreign policy that serves precisely that end.

Counteroffensive against South Africa

Faced with a deteriorating economy and a serious military threat within Mozambique, Frelimo altered its foreign policy in 1982 in order to mount a diplomatic counteroffensive against South African and MNR attacks.[35] Without breaking its ties with Soviet bloc countries, Frelimo sought to reopen diplomatic relations with Western countries. The objective of this new initiative was twofold. First Frelimo recognized that with the exception of their MIG-equipped air force, the communist countries were unprepared or unwilling to provide the military arms and training necessary to combat the MNR threat. However, the Portuguese government was prepared to make large-scale arms sales to Mozambique and to provide counterinsurgency training for units of the Mozambican army. Frelimo also sought Western economic aid and assistance. The Mozambican government has agreed to guarantee commercial investments, for example, for West Germany. It also joined the International Monetary Fund, the World Bank, and the African, Caribbean, and Pacific group (ACP), all of which were designed to encourage Western capital investment and trade with the country.

Second, Frelimo's new initiative toward Western governments was designed to gain diplomatic leverage against

[35] This section relies heavily upon Allen Isaacman's "Mozambique and South Africa, 1900-1983: Tugging at the Chains of Dependency," Bender (1985). I am grateful to the author for making an advance copy available to me.

South Africa and through it the MNR. While South African officials still mention the possible necessity for more "Lebanese-type" raids against Mozambique, and while the MNR remains a major security threat to Frelimo, Mozambique has had some success in its Western diplomatic initiative. In fact, the Nkomati Accord of March 1984 was largely a diplomatic victory for Frelimo.

According to Isaacman (1985), Frelimo had been trying to reach a political accommodation with South Africa in order to relieve growing MNR military pressure upon the party. The Frelimo leadership reportedly sought to exploit the recession-ridden South African economy to extract a concession from South Africa to cease supporting the MNR. Frelimo recognized that South Africa's growing external payments deficit and foreign debt of $15 billion in 1983 gave them some economic bargaining power in gaining a political-military concession from South Africa. Thus the party threatened to deny South African firms in the Transvaal access both to the less costly Maputo harbor and the Mozambican market. In fact, even after the Nkomati agreement was signed in March 1984, Frelimo withheld finalizing economic agreements with South African firms until they received assurances that the South African government would honor the terms of the agreement and put an end to its MNR-sponsored insurgency within Mozambique. Thus, the party sought to use its economic ties with South Africa as political leverage against RSA.

Sensing South Africa's vulnerability to economic pressure and skillfully mobilizing Western diplomatic pressure upon South Africa brought a reversal of South Africa's initial refusal to sign a nonaggression pact, instead offering economic assistance in return for Frelimo's expulsion of the African National Congress. The party rejected this condition and thus maintained its commitment to its internationalist duty. In this way Frelimo successfully brought Western diplomatic pressure to bear on South Africa to agree to sign a nonaggression pact in which South Africa promised not to allow its territory to be used to launch attacks or acts of sabotage against Mozambique.

While attacks by the MNR in Mozambique have increased rather than decreased, and while Frelimo recognizes that only it can put an end to the MNR's security threat, Nkomati has given Mozambique diplomatic leverage over South Africa. Western powers wish to avoid widening the conflict in Southern Africa fearing that this can play into the hands of the Soviet Union, the principal backer of the ANC and SWAPO. Therefore, South Africa's Western allies have an interest in restraining the country's regional military action. This has given Frelimo an important diplomatic card to play against South Africa.

While Mozambique is heavily dependent upon South Africa for much of its governmental revenues and foreign exchange, this did not not interfere with its internationalist duty to support Southern African liberation movements. Nor has it prevented Frelimo from undertaking political action to secure the party's political control of the country. In fact, in the midst of a crisis situation, Frelimo has demonstrated great flexibility and skill in shifting from a Soviet-inspired model of development and foreign assistance to a diplomatic strategy of mobilizing Western pressure on South Africa to respect Mozambique's national sovereignty.

Whether this strategy will ultimately prove more successful than Frelimo's reliance upon its "natural allies" remains to be seen. However, what is clear is that far from losing its political independence due to Mozambique's economic dependence upon South Africa, Frelimo has demonstrated considerable scope of autonomous political action both in its domestic and foreign policies.

ZAMBIA

Zambia illustrates the strategic use of a state's regional economic ties when a regime is threatened by domestic political opposition. The leadership of the ruling United National Independence party adopted a doctrinaire foreign policy of complying with United Nations Security Council Resolution 232 against Rhodesia for declaring Unilateral Declaration of Independence despite Zambia's exemption. Zambia complied with the sanctions from 1973 to 1978 by discontinuing its trade with Rhodesia. This action involved great economic costs to Zambia since Rhodesia was the country's major lowest-cost supplier.

When Zambia's means of paying for its imports—the sale of copper on world markets—declined seriously beginning in 1975, the government was forced to drastically curtail its imports. The reduction significantly affected the availability of consumer goods for the large urban wage-earning population, resulting in severe shortages of consumer goods, high unemployment, inflation, and industrial strikes.

The pressure of urban dissatisfaction with the ruling party's foreign economic policy grew and found political expression during the third general and presidential election campaign in 1978. Rival political leaders challenged UNIP's leadership of the country by appealing for urban political support on the basis of a promise to resume trading with Rhodesia. The election threat to the party ultimately forced a reversal of the original decision to discontinue trading with Rhodesia, and the border between the two countries was reopened just prior to scheduled elections.

Mining and Urbanization

As early as 1933, representatives of the mining industry called for the stabilization of the African work force[36]

[36] Two large transnational mining companies, Zambian Anglo American (later Nchanga Consolidated Copper Mines, Ltd.—NCCM) and Roan Selection Trust (later RCM), developed Zambia's mining industry. Anglo American is a South African corporation, and RCM was dominated by

(Heisler 1971:129). The pressure for the establishment of a permanently industrialized community at the mines was also evident in the Pim Commission Report of 1941, which called upon the government to prepare a plan for the settlement of a permanent urban labor force for the copper industry.

The success of the mining industry's efforts to stablize its labor force at the mining sites is evident in the geographical location of the country's urban centers. For example, it is estimated that about 40 percent of Zambia's total population lives within twenty miles of each side of the railway that was primarily designed to serve the copper industry (UNDP 1976:32). In 1981, it was estimated that about 50 percent of Zambia's total population of 5.8 million lived in the so-called line-of-rail provinces (the Copperbelt, Central—including Lusaka—and Southern provinces). Rothchild (1972:224) has noted the fact that in 1969 (the year of the first national census), the line-of-rail provinces accounted for 84 percent of the total formal employment and 91 percent of earnings from employment. Likewise, it was estimated that in 1972, over 95 percent of the total number of manufacturing establishments and manufacturing employees were located in the line-of-rail provinces. In 1976, of the estimated 340,520 Zambians who were in salaried employment, 288,180 or 85 percent of them were in Zambia's line-of-rail province. In 1982, the number of wage earners was 396,220 (excluding domestic servants), the bulk of whom were in the urban areas along

American capital. In 1969, the Zambian government signed nationalization agreements with the two groups of companies. The government took a 51 percent state interest in the companies through the agency of a public corporation, the Zambia Industrial and Mining Corp. Ltd. (ZIMCO). In 1982, RCM merged with NCCM to form the Zambia Consolidated Copper Mines (ZCCM), with ZIMCO holding a 60.3 percent controlling interest in the company. In 1984, the U.S. company with an interest in ZCCM, Amax, sold its equity, leaving Zambia Copper Investments (a subsididary of the South African Anglo American Corporation) as the principal foreign mining interest in Zambia (with a 27.3 percent ownership of ZCCM).

the line-of-rail. They were located primarily in the capital city, Lusaka, and the Copperbelt cities of Kitwe and Ndola (*Africa South of the Sahara* 1984:966).

The average annual income of all Zambian wage earners in 1976 was 1,469 kawcha (U.S. $1,689). The lowest wage was 604 kwacha (U.S. $695) in the agricultural forestry, and fisheries sector, while the highest annual wage was 2,507 kwacha (U.S. $2,883) in mining and quarrying. Mining was the single largest employer with 55,580 (Zambia 1978).[37] By 1980 an estimated 100,000 households (mostly in urban areas) had an average annual income of 1,800 kwacha or more. By African standards, this is a large well-paid industrial labor force for a country with a population of about 6 million.

However, industrial expansion has not had the desired result of diversifying Zambia's economy away from its extreme mineral dependence. It has had the opposite result of making the economy even more dependent upon mineral exports. The reason is that the industrial expansion has tended to specialize in consumer production (especially last-stage assembly), which is heavily import dependent. This industry tends to be a net foreign exchange spender rather than an earner. Hence, Zambia's manufacturing industry did not develop as an export industry but has tended to provide consumer goods with low value added and high import costs to a large urban population that itself is dependent upon the copper industry. For example, it was reported that the manufacturing sector contributes less than 1 percent of Zambia's foreign exchange earnings (*Africa* 1984:80).

Rapid urban growth in Zambia has occurred largely in response to the growing gap in income between the stagnant rural subsistence sector and the urban sector, which

---

[37] Employment in the mining sector in 1983 was 59,049, which represents 14 percent of the total labor force in formal employment. This includes an estimated 2,000 highly paid expatriates.

is led by mining. Mwanza (1979:175-176) has estimated, for example, that the subsistance sector's growth rate in Zambia was 0.9 percent a year from 1965 to 1976. By contrast, the manufacturing sector grew at an annual rate of 11.2 percent in real terms during the period. By 1980, it was estimated that approximately 650,000 households (mostly rural) earned an average annual income below the poverty datum line of 500 kwacha (U.S. $600).

High growth rates were also experienced in the commercial agricultural and service sectors, which are concentrated in the urban areas of the country. The growth rate of money wages was estimated to have increased in urban areas by 10.5 percent a year, with real wages growing on average by about 4 percent. By contrast, there was virtually no growth in real income in the subsistence sector. According to United Nations' estimates, the average monthly household income in 1974 in urban areas was 120 kwacha, whereas it was only 29 kwacha for rural households.[38]

The gap between urban wages and rural income has accelerated the migration to urban areas, making Zambia one of the most highly urbanized countries in Africa. In 1982, for example, it was estimated that 45 percent of the population lived in urban areas (towns of five thousand or more). It is the rapid urbanization in Zambia based upon the prosperity of its mining industry that constitutes the most explosive political threat to the regime. Mwanza (1979:176) estimates that urban unemployment (including the disguised unemployment in the informal sector) grew

[38] Zambia's 1983 per capita income was estimated to be 17 percent above the 1970 level (in 1970 constant prices). However, if the decline in purchasing power due to adverse terms of trade (import costs in relation to export values) is taken into account, GDP per capita income has actually declined by an estimated 22 percent (in constant prices) (*Africa South of the Sahara* 1984:966). The decline in living standards for the majority of rural subsistence households has been even greater, with many unable to provide for their basic needs of food, shelter, and clothing.

by 48.3 percent from 201,000 to 298,000 between 1969 and 1974. In 1977, the unemployment was estimated to have risen to 381,750 or 25 percent of the entire wage-earning labor force. The migration to urban areas has involved the movement of about one million people in search of employment from 1964 to 1984.

However, most industries are operating at below 30 percent of capacity due to a severe shortage of imported materials. The smaller unprofitable mines have been closed, and the larger ones are threatened with closure. There is a high annual population growth rate of 3.3 percent, and over a hundred thousand political refugees from Angola alone are in Zambia. The country's unemployment rate is probably in the range of 40 percent or more.

In addition to the growing army of indigents in urban areas, the decline in earnings from copper sales has substantially lowered the real wage income of urban sector workers. It is estimated, for example, that in 1984, the real average income of Zambian wage earners was only 80 percent of what it was in 1974 (*African Business* 1984x:20). The annual rate of inflation rose to 23.5 percent in 1984, and real GDP per capita declined to only 230 kwacha in 1983. In 1983 alone, the consumer price index rose by between 11.6 percent and 19.1 percent (*African Business* 1984v:60).

In the face of this serious decline in the living standards of urban wage earners, the unions have been prevented by the government from engaging in free collective bargaining.[39] The trade union movement (representing about

[39] Between 1976 and 1979, the government froze money wages with most wage earners receiving a flat-rate increase as part of the government's incomes policy. In 1982, the government suspended free collective bargaining and in its place imposed a 10 percent wage increase limit. Under union pressure the system of free collective bargaining was reintroduced in November 1984. However, following the reintroduction of collective bargaining, the government again set a 10 percent ceiling on wage increases.

400,000 workers) has been particularly angered by the un-controlled escalation in prices while wages are frozen or controlled. This virtually guarantees further declines in workers' real living standards.[40]

The union response to this situation has been to engage in industrial strikes.[41] In 1980, President Kaunda esti-mated that during the previous sixteen months, 698,072 man hours had been lost in 120 strikes, and there had been slowdowns involving 29,876 workers (*Africa* 1980b:55). Sporadic illegal strikes have continued during the suspen-sion of free collective bargaining. For example, in Septem-ber 1983, the employees of Zambia Railways went on strike protesting a 10 percent wage ceiling, and during the first quarter of 1984, the minister of labour reported that 14,503 workers went on illegal strike resulting in a loss of 64,954 man days (*African Business* 1985b:36). The indus-trial unrest centers upon workers' grievances regarding their declining real wages in the face of the withdrawal of governmental and company subsidies on consumer goods and fringe benefits (such as the right to purchase family

[40] The most tangible indication of the declining living standards of wage earners in Zambia is the price of the principal staple food—maize meal. For example, in July 1984, the government announced a 70 percent increase in the price of maize meal resulting from the reduction in gov-ernmental food subsidies, which was a condition for IMF standby loans. It is estimated that between 1979 and 1983, 362.9 million kwacha was spent on subsidizing maize imports (*African Business* 1984u:78). The high cost of maize subsidy was due to the serious decline in domestic maize production caused by a two-year drought and the fact that it was necessary to import maize from as far away as Thailand, Indonesia, and Argentina since the drought also reduced maize production in Zimbabwe and South Africa (Zambia's traditional suppliers).

[41] Gertzel (1975) points out that "its [i.e., the Mineworkers' Union] sound organization . . . and its secure financial situation . . . made the Union a powerful body that any government had at independence, to take into account. Eighteen months after independence, in the strikes of Au-gust 1966, the Mineworkers' Union showed it retained the power and the ability to challenge the independent government as it had once its colo-nial predecessor."

food staples from company stores and transportation subsidies). At the same time the prices of "essential commodities" are "decontrolled" and are allowed to rise by huge margins.

Strike action came to a head in January 1981 when the Mineworkers' Union of Zambia (MUZ) directly challenged the ruling party. The confrontation was over the government's authority to overrule the union's right to engage in free collective bargaining. The trade union's disputed UNIP's authority to approve the mining companies' reduction in worker fringe benefits. The MUZ refused to accede to the party's ruling (which favored the companies) without first consulting with the union. In the ensuing controversy the government arrested the entire leadership of the MUZ (seventeen in all). However, within days of the action, all 56,000 miners went out on strike demanding the release and reinstatement of their trade union leaders. In sympathy with the MUZ strike, other unions that are affiliated with the Zambia Congress of Trade Unions (ZCTU) in the key banking, insurance, and building societies joined the strike, with more workers threatening to strike if the government did not reverse its action.

While the government was ultimately successful in handling the strike, the unions continue to pose a major political threat to the ruling party. For example, in 1984, the ZCTU threatened to boycott a national convention called by the president to build national support for tough austerity policies. Union leaders also called for the reintroduction of price controls and the elimination of government ceilings on wage increases. They have demanded the dismantling of "unproductive middlemen" such as wholesalers, retailers, and the state marketing boards on grounds that they unnecessarily add to the price of essential commodities (African Business 1984r:78). With the real value of wages falling by as much as 50 percent during the past decade and with government wage ceilings, the stage has been set for confrontation between UNIP and the powerful trade unions.

"Disengagement" from Rhodesia

Rhodesia and South Africa have historically blocked Zambia's industrialization. Between 1930 and 1953, for example, a customs agreement between South Africa and the two Rhodesias prevented Northern Rhodesia (Zambia) from using tariffs to promote its industrial development. During the federal period from 1953 to 1963, industrial development occurred in Southern Rhodesia due in large measure to the diversion of Northern Rhodesia's imports from South Africa and Great Britain to Southern Rhodesia. At the time of Zambia's independence in 1965, therefore, the country's manufacturing sector contributed less than 7 percent to GDP. This virtually ensured that Zambia would be heavily dependent upon Rhodesia and South Africa for its imported intermediate and capital goods and for consumer commodities.

Between 1964 and 1969, the positions of Rhodesia and South Africa as Zambia's principal supplier were reversed so that South Africa became more important than Rhodesia in supplying Zambian imports (see Table 4.7). This was due to Zambia's voluntary compliance with United Nations Security Council Resolution 232 of 1966, which imposed mandatory sanctions against Rhodesia for its Unilateral Declaration of Independence. After 1973, when Zambia officially closed its border with Rhodesia, trading figures between the two countries ceased to be reported. However, official remittances by Zambia to Rhodesia continued, and the Rhodesian Railways continued to operate in Zambia, indicating that at least some trade continued between the two countries.

From 1969 to 1978 (the date of the border reopening), Zambia substituted the United Kingdom for Rhodesia as its principal supplier (see Table 4.7). However, after the re-

Table 4.7   Zambia's Imports by Major Supplier (in thousands of kwacha)

Country	1964	1969	1974	1978	1981
Rhodesia (Zimbabwe)	61,737	21,772	NA	NA	NA
South Africa	32,406	69,946	38,716	31,476	139,631
U.K.	26,832	71,407	99,435	122,294	144,110
U.S.A	8,050	30,083	39,652	38,679	76,629
Japan	3,193	22,588	48,571	21,832	55,203
West Germany	4,216	12,151	40,949	54,700	72,286
East African Countries	715	11,180	15,468	5,019	8,148

SOURCES: UNDP (1976:15), and Zambia (1984:22).
NOTES: NA = not available.
1 Zambian kwacha = U.S. $1.400 in 1964 and 1969, $1.554 in 1974, $1.2704 in 1978, and $1.1328 in 1981.

opening of the border with Rhodesia South Africa rivaled Britain as Zambia's chief supplier.[42] Although Zimbabwe has tried to restore its former place as Zambia's principal supplier, it has encountered difficulty because South African exports are on the whole cheaper (*African Business* 1984z:31). In 1982, for example, Zimbabwe exported commodities to Zambia valued at only U.S. $25 million—less than one third of its exports in 1964.

The high economic cost of having the United Kingdom as Zambia's major supplier instead of Rhodesia or South

[42] The bulk of Zambia's imports are for mining and transport equipment and intermediate and consumer durables. The end use of Zambia's imports in 1974 included intermediate goods (50 percent), capital equipment (20.9), and durable and other consumer goods (17.4 percent; UNDP 1976:14). In 1980, machinery and transport equipment and basic manufacturers constituted about 55 percent of the country's total imports (*Africa South of the Sahara* 1984:976). South Africa supplies Zambia with mining equipment, medicines, cooking oil, detergents, maize, butter, cheese, and a wide range of consumer items including beer bottles and sports equipment.

Africa made Zambia highly vulnerable to economic shocks to its urban wage-earning population. Such shocks could be temporarily avoided by the cushion of high world prices for Zambia's copper exports. However, when the world price of copper plunged after 1975, the results were shortages of essential commodities.[43] This fueled worker dissatisfaction, particularly within the urban areas.

When the economic status of the wage-earning urban population began to deteriorate seriously (measured by shortages of consumer goods, declining real wages, and high unemployment), opposition politicans began to mobilize them against the government's policy of disengaging its economic ties with Rhodesia.

Opposition to Disengagement

Beginning in 1975, Zambia suffered a severe and prolonged decline in the earnings of its major export industry—copper production. In 1976, for example, Nchanga Consolidated Copper Mines Ltd. (the country's most cost-efficient mining company) lost 113.8 kwacha per metric ton of copper sold on the world market. The situation improved somewhat, but the companies failed to make profits in 1977 and through most of 1978 (NCCM 1975-1978). The mining industry continued its decline, with Zambia Consolidated Copper Mines losing 173.6 million kwacha

---

[43] Zambia's wage-earning urban population has imbibed a highly Westernized life style, with the third highest per capita income in black Africa, one of the highest per capita ratios of passenger cars and hospital beds, one of the most highly developed public transporation systems in Africa, high standards of drinking water, and an extensive welfare and education program. The maintenance of this Westernized life style requires a high level of consumer goods that extends to such things as clothing and cosmetics, drinks and food. For example, Zambia is among the few black African countries where imported wheat, cooking oil, and washing powder are classified as "essential commodities" by the government.

in 1982 and 127.5 million in 1983 (*African Business* 1984x:20).

The result was that Zambia ran large balance of payments deficits on current account during these years: −$617 million in 1975, −$145 million in 1976, −$115 million in 1977, and −$423 million in 1982. At first the government financed the trade gap (largely with the United Kingdom) by running down the reserves that it had built up since 1970 during the good years of world copper prices. However, by late 1975 and 1976, Zambia had to resort to large-scale international borrowing to meet the costs of continued high levels of importation.[44] This situation continued to deteriorate until Zambia exhausted its normal credit facilities. It was finally forced to take extreme austerity measures in order to get emergency assistance from the International Monetary Fund.

The impact of Zambia's economic crisis upon urban wage earners has been severe and long-lasting. It was estimated, for example, that beginning in December of 1975 there was an average of twenty thousand new jobless each month (mostly unskilled), with an estimated 25 percent of the total urban work force unemployed by 1977 (Kauseni 1977:141). Reductions in imports and governmental spending produced severe shortages of consumer commodities in the urban centers.[45] Shortages of imported

[44] In 1985, the country's total foreign debt stood at over $2.8 billion, which is a crippling debt burden for a poor country of only 6 million people.

[45] In real terms the volume of imports fell during the 1980s due largely to increased foreign exchange requirements for the importation of oil. Under intense pressure from the IMF, Zambia actually cut back its imports from 920 million kwacha in 1982 (U.S. $991) to 874 million in 1983 (U.S. $698)—a steep reduction in real terms (*New African* 1984b:69). The decrease in governmental subsidies for "essential commodities" and the increased sales tax for nonessential commodities such as petrol and diesel fuel had the result of increasing the cost of living to urban wage earners by raising the prices of public transport, maize meal, cooking oil, sugar, and clothing (*African Business* 1984v:59, and Zambia 1984:29).

equipment and spare parts also forced industries to close, thus laying off more workers.

Public disaffection with the government mounted as it was forced to take more stringent action to satisfy its international creditors, donor countries, and international financial and development agencies. There was a devaluation in July 1976 of 20 percent, which raised the cost of imports and the Consumer Price Index for low-income urban dwellers by 18.6 percent (Hodges 1977a: 1,049). In March 1978, there was a further devaluation of 10 percent.[46] The government also imposed wage controls (including a one-year freeze on civil servants and parastatal employees). There were major cuts in spending by both the government and the mining companies, which produced severe shortages of consumer commodities in the urban centers. The pressure on the government from urban wage earners reached the point where the Minister of Finance John Mwanakatwe was forced to acknowledge that the shortages of essential commodities were the most sensitive political issue in the country (Hodges 1977a: 1,051). Zambia's third general and presidential election, scheduled for December 1978, gave urban voters an opportunity to protest the government's economic policy.

In 1972, Zambia was declared a one-party state. The ruling party was the United National Independence party (UNIP). According to the constitution, only one presidential candidate can be nominated. There was a danger therefore that public unhappiness with the state of the economy could produce a strong "no" protest vote against UNIP's presidential nominee in 1978. If the party's candidate did not receive a majority of "yes" votes from the total votes

[46] In January 1983, there was an additional devaluation of 20 percent against the International Monetary Fund's special drawing right (SDR). In 1976, Zambia broke its link with the U.S. dollar when it devalued, and the kwacha was then tied to the SDR. As of March 31, 1984, one Zambian kwacha was worth U.S. $0.629.

cast in the presidential plebiscite, it would create a constitutional crisis in the country. In that eventuality the national party congress would have to be reconvened to nominate a new presidential candidate. Another presidential
election would then be held. The process would continue
(theoretically at least) until a candidate received a majority
of the votes cast.

In such an unprecedented position UNIP would be extremely vulnerable. The only serious rival to President
Kaunda, the party's presidential nominee, was Simon
Kapwepwe, an exvice president and leader of the banned
opposition party—the United Progressive party. If President Kauda, who was clearly the most popular UNIP politician, could not win the presidential plebiscite, there was
little hope that any other member of the party could do better. Therefore, if Kaunda lost the election, UNIP would be
faced with the prospect of either nominating the opposition's chief candidate, Kapwepwe, or suspending the constitution and risking civil conflict over an unprecendented
and undoubtedly highly unpopular action.

In challenging the president and UNIP, Kapwepwe
sought to mobilize urban wage earners on the Copperbelt
and in the Central and Lusaka provinces on the basis of his
promise to end the shortages by reopening the border for
trade with Rhodesia. Another prominent Zambian politician, Harry Nkumbula, the head of the banned Zambian
African National Congress, who had his base of support in
the commercial, agricultural, Southern province, also declared his candidacy for the presidency. Nkumbula's popularity with the urban wage earners in the Southern province constituted an additional threat to UNIP. The
combination of Kapwepwe and Nkumbula challenging
UNIP's popularity in a presidential race therefore combined to constitute a serious threat to the ruling party. An
examination of UNIP's base of political support in the
country reveals the reason for their apprehension. Table

Table 4.8   United National Independence Party's Official Membership and Total Population by Province, 1978

Province	Population[a]	UNIP Membership
Copperbelt	1,046	39,404
Central (including Lusaka)	920	54,971
Southern	540	28,742
Eastern	568	34,329
Northern	580	17,347
Western	463	8,408
North-Western	256	20,393
Total	4,373	203,594

SOURCE: UNIP party headquarters, Lusaka, Zambia, 1978.
NOTE: [a] In thousands.

4.8 shows UNIP's official party membership by province in 1978.

With the exception of the Eastern province, UNIP's membership tends to be concentrated in the line-of-rail (the Copperbelt, Central-Lusaka, and Southern provinces) where the majority of the country's urban wage earners work and live (see Table 4.8). Kapwepwe and Nkumbula's challenge to UNIP was, therefore, an appeal for support from the very social elements on which the ruling party depends for its political support. They directly challenged UNIP by opposing the president's decision in 1973 to close Zambia's border with Rhodesia for reasons of "principle" (until the Rhodesian government was dissolved and a legal black majority government was installed in power). Kapwepwe pointed out in his campaign, for example, that the United Nations had exempted Zambia from complying with U.N. mandatory sanctions. Therefore, the government's refusal to use the southern transport route unnecessarily cost Zambia a staggering U.S. $744 million.[47]

[47] Sir Robert Jackson, the excoordinator of U.N. Assistance to Zambia,

Although Kapwepwe and Nkumbula's political challenge did not remove UNIP nor President Kaunda from power, it did succeed in persuading the government to reverse its disengagement policy in October of 1978 (two months before the national and presidential elections). Zambia's border with Rhodesia was reopened, and trade with South Africa was officially encouraged.[48] The government declared that henceforth the cheapest source of imports (implying its regional trading partners—Rhodesia and South Africa) would be Zambia's guide in allocating future licenses to import.

In reversing the disengagement policy, the president and UNIP had thus undercut the major source of urban grievances that their political rivals sought to use against them. The reestablishment of Zambia's regional trading pattern was designed primarily to serve the interests of the state's base of political support—urban wage earners.

This would suggest that in order for UNIP to remain secure in power it must continue to protect and advance the interests of the large and growing urban population, which would almost certainly rule out any attempts to disengage Zambia from its economic ties with South Africa.[49] The

---

gave this figure for the years 1966 to 1977 in his report to ECOSOC on behalf of the secretary general of the United Nations following Zambia's decision to comply with the sanctions. However, the figure actually deflates the real cost to Zambia. It does not include the extra recurrent and capital costs arising from rerouting Zambia's external trade, the congestion surcharges at Indian and Atlantic ocean ports, increased storage charges, nor state subsides paid to transport agencies such as Zambia Railways.

[48] The official reason given for the decision to reopen the border with Rhodesia was to expedite desperately needed fertilizer from South Africa in time for the new planting season in Zambia (August to October). However, once the border was open, unrestricted trade with Rhodesia and South Africa was encouraged, and after the fertilizer shipment was delivered to Zambia the border remained open.

[49] In 1965, the newly independent Zambian government gave twelve months notice of its intention to terminate trade agreements with South Africa (Spence 1965:76ff).

danger of massive urban unrest and trade union opposition to UNIP is simply too risky politically to contemplate
disengagement without assured high revenues from exports to buffer the urban wage earner against the shock of
world economic downturn.[50]

[50] Kaunda easily retained his position in the fourth general and presidential elections held in October 1983, running unopposed and receiving
93 percent of the votes cast compared to 81 percent of the total votes cast
for the presidency in 1978. However, this in no way removed urban dissatisfaction with the government's economic austerity policies nor less-
ened trade union opposition to policies adversely affecting urban wage
earners. The election outcome largely recorded Kaunda's widespread
popularity and the fact that he is the leader most people would prefer to
have in the presidency during times of crisis.

CHAPTER FIVE

Marginal State Involvement in the Regional Economy: Tanzania and Zaire

THE FOURTH CATEGORY of state action in the regional economy is marginal involvement. Unlike the states in the other categories of state action, the regimes of Tanzania and Zaire were not forced to deal with the constraints and opportunities presented by the regional economy. Because the economies of these states were not significantly influenced, at least initially, by the regional economy, it was only as a result of deliberate state action that they elected to become involved. They took this action in order to shore up declining domestic political support or to carry out foreign policy objectives toward Southern Africa.

Tanzania became involved in the regional economy in response to the regime's foreign policy commitment to remove the minority regimes of Rhodesia and South Africa from power. However, in the process of carrying out this policy, the country incurred major political costs resulting from a neglect of domestic national development in favor of fulfilling doctrinaire foreign policy objectives. Another major cost is that Tanzania's foreign policy opened its economy to competitive threats from states in the regional economy.

By contrast, Zaire became involved in the regional economy when it was faced with an economic crisis stemming from the Angolan civil war. This conflict had the effect of disrupting the country's primary rail transit route for its major export—minerals—through Angola. Faced with this crisis, the regime decided to reroute its exports through South Africa in order to guarantee a reliable transit route.

The political significance of this action for the Zairian regime is that it guaranteed foreign exchange earnings and state revenues on which the regime depends for its survival. In the case of Tanzania, by contrast, its involvement in the regional economy has tended to undermine the regime's domestic base of power.

TANZANIA

Tanzania's involvement in the Southern African economy resulted from the ruling Chama Cha Mapinduzi (CCM) party's overriding foreign policy commitment to liberate Southern Africa from white minority regimes.[1] The CCM devoted itself to two major foreign policy principles: the liberation of minority regimes in Southern Africa and non-alignment in East-West affairs. On the issue of liberation, Tanzania committed itself to supporting movements in Angola, Mozambique, Namibia, Rhodesia, and South Africa. In lending support, both diplomatic and material, to the Southern African liberation movements, however, the country tended to be guided by pragmatic considerations. That is, they supported movements which were prepared to fight and had the best prospects of taking over these countries (Coulson 1982:306). In assuming this principled stance, Tanzania was accorded the status of being the headquarters of the African Liberation Committee of the Organization of African States and was also given the chairmanship of the Frontline States.

Tanzania's commitment to the liberation of Southern Africa led to a major reorientation of the country's transportation trunk lines toward the south. This occurred after

[1] In 1977, the Tanganyika African National Union and Zanzibar's ruling party, the Afro-Shirazi party, merged to form one ruling party called the Chama Cha Mapinduzi, which in English means Revolutionary party of Tanzania.

1965 when the Rhodesian regime declared UDI. Tanzania's reaction was to provide landlocked Zambia with an "economic lifeline" to the sea by undertaking major transportation projects to establish trunk routes to Zambia.

At the time of Zambia's independence from British colonial rule in October 1964, the country's transportation links were almost entirely oriented toward the southern rail routes through Rhodesia to Cape Town and Beira and through Zaire and Angola to Lobito. These routes were all under the control of white minority regimes at the time. After UDI in 1965, and after Rhodesia temporarily closed its border to Zambian traffic in 1973, the Zambian government felt vulnerable to political pressure from "hostile" bordering states. In this situation, Zambia sought to develop transport routes to the sea through northern states (particularly Tanzania). Since Zambia had cordial relations with Tanzania, the Zambians felt that that would guarantee them a stable and reliable transport route.

Tanzania responded to Zambia's efforts to break its dependence upon southern transport routes by undertaking three major projects designed to cement trunk routes to Zambia. These included the Tanzania-Zambian Highway (TANZAM road), the TAZAMA oil pipeline, and the Tanzania-Zambia Railway (TAZARA). The TANZAM road and the TAZARA were primarily designed to provide Zambia with an alternative outlet to the sea, and the TAZAMA pipeline was designed to supply the country with crude oil.

The success of these projects in redirecting Zambia's import-export traffic away from southern transport routes and toward northern routes is evident in Table 5.1. The data reveal that after the closure of the border with Rhodesia in 1973, and after the virtual closure of the Lobito-Zaire route due to the Angolan war in 1975, Dar es Salaam became Zambia's principal outlet to the sea (see Map 13). In fact, between 1970 and 1976, the Rhodesian and Dar es Salaam routes reversed positions in terms of their impor-

Table 5.1 Zambia's Imports and Exports by Routes, 1970-1976 (in thousands of tons)

Area	1970 Import	1970 Export	1971 Import	1971 Export	1972 Import	1972 Export	1973 Import	1973 Export	1974 Import	1974 Export	1975 Import	1975 Export	1976 Import	1976 Export
Rhodesia	1,293 (76.9)[a]	398 (46.9)	1,048 (63.8)	390 (48.9)	864 (68.7)	467 (54.7)	35 (3.9)	5 (0.6)	— (0.0)	— (0.0)	— (0.0)	— (0.0)	— (0.0)	— (0.0)
Dar es Salaam	248 (14.8)	253 (29.8)	295 (17.9)	221 (27.7)	202 (16.1)	210 (24.6)	232 (25.7)	284 (34.7)	289 (29.4)	319 (34.5)	379 (43.1)	395 (50.4)	575 (75.5)	676 (74.9)
Lobito-Zaire	118 (7.0)	187 (22.1)	269 (16.3)	176 (22.1)	144 (11.5)	170 (19.9)	424 (47.0)	438 (53.6)	438 (44.6)	509 (55.1)	257 (29.2)	309 (39.5)	4 (0.5)	131 (14.5)
Beira-Nacala	18 (1.1)	6 (0.7)	29 (1.8)	9 (1.1)	39 (3.1)	7 (0.8)	102 (11.3)	39 (4.8)	125 (12.7)	10 (0.1)	159 (18.1)	77 (9.8)	129 (17.0)	83 (9.2)

SOURCES: Ministry of Power, Transport, and Works. Transport Inventory Series (3): Zambia's External Transportation by Routes, 1969-74 (Lusaka: December 1974), and Contingency Planning Unit figures for 1975 and 1976, as reported in IBRD (1977:200-201).
NOTE: [a] Percentages of totals in parentheses.

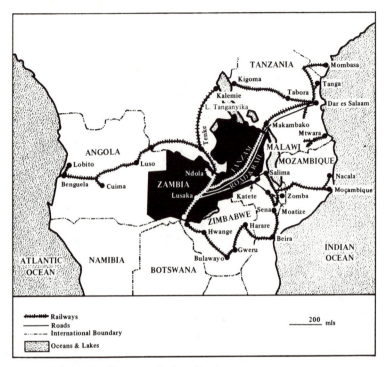

Map 13. Alternative Transport Outlets: Zambia

tance as outlets for Zambia's trade. In 1970, the Rhodesian route accounted for 76.9 percent of Zambia's imports and 46.9 percent of its exports. Dar es Salaam accounted for only 14.8 percent of Zambia's imports and 29.8 percent of its exports. However, by 1976, none of Zambia's trade was reported on the Rhodesian route, while Dar es Salaam accounted for 75.5 percent of Zambia's imports and 74.9 percent of its exports. During 1977 and 1978, Dar es Salaam became even more important to Zambia. In 1977 and during the first nine months of 1978, the Dar es Salaam route accounted for 83 percent of Zambia's entire cargo (Zambia 1979:9).

Economic Lifeline to Zambia

While there can be no doubt about the success of Tanzania's economic lifeline to Zambia in terms of providing an alternative outlet to the sea, the costs to Tanzania of reorienting its transportation trunk lines to Zambia were high. For example, it was estimated that between 1966 and 1973, the structure of Tanzania's investment was oriented toward long-term infrastructure rather than toward manufacturing and agricultural projects, which would have had a shorter pay-off period. The Commonwealth Secretariat (1978:18) has estimated that 43 percent of all fixed capital formation during the 1966 to 1973 period went for transportation and communication.

Under the terms of the Second Five-Year Plan (1969-1974), projects such as the TANZAM road and the TAZARA meant that the economy would experience a lower rate of growth in output. It also meant that other projects of national economic importance had to be postponed in favor of projects that had the political liberation of Southern Africa as the principal objective. For example, the 1969 to 1974 plan states that because of the "massive allocation of resources" to the Tanzania-Zambia rail and road projects, it was necessary to postpone a new trunk highway from Dar es Salaam to Mtwara.

The Commonwealth Secretariat (1978:20) also estimated that a total of 2,500 million shillings (or over U.S. $300 million) was spent by Tanzania for capital expenditure for Zambia-related transport projects during the period 1965 to 1975. In addition, an estimated 1,500 million shillings (one-half the Chinese loan to Tanzania and Zambia for the construction of the TAZARA) was added to Tanzania's external debt. The TANZAM highway was estimated to have cost approximately 600 million shillings, with a further outlay of 400 million for port development at Dar es Salaam to handle the massive increase in Zambian traffic. One indication of just how important these projects were in terms of Tanzania's total developmental budget is evident in the fact that the estimated cost of the TANZAM road in the Second Five-Year Plan was 394 million shillings. This was more than one-half of the total allocated for the country's entire road system (785,421,000 shillings) during the period of the plan. Recurrent costs of maintaining the TANZAM road were also estimated to be in the order of 250 million shillings during the 1965 to 1975 period, with maintenance costs running at about 30 million shillings per annum.[2]

POLITICAL IMPLICATIONS

The domestic political implications of Tanzania's commitment to the liberation of Southern Africa are related to an emerging political threat to the CCM. The economic costs of the construction of major transport links with Zambia has (along with the country's agricultural crisis and declining output) deprived the government of revenues to finance social services and economic infrastructure for peasant farmers.

In 1967, Tanzania's ruling party adopted a policy in the Arusha Declaration of establishing a socialist state where workers and peasants controlled and owned the means of production.[3] The Arusha Declaration encouraged self-re-

---

[2] The recurrent revenue earned by Tanzania from Zambian traffic was estimated to be equal to, or slightly greater than, the recurrent expenditure for operating Tanzania's railway and harbors. It was estimated, for example, that the foreign exchange earned from rail, port, and other services doubled during the period 1971 to 1976 to 1,531 million shillings (or U.S. $184 million) in 1976. The increased foreign exchange earned by Tanzania's service sector was due to usage by neighboring countries—Rwanda, Burundi, Zaire, and Zambia—which accounted for about 67 percent of the increased earnings. However, Zambia's continuing foreign exchange shortage, beginning in 1975 with the collapse of world copper prices, made it difficult for the country to pay for the freight charges and operating costs of the TAZARA (Commonwealth Secretariat 1978:20).

[3] For a description of the Arusha developmental strategy, see Rweyemamu (1973:57-74) and Shivji (1976:79-99).

liance primarily by expanding agricultural production for domestic consumption. In order to realize these goals the government nationalized banks, insurance companies, and foreign trading companies. They also nationalized major industries such as the large agricultural estates, which produced an estimated 70 percent of the country's tea, over half of the sisal, coffee and tobacco.

President Nyerere followed up the Arusha Declaration with a policy statement on "socialism and rural development." The impetus behind this statement was a concern that the growth of cash crop production by individual peasant farmers would lead to class formation and conflict between farmers and laborers. To obviate such a development, Nyerere proposed the establishment of "Ujamaa villages" in which the rural population would collectively live and work together and share in the increased agricultural production. Between 1967 and 1973, the number of rural villagers who were officially designated as residing in Ujamaa villages increased from approximately one-half million to about two million (or an estimated 15 percent of the rural population).[4] In the next several years after 1973, a major drive to bring rural Tanzanians into villages resulted in the creation of villages throughout the entire country. However, this accomplishment involved an extensive show of force and widespread peasant dislocation and discontent. Concurrent with this emphasis on the collection of peasants into villages there was a significant

[4] A major reason for the government's focus upon villagization and cooperative nucleated settlements (that is, Ujamaa or "familyhood" villages, which numbered 8,200 in mainland Tanzania in 1982) was the scattered nature of the rural population. With an estimated population of 19.2 million (according to the 1981 census) and a small urban population (6 percent in 1967), the country was characterized by low population density in the interior and by rural settlements comprised of scattered homesteads instead of villages. Hence, without permanent planned villages it was impossible for the government to implement policies designed to raise peasant agricultural output through collectivization and large-scale production.

downplaying of the earlier emphasis upon communal farming and a corresponding emphasis upon social benefits. Hence, Ujamaa villages came to be seen increasingly as centers for infrastructure and social services.

There is a difference of scholarly opinion regarding the underlying causes of the failure of Tanzania's Ujamaa policy of rural collectivization.[5] However, there can be no disagreement that the widespread dislocation caused by the villagization drive seriously contributed to the decline in agricultural production during these years. Almost all of Tanzania's marketed crops during the 1973 to 1975 period declined. For example, cotton production fell from 77,000 tons in 1973 to 42,500 tons in 1976, and cashew nut output decreased by a third during this period. There were also serious shortfalls in the production of food crops leading to food deficits, particularly in the urban areas of the country. The towns and cities had to be supplied by massive imports of grain costing an estimated 2,000 million shillings.[6]

[5] For example, Lofchie (1978:465) argues that the absence of capitalist incentives in the form of high producer prices for peasant farmers was a major reason for the failure of Ujamaa. Coulson (1982:235-262) takes the position that the bulk of the villagization program discouraged grassroots participation, failed to emphasize communal work, and incurred enormous costs in terms of staffing, vehicles, property losses, unplanted or unharvested crops, and large food imports to compensate for the decline in food production. Samoff (1981) argues that since the villagization program in Tanzania failed to achieve communal socialist goals in the rural areas, it was the absence of socialism rather than its presence that brought on the agrarian crisis of 1973 to 1975. Shivji (1976) argues that Ujamaa failed because the Tanzanian ruling "bureaucratic bourgeoisie" formed a class alliance with rich peasants, which had the effect of dominating and exploiting the poor and "middle" peasants. Hyden (1980) explains the failure of Ujamaa in terms of the peasantry's resistance to attempts by other social classes to transform to capitalist or socialist modes of production. There is also a tendency for writers to blame the failure of the economic program on bad luck such as drought (Green, private communication 1985), the collapse of the sisal market during the 1960s, the Mozambican liberation struggle, increased petroleum prices, and the war with Uganda (Freund 1981:485).

[6] In 1971/1972, Tanzania's grain imports (the basic food staple grown

The effect of this was to exhaust Tanzania's foreign exchange reserves and to make the country dependent upon Western food aid.

Faced with an agrarian crisis, the Tanzanian government began to reorient its rural development strategy away from communal work and toward small-scale peasant farming. This was done to reverse the decline in agricultural production. For example, the new agricultural policy in 1983 reaffirmed the practice of paying farmers immediately upon receipt of their produce instead of waiting for months as was increasingly the case after 1977. This measure along with government subsidies of agricultural inputs (abolished in 1984 under IMF pressure) was expected to increase export crop earnings in real terms by 35 percent during the 1983 to 1986 period.

The government's previous emphasis upon communal production was replaced with "block farming" in which peasants cultivated their own individual plots that joined other plots to form a "block" of village farming land.[7] The objective of the new rural development strategy was to organize peasant village agricultural production on the basis of individual initiative according to economies of scale. Block-farming villages were expected to become the principal peasant agricultural production unit. They were to function within a centralized administrative organization that would make available tractors and other agricultural inputs at the village level (Bryceson 1982).

However, from the point of view of the peasantry (who

---

primarily by hoe-wielding smallholder peasants) were estimated to be 135,000 tons, including 90,000 tons of maize. In 1972/1973, grain imports were 90,000 tons of which 80,000 tons were maize. However, during the next two years from August 1973 to July 1975, Tanzania was forced to import over 500,000 tons of maize (*African Business* 1979:21).

[7] Reginald Green argues that both communal Ujamaa and block-farming policies were largely rhetoric, with communal farming acreage covering only between 3 to 5 percent of the total and block farms covering even less (private communication 1985).

constitute about 80 percent of the population and cultivate about 90 percent of all farmland), the principal attraction of the development villages (as well as the Ujamaa villages) was the promise of state subsidies. This took the form of clean water, health clinics, schools, roads, livestock facilities and slaughter houses, plus seeds and fertilizers. The political significance of massive infusions of social services and economic infrastructure to the peasantry is that it constitutes the state's principal claim to legitimacy.

For example, the regime lays claim to having brought piped water to between 40 and 50 percent of Tanzania's villages (although about half have broken down), to having brought electricity and roads to the rural areas, and to having provided 40 percent more physicians and nurses than surrounding African countries. They also claim to have expanded the country's educational program to the point where Tanzania has one of the highest literacy rates in Africa.[8]

The dilemma that the agricultural crisis poses to the regime is that the costly state programs cannot be sustained in the face of the decline in Tanzania's export earnings. Tanzania's export crops have declined by an estimated 40 percent in volume since 1971/1972. Cashew production declined from 125,600 metric tons in 1972/1973 to 30,000 metric tons in 1983. Sisal production also fell from 155,000 metric tons in 1982 to only 61,200 metric tons in 1983. The country has continued to suffer from food shortages. For example, the gap between Tanzania's cereal requirements and production was 340,000 metric tons in

[8] Speaking in an interview in 1984, Prime Minister Salim Ahmed Salim identified Ujamaa as Tanzania's political ideology and stated that Ujamaa has been behind the achievements of the nation in providing social services to uplift the quality of life of the average Tanzanian (*Africa* 1984b:17). Seushi and Loxley have estimated that the cost to the government of its investments in Ujamaa villages was 250 million shillings each year from 1971 to 1973 (Barker 1974).

1984 (*New African* 1984a:42). This made Tanzania the only country on the Food and Agricultural Organization's list of twenty-four countries in Africa experiencing food emergencies not incurred by drought. Likewise, Tanzania's industrial output has declined seriously. In 1982, for example, it was estimated that the country's factories were only operating at between 15 and 30 percent of capacity. This was largely due to severe shortages of raw materials and spare parts. During 1984, industry was estimated to be running at only 25 percent of capacity.

The government's response to the agricultural crisis was to rely upon outside sources of aid. Foreign donors such as the World Bank, Sweden, Norway, West Germany, Holland, and Britain provided over 60 percent (U.S. $650 million) of Tanzania's 1981/1982 development budget. This has made Tanzania heavily dependent upon Western aid (*African Business* 1984e:22). Another indication of just how dependent Tanzania is upon Western aid to avoid a collapse of the economy is the fact that the country's commercial credit has virtually evaporated. For example, in 1981 Tanzania received 800 million shillings in commercial supplier credits, whereas in 1983 it only received 6 million.

The provision of social services and economic infrastructure to rural peasant farmers is critically important to the ruling party in terms of legitimating the regime. However, there does not appear to be any correlation between the provision of social services and increases in the output of peasant commodity production. In fact, the majority of Ujamaa villages were situated in the poorest areas of the country outside of the cash crop (domestic and export) agricultural areas. And significantly, the formation of Ujamaa settlements was frequently for noneconomic reasons.

For example, the heavy concentration of Ujamaa villages in Mtwara and Ruvuma regions was largely due to the urgency of establishing "self-defense" organizations in the face of Portuguese attacks during the Mozambican independence war. In addition, since the resistance to Ujamaa was strongest in the high income areas of the country, the villages tended to be concentrated in the poorer, subsistence farming areas (Barker 1974:445). Hence, Ujamaa villages came to be associated with the less productive subsistence peasant farmers, which tended to relegate the program to a welfare function.[9] Barker suggests that in the face of an agricultural crisis, the welfare-oriented Ujamaa program was likely to give way in favor of concentrating agricultural inputs in the more prosperous and productive private cash crop farms. There is evidence that this is, in fact, beginning to occur.[10]

The government's heavy reliance upon Western private-sector-oriented foreign donors for its development budget however, threatens to reverse the substantial benefits that a large number of peasants who participated in the Ujamaa program enjoyed.[11] The Tanzanian leadership is under-

[9] Hyden (1980:119) notes the absence of an association between Ujamaa villagization and increases in the output of peasant farmers. For example, governmental provision of mechanized farming equipment to Ujamaa peasant farmers merely freed peasants from their Ujamaa work assignments and gave them more time to work their own private plots. The peasants in Ujamaa villages also neglected farm machinery, which was often abandoned in the fields when it became defective. Green takes the position that weather was the dominant factor in determining peasant production and that "logically, villagization should improve the output record." He argues that other factors account for only about 1 to 2 percent loss of output growth per year. (Private communication 1985.)

[10] Under pressure from the IMF and aid donors the Tanzanian government began to provide greater incentives to private farmers in contradiction of its Ujamaa socialist policy. For example, in 1983 the government raised producer prices and encouraged private peasant farmers. It also agreed to allow eighteen major agricultural companies to retain between 10 and 15 percent of the foreign exchange that their exports earned for their own import needs (*African Business* 1984e:22, and *African Business* 1984m:53).

[11] It was estimated, for example, that out of the 8,320 Ujamaa villages, 6,000 have village shops, 2,900 have dispensaries, 7,600 have elementary schools, and 3,100 have clean water supplies. Life expectancy has also risen from thirty-seven years in 1961 to fifty-one years in 1983. An esti-

standably concerned about the political fallout of eliminating social programs, which are widely perceived by the peasantry to be theirs as a matter of right under a socialist state.

The post-1980 forced cutbacks in social programs that the IMF and other Western donor countries made as a condition for further financial assistance have heightened the Tanzanian leadership's fears of political disruption.[12] The specter of rioting in other third world countries such as Ghana, Peru, Egypt, and the Dominican Republic is a matter of grave concern to the ruling party. Equally worrisome to the CCM are signs of bureaucratic-business opposition to the party's socialist policies favoring the orthodox policies of the IMF and donor countries. The abortive coup attempt in 1983 led by middle-ranking army officers, a State House official, and a prominent industrialist was seen in that light.

---

mated 95 percent of all school-aged children in Tanzania receive seven years of schooling, and infant mortality has fallen from 175 per 1,000 to 140 per 1,000 in 1983 (*New African* 1983:42).

[12] Tanzania made a drawing of funds from the IMF in September 1980 (based upon an agreement in August 1980 for $200 million in SDRs over a two-year period). The government was forced to approach the IMF again for further financial assistance to help cover the cost of its imports because only 40 percent was being met by the earnings from Tanzanian exports in 1983. The IMF insisted upon the following conditions for its financial assistance to Tanzania: a 70 percent devaluation of the Tanzanian shilling, dropping subsidies on such commodities as maize meal (the food staple), lifting import controls and increasing the prices paid to cash crop producers by 45 percent over the 1981/1982 prices, and cuts in governmental spending. The abolition of subventions on maize meal, which was subsidized at 8 shillings per kilogram, would result in a rise to 25 shillings per killogram. This is well beyond the average daily wage of peasant laborers. Under IMF pressure the government eliminated an estimated two hundred projects, many of which were in the "nonproductive" rural sector. However, despite Tanzania's partial concessions to IMF demands, such as a devaluation, increases in producer prices, and a drop in food subsidies, as of early 1985 no agreement had been reached with the IMF to provide desperately needed financial assistance (*African Business* 1985a:19).

OVERCOMING ECONOMIC CRISIS

Tanzania initially became involved in the Southern African economy through its commitment to the liberation of white minority regimes. It subsequently sought to use the southern transport route to help cope with its economic crisis. The regime has attempted to use its transport links with Zambia to stimulate industrial exports to SADCC countries and to stimulate the growth of agricultural production and processing industries in southern Tanzania along the TAZARA line-of-rail—the Uhuru Corridor.

In principal, at least, the CCM has sought to reorient the country's manufacturing exports away from East Africa and toward Southern Africa. It has attempted to do this in Tanzania's capacity as the coordinating country for SADCC's industrial development. Tanzania has also concluded special trading agreements with Zambia and Mozambique in order to secure markets in the region for its exports.

The significance of Tanzania's efforts to penetrate SADCC markets is evident in the country's highly unfavorable trading relationship with its chief East African trading partner—Kenya.[13] For example, in 1976, the year before the dissolutionment of the East African Community (EAC), Tanzania imported 461 million shillings in goods from Kenya while only exporting 235 million shillings in value. In 1977, it was estimated that trade with Kenya was responsible for over 10 percent of Tanzania's trade deficit. During most of the EAC period, in fact, Tanzania ran persistent trade deficits with Kenya.

In 1972, Tanzania began to replace Zambia's distant sup-

[13] A likely reason that Tanzania was a holdout from joining the Preferential Trade Area for countries of Eastern and Southern Africa for almost eight years was that it included Kenya as well as most SADCC countries. This was undoubtedly perceived by the Tanzanians as a potential threat to their strategy to secure access to markets in SADCC countries. Although Tanzania finally signed the PTA articles of agreement in 1985, they have yet to ratify the agreement.

pliers, such as Argentina (corned beef) and Switzerland and the Ivory Coast (coffee). In addition, Tanzania exported a range of manufactured goods to Mozambique under the terms of the Mozambique-Tanzania Permanent Commission of cooperation, which was established in 1976. In 1983, Tanzania also signed barter trade agreements with Zambia and Mozambique, enabling them to settle their accounts in local currencies instead of foreign currency, which is in critically short supply (*African Business* 1983:5). However, not only are Tanzania's export markets within SADCC limited largely to Mozambique and Zambia but Tanzania has had adverse terms of trade with SADCC countries (SADCC 1984a:I, 3).

Of equal potential importance to Tanzania stemming from its involvement in the regional economy is the Uhuru Corridor, which flanks the TAZARA line-of-rail. It was hoped that the TAZARA would open up major development projects, including the expansion of agricultural production, by providing cheap transport facilities along the 1,155 miles of track between Dar es Salaam and Kapiri Mposhi in the Zambian copperbelt. It was also hoped that the railway would make it economical to transport agricultural products to market and to storage and processing centers and to supply farmers with agricultural inputs such as fertilizers and machinery. Before the TAZARA was opened, there were no industries along the route, with the exception of the Kilombero sugar refinery, and there were no industries at all in the southern portion of the country.

These expectations for the TAZARA, however, have to date at least, not been fulfilled. The only major project is a massive pulp and paper mill at Mufindi. Green (private communication 1985) notes in this regard that Tazania's largely obsolete internal railway system (Tanzania Railway Corporation) and its highway system and vehicle fleet (which is also in a poor state) are probably more important than the TAZARA in the agricultural corridor.

By tying its development strategy to participation in the

Southern African regional economy, the regime has inadvertently made itself vulnerable to competitive threats originating from within the region. For example, in order to earn large and continuing foreign exchange, the TAN-ZAM road, the TAZARA, and the port of Dar es Salaam must compete with other regional road, rail, and port facilities for traffic. Likewise, Tanzania's success in penetrating Southern African markets will depend in large measure upon how competitive its goods are compared with the economical and efficient South African and Zimbabwean manufacturers who now dominate regional markets.

If successful, this strategy could reduce the pressure upon the government to accept the austerity policies of the IMF and Western donors (invariably requiring further cuts in social welfare programs) that would undermine peasant support for the ruling party. On the other hand, if the strategy fails, Tanzania could find itself in a disadvantageous position comparable to its experience in the EAC. If this happens, it could further erode political support for the CCM.

ZAIRE

Zaire's economy is involved in the Southern African regional economy in two important ways. One, the southern transport route is essential to guarantee the shipment of Zaire's chief export—minerals—to world markets; and two, the urban areas of Zaire (especially Shaba province) are dependent upon South Africa and to a lesser extent Zimbabwe for food supplies, consumer goods, and industrial inputs. The significance of Zaire's participation in the regional economy is that it helps to stabilize the country's mining industry, which generates the economic surplus binding together the ruling class and provides the patronage the regime needs to remain in power.

Any serious interruption of Zaire's mining operations (which comprise about 25 percent of GDP, 85 percent of the country's foreign exchange, and almost 50 percent of the government's total revenues) constitutes a major threat to the regime. Hence, Zaire's involvement in the regional economy (especially its economic ties with South Africa) tends to support the regime.

The Southern Transport Route

Zaire's reliance upon the southern transport route through Zambia, Zimbabwe, and South Africa (see Map 1) is due in large part to the continuing civil conflict within Angola and to the economic deterioration of Zaire's transport infrastructure.[14] Before the outbreak of the Angolan civil war in 1975, approximately 50 percent of Zaire's cargo traveled on the Benguela railway line, which passed through Angola en route to the Atlantic coast. As the least expensive and quickest export route for Shaba's mineral production, the Angolan Benguela railway transported the bulk of Zaire's minerals to the Atlantic port of Lobito for shipment to world markets.

However, in August 1975, the Angolan civil war resulted in the disruption of the Benguela line. The principal obstacle to restoring the operation of the line is the sabotage being carried out by guerillas in the National Union

[14] Zaire's *voie nationale* (national way) connects Shaba province to the port city of Matadi. While it is the only route that lies entirely within Zaire, its tortuous network of river and rail routes requires loading and unloading numerous times before reaching Matadi, which has become too silted from neglect to accommodate supply ships. This makes the route uneconomical to use (Bobb 1979:20). The only advantage that the *voie nationale* has over alternative routes is that since it is a domestic route it saves the country foreign exchange, which is in critically short supply. Two additional transport routes for the shipment of Zaire's mineral exports include a route via Kalemie, Lake Tanganyika, and Tanzania to Dar es Salaam and a direct link with the port of Dar es Salaam through Zambia. However, congestion at the port of Dar es Salaam along with inefficiency and slow turn-around time severely limits their potential as alternatives to the Angolan Benguela railway route.

for the Total Independence of Angola (UNITA) led by Dr. Jonas Savimbi. The organization has conducted an effective campaign of guerilla sabotage designed to prevent the Benguela railway from reopening.[15]

UNITA's military strength is concentrated in the eastern and southeastern areas of Angola where it operated against the Portuguese between 1967 and 1974 with the support of South Africa. However, it operated largely on its own in the central highlands where it disrupted road and rail traffic. Map 14 shows that UNITA's operations in October 1984 had spread from southern and central Angola up to Luanda province on the coast and to Uige in the north.[16] In addition to sabotaging infrastructure such as bridges, roads, and the Benguela railway, Savimbi has targeted economic projects such as the diamond- and coffee-producing areas plus the crucial Cabinda oil-rich enclave of Angola.

[15] Even if the Benguela railway line were secured and restored to full operation, however, there would still be doubts about its profitability. For example, the Benguela Railway Company—Companhia Ferroviária de Benguela—estimated that in 1976, even without guerilla sabotage, the line's monthly carrying capacity would be 30,000 tons downwards and between 15,000 and 20,000 tons upwards, which is less than one-third the carrying capacity of the railway line during the Portuguese colonial period. The construction of the TAZARA has also diverted Zambian and Zairian traffic away from the Benguela and therefore will add to the competitive pressure on the Benguela railway line if and when it returns to full operation. An additional reason the Benguela railway line will not be as profitable as it was under colonial rule is that the European "infrastructure" lobby is trying to sell new transport equipment including the construction of a new deep-water harbor at Banana in the context of the rehabilitation of the *voie nationale*. (Jean-Claude Williame, private communication 1985.)

[16] This is not to suggest that UNITA "controls" one-third or one-half of the country. Nor does it suggest that it is merely a "puppet" organization solely dependent upon South African support. However, UNITA's ability to survive operations against it by the Angolan armed forces (the People's Armed Forces for the Liberation of Angola—FAPLA) and to operate in the center of the country (far removed from direct South African support) to sabotage the Benguela railway virtually at will suggests it is a political force in Angola with or without South African support (Bender 1983).

Map 14. UNITA's Guerilla Operations, 1984: Angola
SOURCE: *Africa Confidential* 26, no. 4 (Feb. 13, 1985), p. 3.

UNITA's objective is to deprive the MPLA (Popular Movement for the Liberation of Angola) government of vital foreign exchange on which it depends heavily for defense expenditures (including the cost of maintaining Cuban troops) and public revenues. An indication that the Benguela railway continues to be regarded as an unreliable transport outlet for Zaire's mineral output was a communiqué issued by Angola's President Dos Santos, Zaire's President Mobutu, and Zambia's President Kaunda in June 1983. The leaders pledged themselves at that meeting to "rehabilitate" the Benguela railroad (*Africa News* 1983a:3).

The severe economic deterioration of Zaire's own transport system is the second major reason for its reliance upon the southern transport route. The breakdown of the country's economic infrastructure, especially after the second Shaba war in May 1978, made the southern route for the transport of Zaire's mineral exports and for imports from Zimbabwe and South Africa crucial. For example, before independence in 1960, trucks were able to traverse the entire country within two to three days. Prior to Shaba II,[17]

---

[17] The invasions of Shaba in 1977 and 1978 (called Shaba I and Shaba II) were made by the Front de Libération Nationale du Congo (FLNC), which was comprised largely of former Katangan provincial police (primarily of Lunda ethnicity) who took refuge in Angola after Mobutu came to power. The attacks were part of the MPLA's counterstrategy against the Mobutu regime's support for the anti-MPLA movements: the Front for the Liberation of the Cabinda Enclave (FLEC), the Front for the National Liberation of Angola (FLNA), and UNITA. After the Shaba II invasion Mobutu sought a rapprochement with the Angolan government in order to obviate a possible Shaba III. The so-called Brazzaville agreements were concluded, with both sides assenting to discontinue their support for opposition insurgent movements. In return for Angola's agreement to curb the operations of the Katangese, Mobutu agreed to close FNLA bases in Zaire and expel its leader Holden Roberto. Bender (1983) has argued that although some UNITA officials operate in Kinshasa and while some of their planes have been allowed to land in Zaire, Mobutu has not actively supported their operations against Angola for fear of a Shaba III retaliation. An indication of the improved relations between Angola and Zaire

trucks traveled between Lubmumbashi in Shaba and Kinshasa, the capital, in twelve days. After 1978, however, few if any such trips were undertaken. The route between the provincial capitals of Bukavu and Kisangani (a day's trip before independence) was completely impassable, and river transport was severely curtailed by the breakdown of steamer boats. Only one out of four Air Zaire flights departed on scheduled days. One-half of the country's locomotives and about three-fourths of all road trucks were inoperative due to a lack of spare parts. In addition, there was a severe shortage of petrol, which made long distance road transport uneconomic. It was estimated, for example, that the country could only afford to pay for about 60 percent of its petrol requirements, and most of the available petroleum is in Kinshasa and in the remote mining centers of the country.

Callaghy (1983:383-385) notes the fact that the Zairian government has consistently preferred the southern route since the breakdown of the Benguela railroad line because of its greater efficiency and superior facilities. It was estimated, for example, that in 1981 roughly one-half of Zaire's copper (the principal mineral export) was being exported by rail through the South African ports of East London, Port Elizabeth, and Durban. It was also estimated that it took only about 35 days for imports or exports to travel from South Africa to Zaire, whereas it took 60 days on the *voie nationale* to the port city of Matadi and between 80 and 90 days to travel to the port of Dar es Salaam in Tanzania. South African ports also have excellent storage facilities, and South Africa has reportedly granted to Zaire preferential rates in the shipment of exports through South Africa. Callaghy (1983:384) notes that in 1982, Zaire's now defunct state marketing mining monopoly, SOZACOM,

---

was the presence of President Dos Santos in Kinshasa at the swearing-in of Mobutu for his new seven-year presidential term in December 1984. Dos Santos subsequently returned to Zaire on a state visit in 1985.

concluded an agreement with South Africa to ship its zinc through the country.[18]

The second important reason that Zaire has become involved in the regional economy is that the country's major mining centers of Lubumbashi, Kolwezi, and Mbuji-Mayi, which are located in the remote southeastern part of the country adjoining the Zambian Copperbelt, are supplied primarily by South Africa. According to the International Monetary Fund (IMF), there is a sizable trading relationship between South Africa and Zaire.[19] Official IMF reports indicate that from 1978 to 1980, Zaire's imports from South Africa averaged 10 percent per annum of Zaire's total imports.

Despite the depressed economic conditions of the rural areas and cities such as Kisangani, Mbandaka, Kananga, and Bukavu in the hinterland, most of the imports from South Africa are destined for Kinshasa and Zaire's mining centers, which are heavily dependent upon South Africa and Zimbabwe for foodstuffs, consumer goods, and indus-

[18] Callaghy (1983) also notes the fact that there are unofficial reports of regular air links between Zaire and South Africa involving unrecorded shipments of cobalt, coffee, and diamonds from Kinshasa or Lubumbashi and food and luxury goods returning from South Africa destined for Shaba and Kinshasa.

[19] Neither South Africa nor Zaire publish official statistics on their trading relationship. And since there are reliable reports of substantial and unrecorded trade between them, the IMF estimates of their trade (up to 1980) undoubtedly deflate the actual figures. Nevertheless, the IMF reported that Zaire's imports from South Africa during the years 1978, 1979, and 1980 were U.S. $118.9 million, U.S. $139.5 million, and U.S. $167.4 million respectively. As a percentage of Zaire's total recorded imports, South Africa contributed 9.96 percent in 1978, 9.66 percent in 1979, and 9.46 percent in 1980. This placed South Africa fourth in terms of Zaire's most important supplier country. The comparable figures for Zaire's imports from Zimbabwe during this period were U.S. $78.8 million for 1978, U.S. $90.9 million for 1979, and U.S. $109 million for 1980. As a percentage of Zaire's total imports during this period, Zimbabwe supplied 6.6 percent in 1978, 6.3 percent in 1979, and 6.2 percent in 1980 (IMF 1981:406).

trial inputs.[20] For example, the stores and markets in these cities have food supplies and imported goods from Europe, Japan, and South Africa.

In addition to the reliance of the mining centers upon South Africa and Zimbabwe for their foodstuffs and consumer merchandise, nearly all of Shaba's industrial imports come from the two countries. For example, Shaba depends upon them for its coke, coal, and sulfur requirements. One important consequence of these imports is that they have contributed to the formation of a small group of extremely rich businessmen who have managed to amass great wealth by importing products largely to Shaba and Kinshasa. Businessmen purchase foreign exchange from the Zairian government at the official exchange rate and then sell the goods at substantially higher black market prices. In the face of depressed world prices for Zaire's mineral exports, Zairian businessmen have been able to secure credit in South Africa for imports while being denied credit elsewhere (Callaghy 1983:385). This has enabled the commercial elite to enjoy a sumptuous Western life style (in the midst of depression), which includes expensive cars, digital watches, and videotape machines.

[20] An indication of the importance of South African and Zimbabwean supplies to Zaire's mining areas is the fact that even during the chaotic conditions prevailing throughout most of the country during the 1960s and late 1970s, the mining areas remained largely unaffected and the mining companies continued profitable operations. For example, at the annual general meeting of shareholders of Union Minière du Haut-Katanga held on May 25, 1961, the chairman of the board of directions, Paul Gillet, reported that the company enjoyed a net profit and that aside from two days interruption of their operations the civil conflict in the Congo had practically no repercussions for Union Minière (*East Africa and Rhodesia* 1961:1,078). Likewise, the state-owned mining monopoly, Gécamines, which succeeded the Union Minière du Haut Katanga, showed a remarkable recovery shortly after the second Shaba invasion in May 1978. In Kolwezi, the country's principal mining center, for example, by July 1978 productivity was 57 percent of prewar-planned output, and by August 1978 it had risen to 81 percent of prewar production. By January of 1979 mining operations were 90 percent of prewar levels.

The Zairian Ruling Class

There is scholarly disagreement over whether Zaire's ruling class is a commercial bourgeoisie, a bureaucratic or state bourgeoisie, a comprador "local branch" of the international bourgeoisie, or simply a political class with specific class interests. Likewise, there is disagreement over whether the Zairian state corresponds to the French Bonapartist or absolutist pattern of statehood. Indeed, apart from its status as a major international debtor and the legal fiction of statehood, there is a question of whether it is a state at all.[21]

However, there is little disagreement about the existence of a ruling class in Zaire. Peemans (1975), Depelchin (1981), and Gould (1979:93) argue, for example, that a "bureaucratic bourgeoisie" is the dominant ruling class in Zaire. It controls the state apparatus including the party, army, civil service, public corporations, and state-licensed companies.

Rymenan (1977:8-9) divides the Zairian ruling class into two categories: one, a presidential clique of roughly fifty Mobutu family members, kinsmen, and friends who occupy the most important positions in the state apparatus such as head of the Judiciary Council, Secret Police, Interior Ministry, and President's Office, and two, a few hundred elites who hold the next most important positions under the presidential clique. This group is said to include every major tribe and interest in the country. Beyond these two groups, there is the petite bourgeoisie that is described as a "helper class" comprised of thousands of middle-level civil servants, teachers, university graduates, and small businessmen who aspire to gain access to the bureaucratic bourgeoisie. The bureaucratic bourgeoisie is allied to the petite bourgeoisie, and together they control the state apparatus for their own aggrandisement to the detri-

---

[21] For a discussion of these issues, see Nzongola-Ntalaja (1984:99-102), Young (1984:80-82), Callaghy (1984:184-204), and Schatzberg (1980).

ment of the "masses" who constitute the vast majority of the population and who are denied the class prerogatives of the politico-commercial bourgeoisie.

Nzongola (1970) argues for the existence of five social classes in Zaire: 1) national bourgeoisie, 2) petite bourgeoisie, 3) working class, 4) peasantry, and 5) lumpenproletariat. The national bourgeoisie is the class that holds the position, and performs the roles, that Europeans did before independence. It is the only class that has so far been successful in wielding political power in Zaire. Hence, the national bourgeoisie (also referred to as the politico-administrative bourgeoisie) is Zaire's ruling class. For Nzongola the petite bourgeoisie is the class from which wealthy traders or merchants originated. Many members of the national bourgeoisie whose wives and family engage in business overlap the petite bourgeoisie. Nzongola contends that the petite bourgeoisie was the only class that was prepared to organize itself to represent the people during the anticolonial revolution in the Congo.

Callaghy (1984:184-185) argues that Zaire's "state class" is comprised of three groups. The first is comprised of top-level political, administrative, and military officials, including foreign advisers, which Callaghy refers to as the "presidential family" or "presidential brotherhood." This top echelon of the ruling class includes members of the Political Bureau and Executive Council, state commissioners, Mobutu's relatives, heads of parastatals, and field grade military officers. Those who are closest to Mobutu are said to have unlimited access to state wealth and privileges. They form their own patron-client networks and are themselves part of others' networks. The second group is comprised of middle-level administrative and military officers in Kinshasa who aspire to admission to the "presidential family." The third group includes the territorial prefects and military officers in the regions plus middle- and high-level officials in the moribund regional state services who also wish to move up the class hierarchy.

Young (1985) also argues that there are three groups comprising Zaire's "state bourgeoisie" or state class. The first group is a dominant political class that accumulates capital and is involved in supportive mercantile enterprises. The second group includes individuals who initially derived their assets from politics but have since retired from political life. Nevertheless, they maintain their political connections for insurance and protection of their illegal economic activities. More recently there has emerged a third group comprised of a new *magendo* class of businessmen who fill a niche in the economy created by policies such as "Zairianization" during the 1970s.

SOURCE OF POLITICAL PATRONAGE

The highest echelon of Zaire's ruling class is an inner core of President Mobutu's family and close associates. The small coterie of political allies includes members of the powerful Central Committee of the People's Revolutionary Movement of Zaire (MPR) and advisers to the president, many of whom originated in the president's own Nord Ubangi subregion in northern Equateur. At the center of this political clique is what is pejoratively called the "presidential family." Mobutu is *Luna inter stellas* (moon among stars) in this group in terms of wealth and political power.[22] Closely associated with Mobutu's family and friends and larger in number are his political allies from the Equateur region and adjacent areas that are culturally, linguistically, and ethnically close to the Equateur region.

The center of political power in Zaire is the president

---

[22] The death of Mobutu's fabulously wealthy and venerated uncle, Litho Moboti, in 1982 left a gap in the presidential family. That lacuna was only partially filled by Litho's younger brother, Monenge, and Mobutu's brother-in-law, the brother of his second wife, Bobi Ladawa. Mobutu's nephew, Moleka Liboko, also appeared to gain in influence with the president. However, during 1982 and 1983, Mobutu disposed of the Litho's family fortune by conceding its management to his own Israeli business connection. (Willame, private communication 1985.)

and his personal political allies who have control over vast powers of patronage that originate from the president. For example, the Bank of Zaire, SOZACOM (the now defunct state-owned mining marketing organization), and Gécamines (the state mining company) were under the president's personal control and were administered on his behalf by his family and close political allies.[23] Thus Mobutu and his political allies use their control of the state apparatus not only to enrich themselves but more importantly to bind the ruling class together in support of the regime.

The granting of political patronage permeates every major institution in Zairian society from ministerial bribery to small-scale *matabiche* for postal clerks, telephone operators, and petrol pump attendands. It is particularly instrumental in the ruling political party, the People's Revolutionary Movement, and in the twenty-thousand-man Zairian military (FAZ).

An illustration of the political use of patronage in consolidating political support among the ruling class for the regime was Mobutu's successful strategy for silencing criticism from an increasingly independent-minded elected *commissaires du peuple* in 1979/1980. The president attempted to curtail outspoken members of parliament by creating a 121-member Central Committee of the MPR—the members of whom were appointed personally by Mobutu.

In effect, the Central Committee of the party is above the *commissaires du peuple* and is therefore empowered to overrule its decisions. In order to ensure the allegiance and loyalty of members of the Central Committee, Mobutu authorized huge salaries for them. Nguza Karl-I-Bond esti-

[23] SOZACOM and Gécamines were administered by "yes men" from Kasai and Shaba who could not resist presidential pressures. SOZACOM has ceased to exist since the end of 1984, a requirement imposed by the World Bank, the IMF, and the European Economic Community as a condition for further assistance to the mining sector (Willame, private communication 1985).

mated, for example, that members of the committee are paid at least 15,000 zaires per month (U.S. $5,000 at the time of authorization in March 1981). In contrast, medical doctors earned an average of between 500 to 800 zaires per month (approximately U.S. $200-$250).

Likewise, generals and other ranking officials in the military are well rewarded for their loyalty to Mobutu. Examples of this are as commonplace as they are notorious. Zaire's large and continuing budget overruns (with as much as 60 percent of government revenue used for non-designated purposes) are due to massive political patronage, which includes the Ministry of Defense. The Zairian armed forces have been a continuous drain on the economy largely through misappropriation of funds and food supplies for the personal enrichment of senior officers.

One illustration of this is General Eluki, the former state secretary for national defense. In August 1979, General Eluki along with former Minister of Agriculture Tepatondele were convicted of embezzling government funds. Eluki's wife was reportedly stopped at a roadblock and found to be in possession of seventeen suitcases of money, and a search of Eluki's home resulted in uncovering U.S. $2 million and an additional 2 million zaires. An indication that Eluki was simply a scapegoat among hundreds of other offenders who were not arrested is the fact that General Eluki's twenty-year prison sentence was set aside, and he assumed the position of commander of Shaba region.

However, despite the huge sums that have been funneled through the military, the Zairian armed forces are ineffective, dispirited, and rapacious. This is largely due to the low wages and irregular pay received by the troops, which does not keep pace with the high inflation and devaluations. This situation contributes to soldiers' exploitation of the civilian population in order to supplement their income (Callaghy 1984:293-303). Even the infamous Kamanyola division comprised of soldiers from Equateur province who are better armed and equipped than other army units is poorly paid and is reportedly down to battalion strength. Ironically, however, the pitiful state of the Zairian army as a fighting force has inadvertently contributed to the stability of Mobutu's regime. The low morale of the troops and the lack of cohesion among the officers makes any coup attempt by the military unlikely to succeed. Indeed, one of the hallmarks of Mobutu's rule is the constant rotation of regional military commanders precisely to avoid the formation of local military strongholds that could form the basis of opposition to the regime.

THREATS TO ZAIRE'S RULING CLASS

Callaghy (1984:13) notes the fact that the patron-client networks that bind together the Zairian ruling class are so critical to the regime's survival that any threat to the financial resources available for patronage must be avoided at all costs. Therefore, financial crisis constitutes a serious threat to Zaire's ruling class.

Zaire's fiscal crisis began in 1975 when the country entered a period of chronic external payments deficits and reached a virtually unpayable external debt of about U.S. $4.7 billion in 1985. The principal source of Zaire's financial crisis was the depressed world market price for its mineral exports. For example, copper (the country's principal export earner) fell in terms of price from U.S. $3,000 per ton in 1974 to only U.S. $1,000 per ton in 1975. This produced an acute shortage of financial resources available to the government. Added to this severe shortfall in governmental revenues was an increase in the price of imported goods and a quadrupling of the price of oil imports from $50 million in 1974 to $200 million in 1975.[24]

While the Mobutu regime has been effective in securing

[24] Callaghy (1983:5) attributes Zaire's financial crisis to several factors, including the fall of world copper and commodities prices, closure of the Benguela rail line, the ill-conceived Zairianization measures of 1973 to 1975, increases in the price of oil, and the Shaba invasions of 1977 and 1978.

sufficient international loans and aid from the IMF, aid donors, and commercial banks to avert the financial collapse of his government,[25] assistance has come at a high political cost. The major consequence is that it has weakened the Zairian ruling class by undermining the legitimacy of the regime with the majority of the urban and rural population. While the top echelon of Zaire's ruling class still enjoys the opulence and privileges of great wealth, the diminished economic surplus available to the state (primarily from mineral exports) has not been sufficient to filter down to the urban middle class, to workers, and to the rural population who have been experiencing a catastrophic decline in their standards of living.

The manufacturing industry (concentrated primarily in Kinshasa) was operating well below capacity in the 1980s due to the absence of spare parts and industrial inputs because of the shortage of foreign exchange and the restrictions on industrial imports. No such restrictions have been placed on luxury imports, however. Likewise, the agricultural sector has been shrinking in real terms and in relation to the economy as a whole. Zaire's population has doubled since independence in 1960 (and the urban population has quadrupled). However, agricultural output in the 1980s was below the output in 1960. Hence, while the country was once self-sufficient in food production and indeed was a major exporter of agricultural produce, it has become a major importer of foodstuffs. Hunger and malnutrition have now become widespread.

This has led to a situation in which the so-called "helper class" of civil servants, teachers, university graduates, and small businessmen (as well as the majority of the population) have suffered the worst effects of the virtual collapse

[25] At the end of 1984, Zaire's external debt was rescheduled (payment arrears refinanced and period of repayment extended) for the seventh time—the last one in 1983. Zaire's debt-service payment, due in 1985, was nearly $900 million, which was the third highest (after Nigeria and the Ivory Coast) in sub-Saharan Africa (*African Business* 1984y:7).

of the nonmineral productive sectors of the economy.[26] Workers' salaries have declined to the point where their purchasing power in 1983 was less than 5 percent of what it was in 1960. Their wages have fallen below the so-called "breadline," which is a bare subsistence living wage. Unemployment was estimated to be 50 percent in Kinshasa, with the figure rising to 70 or 80 percent in many of the other towns.

The urban middle class, workers, middle-level civil servants, lower clerical and businessmen in the private sector have all suffered a severe economic setback. They have been left far behind the ruling class, which is still able to afford expensive imported products (including food) and luxury goods. While both internal and external political opposition groups are divided, the country's financial crisis has provoked widespread discontent directed at Zaire's ruling class.[27] Reports of sporadic but growing outbursts of protests suggest that it has become a major threat to the regime.[28]

---

[26] An indication of the expendability of "helper class" interests in order to secure foreign aid to sustain the wealth and prerogatives of Zaire's ruling class was the retrenchment in 1984. Civil servants and teachers were reduced from 260,000 to 178,000, and 80 percent of Air Zaire's staff (of 4,200 employees) was laid off in 1984 as part of the regime's efforts to restore IMF and aid donor governments' confidence in Zaire (ibid., p. 47).

[27] In 1982, seven major opposition parties in exile formed a single front called the Congolese Front for the Restoration of Democracy. Its program included overthrowing Mobutu's regime, forming a transitional government, and rebuilding the economy. Front members agreed not to divide into separate parties until free elections were held in Zaire. However, in the aftermath of the terrorist explosions in Zaire (three in January and two in March 1984) controversy surfaced in the exiled opposition movements (especially within the Congolese National Movement-Lumumba: MNC/L) over whether to take credit for the explosions. There also appears to be doubt about the support that these organizations have within the country (*Africa* 1984d:39, and *New African* 1984:32).

[28] In late 1984, for example, students in Kisangani demonstrated against the state secretary for information and propaganda, and in Lubumbashi students barred him from entering the campus. In Bassako (Up-

The political significance of Zaire's economic ties with South Africa lies in its stabilizing influence on the state's economic surplus. That surplus is necessary to provide patronage to ensure the loyalty and support of the ruling class for the Mobutu regime. By providing a reliable and efficient transport route for Zaire's mineral exports and by supplying the mining areas of the country with foodstuffs, consumer goods, and industrial inputs necessary for the mining industry to operate profitably South Africa ensures the stabilization of Zaire's economic surplus and her economy. Any serious disruption of Zaire's economic relationship with South Africa, therefore, removes an important stabilizing influence upon a crucial source of revenue and foreign exchange that the regime requires to remain in power. Therefore, a disruption of Zaire's economic ties with South Africa weakens political support for Zaire's ruling class.

However, despite the fact that Mobutu and his political allies are dependent upon South Africa as an important source of the regime's economic surplus, this does not mean that Zaire's foreign policy has favored or deferred to South African interests. Callaghy (1983:371-376) has pointed out, for example, that the Mobutu government has taken a consistently hostile diplomatic posture toward South Africa in international fora. Kinshasa has vocally disclaimed any dealings with Pretoria and has condemned South Africa even during periods of growing trade be-

---

per Zaire region) demonstrators protested Mobutu personally for the government's failure to repair a hospital building that had collapsed (*New African* 1984c:55). In March 1984, Zairian soldiers burned their ammunition in N'Djamena (at the Zairian barracks in the Chadian capital) in protest against nonpayment of their salaries and their inability to get loans from local traders (*New African* 1984:33). And in June 1984, businessmen in both Kinshasa and Shaba regions along with members of the banned political opposition movement, the MNC/L, were arrested and charged with exploding two bombs in Kinshasa in March 1984 (*Africa Research Bulletin* 1984:7,286).

tween Zaire and South Africa. In fact, if anything, the only change in Zairian foreign policy toward South Africa has been in the degree of vilification of the apartheid regime, tending to increase when Mobutu was currying favor with other African leaders.

CHAPTER SIX

Namibia's Preindependence Transitional Mode of Involvement

ASSUMING that Namibia achieves independence under a unitary SWAPO-controlled state, the ruling party will be faced with questions concerning the country's involvement in the regional economy comparable with the decision faced by Zambia's ruling party in 1973. SWAPO can make effective use of South African economic inputs in order to build its domestic base of political support or it can refuse to use these inputs and potentially jeopardize that support. Since SWAPO's base of political support is among Ovambo migrant miners, and since South African mining interests are prepared to negotiate with SWAPO in order to continue their operations there, it is unlikely that the party would sever its South African mining ties. However, the party's position on Namibia's other major South African-oriented industries—karakul sheep and cattle ranching—is less clear.

This is a particularly sensitive issue. SWAPO espouses a socialist land reform program. However, non-Ovambo ethnic groups in central and southern Namibia have a long-standing claim to the restoration of their cattle-ranching land, which was forcibly taken from them first by German and then by South African settlers. Therefore, if SWAPO were to collectivize this land ignoring the historic claims of central and southern groups, the latter would likely emerge as a potential source of political opposition to the party. On the other hand, if SWAPO were to continue the country's involvement in the South African ranching industry and make concessions to central and southern groups, a potential political threat to the regime would be avoided.

THE DILEMMA OF AGRARIAN REFORM

Namibia's economy is characterized by two distinct but interconnected sectors[1], a static and impoverished subsistence sector concentrated in the northern areas of the country in the so-called "homelands" of Ovambo, Kavango, Caprivi, Kaokoland, and the Bushman area, and a market or modern sector in the central and southern areas of the country, the so-called "Police Zone." The latter is controlled by whites in collaboration with South African and foreign capital. Namibia's population has been classified according to race into twelve "ethnic" or "population groups,"[2] each (with the exception of whites and coloreds)

---

[1] Reginald Green notes the fact that the subsistence and market sectors of Namibia's economy are integrated, and the former is actually not even subsistence. It is deliberately subsubsistence in order to generate a cheap labor flow to the white economy while partly supporting the workers' "dependents" and keeping them out of the white zones. Hence, the subsistence sector is actually a labor reserve/residual economy created to serve a "market" economy by providing subsidized labor. (Private communication 1985.)

[2] The distribution of Namibia's population has been determined by "ethnical" categorization imposed by South Africa. One-half of the country was allocated to white ranches and towns (including mines, game parks, railways and communications, power and water, coastal waters for fishing, and ports). This included roughly 90 percent of the usable land in the Police Zone, which was comprised of areas of central and southern Namibia that the Germans subdivided and administered at the end of the nineteenth century. The areas that were subjugated by the Germans north of the Police Zone were treated as reserves because they were either densely populated (for example, Ovambo and Kavango) or were unsuited to ranching (Kaokoveld) or they were totally isolated from the rest of the territory (Caprivi). At the conclusion of the World War I when South Africa took possession of Namibia from the Germans, the racial division of the population instituted by the Germans was institutionalized by the South African administration. The majority of the African population still lives in homelands north of the Police Zone, while many others live in reserves within the Police Zone.

having been assigned its own ultimately "self-governing homeland" or tribal reserve. Approximately 40 percent of the country's land area (most of which is arid or semiarid and is of little economic value) has been so designated for the black population as shown in Map 15. Subsistence farms are concentrated in the northeast. The land for these farms was first allocated to each ethnic group for their African homeland and in turn was allocated by the traditional authorities according to tribal custom.

In the north most subsistence agriculture involves mixed livestock and crop agriculture on private plots or communally owned land. Approximately 100,000 subsistence farmers and their families live in the northern homeland areas where rainfall is adequate for some cropping. Likewise, for climatic reasons (that is, low and erratic rainfall) the central and southern homelands are largely restricted to livestock production.

About 50 percent of the economically active population is nominally in the northern subsistence sector. The low productivity of the subsistence sector (estimated to be 2 percent of GDP on normal calculations and not greater than 4 percent on an adjusted price basis) is such that the sector cannot in itself provide subsistence for the peasant population (Green and Kiljunen 1981:33). This has forced black Namibians to leave the homelands in search of employment in the white zones as migrant workers. A study conducted by the United Nations Institute for Namibia in 1978 estimated that out of a total black labor force of 241,500 in 1977 (excluding an estimated 240,000 black people employed in nonwhite-owned or subsistence agriculture) 50,000 were employed on white-owned farms and ranches, 75,000 were employed as domestic servants,[3] and 19,000 worked in the mines (UNIN 1978: Table 4).

[3] Green has revised this estimate downward to about 30,000 to 40,000 domestic servants. While there are probably around 75,000 domestic servants, a high proportion of them work part-time for more than one employer. (Private communication 1985.)

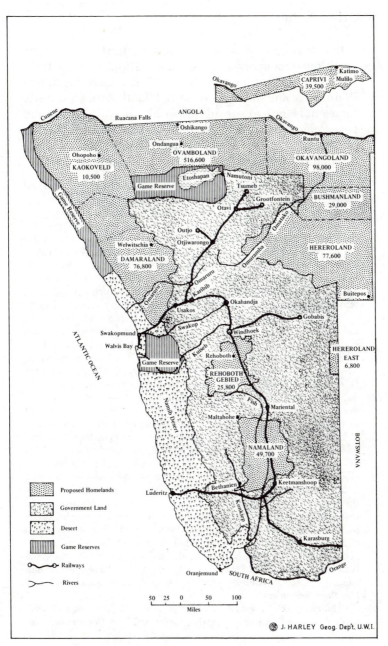

Map 15. Namibia, 1985

In contrast, 43 percent of Namibia's territory has been partitioned for use by the white population.[4] In 1985, there were estimated to be less than 70,000 whites (excluding Walvis Bay and the roughly 90,000 South African security forces in Namibia) spread out within the white areas and government-controlled land as shown in Map 15. Thomas (1978:19-22) estimates that 96 percent of Namibia's white population resides within the white areas[5] (80 percent live

[4] Namibia's homelands were based upon a South African plan that was drafted in 1962/1963 and published in 1964 by the Commission of Enquiry into South West African Affairs, which was set up by the South African government and chaired by F. H. Odendaal. The plan was essentially an elaboration of the German division of Namibia into the "Police Zone," or rich southern region of the country, and the land-poor "native reserves" of the north. The South African government took steps to put the Odendaal Report into effect with the passage of the Development of Self-Government for Native Nations in South West Africa Act of 1968, which created homelands for the Ovambo, Damara, Herero, Kaokolander, Kavango, and East Caprivi. In 1973, the Native Nations Act empowered the state president to grant "self-government" to a Namibian homeland without recourse to the South African Parliament. At the Turnhalle Conference in 1975, and in subsequent attempts by South Africa to resolve the Namibian crisis, the division of the country as envisioned by the Odendaal Report was retained. However, in 1978 there was a major shift in South Africa's position on a constitutional settlement of Namibia under pressure from the contact group of five Western powers represented on the U.N. Security Council. In early 1978 South Africa had in principal, at least, shifted away from its earlier emphasis upon granting independence to Namibia's homelands toward granting independence to Namibia as a whole after U.N.-supervised elections were held in the territory. However, in March 1983 the leader of the all-white National party of South West Africa, Dr. Kosie Pretorius, appealed for support from the National party of South Africa for a plan to divide Namibia into two: an area that would become a unitary state and an area where "the rights of the minority groups would be respected." Blacks would share the first area and whites would control the second. In the light of the recent electoral successes of the Herstigte Nasionale party and the Conservative party, the ruling National party of South Africa was forced to take seriously Pretorius's demand that Namibia's whites must be fully accommodated in any Namibian settlement.

[5] Thomas (1978:22) made the observation that if the northern homelands of Ovambo, Kavango, Caprivi, Kaokoland, and the Bushman re-

Table 6.1 Whites Resident in Namibia, 1977

Temporary residents (RSA domiciled)	15,000
Permanent residents	90,000
German speaking	20,000
English and Portuguese speaking	15,000
Afrikaans speaking	55,000

SOURCE: Thomas (1978:20).

in or near the seven largest towns) and is comprised of three differentiated cultural-linguistic subgroups: German speaking, English and Portuguese speaking, and Afrikaans speaking. Table 6.1 gives a breakdown of the white population by cultural-linguistic group as of 1977. Since 1977, the white population has declined to below 70,000; most of those remaining are Afrikaans speaking.

Namibia's modern sector economy is located in the white areas where production takes place in all of the country's export and tax-earning industries including the lucrative diamond-bearing areas and productive arable and stock-rearing lands. Therefore, the opportunities for gainful employment of blacks in the modern sector are also in the white areas.

THE MINING INDUSTRY

The importance of the mining industry in Namibia's economy is well known. However, in order to appreciate the role of the mineral sector in the political economy of Na-

serve were to be consolidated into one independent homeland, it would constitute an estimated 60 percent of Namibia's total population (those "belonging" to the homelands), leaving an estimated 338,000 people in the so-called white areas (1974 population estimate). The white population of then just over 100,000 would be the largest single "ethnic group," comprising almost 30 percent of the total. This simple arithmetic logic was said to be behind South Africa's strategy of partitioning Namibia.

mibia's transition to political independence it is necessary to describe its salient features.

Namibia's mineral production contributes on average (pre-1980) about 50 percent of the economy's total GDP, constitutes about 80 percent of the country's export earnings, and provides about 70 percent of total domestic government revenue. In terms of value, diamonds lead all other minerals, with uranium oxide from the huge Rössing mining facility second in value. For example, in 1978 taxation from diamonds (98 percent of which are of gem quality) contributed 68 percent of total domestic revenue (down to 39 percent in 1980). In 1984, 40 percent of total government revenue from the sale of minerals came from uranium produced by the Rössing mine (*African Business* 1984u:52, and *Africa South of the Sahara* 1984:634).[6]

Approximately 90 percent of Namibia's mineral production is controlled by four transnational corporations: Consolidated Diamond Mines (CDM) of South West Africa, 98.3 percent owned by De Beers Consolidated Mines Ltd. of South Africa (a subsidiary of Anglo American Corporation); Rössing uranium mine, 46.5 percent owned by the British-based Rio Tinto Zinc and others (South African and European); the Tsumeb Corporation, Ltd. (TCL), controlled by Gold Fields of South Africa (GFSA), also a subsidiary of Anglo American Corporation (with a 43 percent stake) and Newmont Mining of the United States (with a 30 percent interest); and South-West African Co., Ltd. (SWACO), which is owned by Anglo American and other South African interests. There are no major all-Namibian mining companies, nor are there any Namibians (white or

---

[6] The decline in government revenues derived from mineral tax was largely due to the depressed world market for diamonds, uranium, and copper (Namibia's major mineral exports) during the early 1980s. For example, in 1979, taxation from Namibia's mining industry was 142 million rands, whereas in 1982, mineral tax contributed only 20 million rands (*African Business* 1984u: 52).

black) who are known to have any significant investment in the major mining companies in the country.

Therefore, Namibia's mining industry is related to the South African economy through the medium of transnational corporations that are based in South Africa. Thomas (1978:81) has estimated that South African shareholders or wholly owned South African companies have approximately 40 percent of all share capital in Namibian mines. Of particular importance in this regard is the strategic role of diamond production in Namibia's mining sector. Ninety-nine percent of the country's diamond output is controlled by De Beers Consolidated Mines Ltd. of South Africa.

Among South Africa's seven major mining houses, the Anglo-De Beers group occupies a dominant position of leadership.[7] The Anglo group is by far the largest mining corporation, with assets of about 694 million rands (*Moody's International Manual* 1984:3,176) in 1983, which is approximately 9 percent of South Africa's total GDP (Nedbank Group, Ltd. 1983:87). It also has significant holdings in all of the other major mining houses in South Africa. Even more significant for present purposes is Anglo's reliance upon investments in Southern Africa as a whole for the success of its operations. For example, Anglo not only controls Namibia's diamond and base metal (copper and lead) industries but it has major interests in Angola, Botswana, Lesotho, Swaziland, Tanzania, and Zambia.[8] Until the 1960s, Anglo American was primarily

---

[7] A mining house is a group of loosely organized companies with centralized services, such as financial, secretarial and administrative, purchasing, research and marketing, that are provided by a holding company. The seven major houses in South Africa are the Anglo American Corporation of South Africa, Ltd., Anglo Transvaal Consolidated Investment, Ltd., the General Mining and Finance Corporation, Ltd., Gold Fields of South Africa, Ltd., Johannesburg Consolidated Investment Company, Ltd., and Rand Mines, Ltd. (UNCTC 1980:41ff.).

[8] Anglo-De Beers' control of Namibia's rich diamond mines goes beyond ownership. Anglo controls the entire chain of Namibia's diamond

oriented toward expanding its operations in the Southern African region. Since the 1960s, it has become a global corporation with worldwide mining and financial interests (Metzger 1978).

The principal source of conflict to date between the mining industry and the South African government centers upon the government's labor policy for Africans.[9] In this regard there are two key elements that concern the mining companies. The first is the uneconomic nature of the "contract labor" or migrant labor system, especially for skilled jobs in an industry that is heavily capital-intensive and increasingly mechanized. It is uneconomic for the mining industry to continually train migrant labor to fill skilled positions only to have them leave the company at the conclusion of their labor contracts. They also have difficulty attracting educated blacks into the industry without being able to offer them family housing (Lipton 1980:118).

The second major concern of the mining industry regarding the government's labor policy is to ensure that their mining compounds, which have historically been effective instruments of social control over their labor force, do not become bases of political opposition or subver-

---

production through its Central Selling Organization (CSO). Its control extends from the mining stage through wholesaling and marketing. Since CSO sells most of the world's precious diamonds, it has complete control of Namibia's diamond production, including determining the production output and pricing of the gems. During the hearings of the Thirion Commission investigating corruption in Namibia's second-tier ethnic authorities, it was revealed that the territory's diamond board did not exercise independent control of the industry and that most of the key functions of the board were delegated to De Beers (*African Business* 1984h: 57).

[9] Green points out another area of conflict between the mining industry in Namibia (especially Anglo-De Beers) and the South African government: the industry's wish for an early political settlement of the conflict even if it leads to a SWAPO government. Major mining interests in Namibia want a settlement to ensure a stable and attractive business climate (private communication 1985). They also wish to avoid the radicalization of the liberation movements that inevitably accompany a prolonged military conflict.

sion.[10] In order to defuse what the mining industry sees as an explosive situation in the white (urban) areas the Chamber of Mines has called for recognizing black unions in the mines, stabilizing an increasing proportion of their labor force, and improving the living conditions of the miners generally.

Historically, the chief constraint on the mining industry has been the cost of labor. As Trapido (1971) and Wolpe (1972) have demonstrated, apartheid is essentially a system of repressive labor control. Hence, the major elements of apartheid such as population influx control into urban areas, the homelands policy, and the contract labor system that makes Africans "temporary 'foreign' sojourners" in their own country were designed to supply cheap immobilized labor to South African industry. However, certain industries require cheap labor more than others. In the case of the mining industry, the very high profitability of gold, diamonds, and uranium sales beginning in the mid-1970s removed (at least in the short term) their need for a labor repressive system. South African mining during the past decade has been in the position it was in briefly in 1932 when the world price of gold soared. During this period, it was not necessary for the industry to rely upon the repressive labor "compound system"[11] to guarantee its profitability.

[10] According to Green, the general manager of Anglo American's Consolidated Diamond Mines reportedly stated that mining labor compounds are the best recruiting ground for SWAPO that could be devised (private communication 1985).

[11] Trapido (1971:312-313) describes the mining compound system as a form of "labour barracks" that imposes "a quasi-military pattern of conduct" comparable to the management of European serfs during the feudal period. It gave mining industry the power to stabilize their laborers through total supervision and the power to penalize. The wages of African workers were kept low by the creation of Monopsonistic labor-recruiting agencies such as Wenela in South Africa and the South West Africa Nature Labour Association (SWANLA). The constant use of non-

The mining industry's disagreements with South African state policies over the continued reliance upon labor repressive policies to control its labor force are due largely to four factors: 1) their success operating in black African countries in the region without relying upon labor repressive policies; 2) the prolonged period of high profitability in the industry; 3) the apparent inability of the South African state to guarantee an adequate and reliable labor force through labor repressive methods; and 4) for high technology mining such as the new South African platinum and coal mines, the benefits of the productivity gains of a settled, stable, family based labor force.

Labor repressive state coercion to supply cheap labor for the mining industry has, in fact, produced a potentially explosive problem. For example, it made possible the only effective national strike in Namibia in 1971/1972 involving an estimated 13,500 Ovambo contract workers. The strike action originated in Walvis Bay and the Katutura compound outside of Windhoek and spread to the mining compounds until the country's seven or eight major mines were at a standstill (Kane-Berman 1972:5-6).

In order to ensure Anglo's continued involvement in Namibia after a black nationalist regime secures power in independent Namibia, CDM has been at the forefront in breaking with the hated contract labor system.[12] For ex-

---

South African laborers in the mines has made it extremely difficult to organize unions, and it has depressed the wage levels of African workers.

[12] CDM also supports miners' visits home and visits by wives to Oranjemund at company expense during periods of contract service, and they provide technical training on the job and funding for technical and secondary schools. In addition, CDM has negotiated with workers' committees, which the company must suspect to be SWAPO, and they have made concessions to workers' grievances. CDM has also refused to help the SWA administration politically. For example, the company refused to compel its workers to register to vote in the 1978 "election." In contrast, Rio Tinto Zinc (RTZ), which is a major participant in the Rössing uranium mine, has not demonstrated the same political acumen. For example, RTZ has refused to deal with unionists in the same manner as CDM.

ample, rather than rely upon the labor bureaus in the northern homelands, particularly in Ovambo, CDM mounts its own recruitment campaigns in Ovambo. This addresses one of the major grievances of contract workers—that they cannot determine in advance of signing their labor contract (usually between twelve to eighteen months) the conditions of service and wages at the company's mine at Oranjemund. An indication of the success of this deviation from the normal contract labor system is that positions with CDM, which also has the highest wages and best working conditions in the industry,[13] are highly sought after. CDM has no shortage of applicants.

Taking the lead of CDM, the other major profit-making mine, the Rössing mine, which is the largest uranium mine in the world, has followed suit in declaring its opposition to the contract labor system. For example, at the company's annual general meeting in London in 1972, the chairman, Sir Val Duncan, stated that his company was "totally opposed to the contract labour system and will have nothing whatever to do with it. . . . We are going to employ our labour without the contract system" (Cronje and Cronje 1979:56).

CDM has also taken the lead in attempting to accommodate the efforts of the "radical" nationalist SWAPO leadership to unionize black workers. Since 1977 (two years before the Administrator-General Justice Marthinus Steyn announced that black workers could legally join trade

Rio Tinto Zinc's public relations is primarily oriented toward the British press, whereas CDM's public relations is low-keyed and is oriented primarily toward its own workers and their families.

[13] Consolidated Diamond Mines has raised the salaries of Africans to between 400 and 500 rands per month, has guaranteed permanent jobs for its workers subject only to output cutbacks, and has made some efforts to desegregate facilities and provide some family housing for workers. However, the corporation has made at best only modest reforms in its announced nonracial wages and salaries policy. The living and working conditions for most black workers in its mines (particularly Ovambo contract workers) remain far below those of whites and coloreds.

unions) SWAPO members have organized branches of the National Union of Namibian Workers (NUNW), and they have actively recruited at CDM's Oranjemund headquarters.[14] In addition, Consolidated Mines has tried to meet some of the criticism mounted against them by SWAPO. For example, in response to SWAPO charges that Anglo was simply exploiting Namibia and had no intention of expanding and developing the country's mining industry, the CDM resident director announced in May 1981 the company's intention to double its prospecting outlay.[15] The estimated prospecting expenditure for 1981 was 27 million rands compared to 17 million rands in previous years. The increased prospecting expenditure was said to represent Anglo's efforts to extend the life of the CDM diamond deposits. It was also designed to affirm Anglo's commitment to participate in Namibia's future development. Anglo has also sought to demonstrate its commitment to Namibia's future by building the Consolidated Diamond Mines (CDM) prestige office tower in Windhoek in 1981, a project that they undertook in the midst of a general lack of investment confidence and a virtual absence of any new foreign investment in the country.[16]

[14] Green speculates that CDM believes 90 percent of all NUNW members are SWAPO supporters (private communication 1985).

[15] In 1984, CDM company documents concerning the company's mining strategy during the 1970s raised new suspicions concerning CDM's commitment to fully developing and expanding its operations in Namibia. The leaked documents revealed company plans to maximize the extraction of higher grade deposits and thereby shorten the life of the diamond deposits (*African Business* 1984h:57). However, Green notes the fact that De Beers never provides more than twelve to fifteen years capacity output ahead. Furthermore, since the Oranjemund is currently operating at no more that 60 percent of normal output, that would probably leave the mine with a life of between thirty to fifty years. (Private communication 1985.)

[16] Anglo's takeover of Tsumeb during 1982 along with their expressed interest in possibly developing uranium, coal, and other deposits in Namibia suggest that Anglo American feels confident they can operate profitably under a SWAPO government.

A further indication of Anglo's efforts to reach an accommodation with SWAPO was a meeting in late 1982 between executives of De Beers, Rio Tinto Zinc, and other major companies with a delegation from the United Nations Council for Namibia.[17] The companies reportedly sought information about SWAPO's likely policies once it achieved power after an internationally supervised election. SWAPO is reported to have informed the mining companies that their government would acquire a 70 percent controlling interest in the mines. However when pressed on the issue they equivocated and said that the extent of government ownership by a SWAPO government would be decided after the transition to independence. SWAPO spokesmen have since stated that an independent state under a SWAPO government would follow a pragmatic nationalist policy comparable with the Zimbabwean government of Robert Mugabe.

COMMERCIAL AGRICULTURE

The commercial agricultural sector is the most strategic sector of the Namibian economy in terms of the political economy of the transition to independence. While the entire agricultural sector (commercial and subsistence) only contributes an estimated 14 percent to the country's GDP (9 percent in 1983) and 16 percent to total exports, it is the major employer of African labor. According to official South African sources, in 1970 an estimated 36.6 percent of economically active black farmers (excluding about 200,000 peasants) worked on white-owned farms in the Police Zone. A 1967 estimate placed that figure at 40 percent (Cronje and Cronje 1979:64). Thomas (1978:94) estimates that in 1977 the modern agricultural sector (largely

---

[17] Green notes the fact that there have been a number of such contacts between the mining companies and SWAPO (private communication 1985).

6,800 white farm owners, down to 4,500 in 1985) employed about 46,000 African workers.

Namibia's commercial farms are concentrated in the central and southern parts of the country, typically along rail or road lines and near large townships. Cattle and sheep production accounts for about 90 percent of the total value of the country's agricultural output. Almost all of this production is for export. The sheep are bred for karakul (Persian lamb) fur pelts and wool by-products and are marketed primarily in London (about 60 percent of the finished pelts are normally sold in West Germany, with the rest going to Italy, France, Japan, Scandinavia, and the United States).[18] Innes (1981:71-72) estimates that since 1961 between two-thirds and three-fourths of all cattle marketed by Namibian ranchers was sold in South Africa with less than 10 percent consumed in Namibia annually.

For present purposes there are two major structural differences that distinguish Namibia's livestock industry from its mining industry. The first is that nationally oriented rather than regionally oriented corporations based in South Africa dominate Namibia's ranching industry. The second is that non-Ovambo, nonmigrant African laborers and producers predominate on the white commercial farms in the Police Zone.[19]

Three South African companies, Suidafrikaase Vleis-

[18] The karakul industry is dependent upon the fashion market, which has experienced a drastic decline in demand since 1976. During the past few years, the pelts have been sacrificed at below-cost prices. The greatest decline in demand has occurred in West Germany, which normally takes between 60 and 70 percent of the total output. While the smaller markets for the pelts in Italy, France, and Spain have remained stable, no replacement has been found for the West German market (*African Business* 1983b:69).

[19] Green notes in this regard that the single largest group in the commercial farming labor force is Ovambo. He speculates that from Windhoek north the Ovambo probably are the majority of agricultural laborers. (Private communication 1985.) Nevertheless, the majority of laborers and producers on commercial ranches and farms as a whole are non-Ovambo.

produsent, Vleis-Sentraal Kooperatief, and Afrikaase Sake Ontwikkeiings-Korporasie, along with the South African financed FNDC (the "Bantu" Development corporation of Namibia) and a French company in Walvis Bay, control the slaughtering, meat processing, and marketing of Namibia's livestock. They also dominate the marketing of Namibian beef exports to Europe. Namibia's karakul pelt industry is controlled by one British corporation, Eastwood and Hold, Ltd., that purchases and exports the karakul through South Africa.

What distinguishes these companies from Anglo American is that their production is geared primarily to the South African economy; it does not depend upon the success of operations within Southern Africa as a whole. In the case of both cattle and karakul sheep, Namibian and South African production is fully integrated. For example, the production of cattle in Namibia is strictly controlled by South African livestock producers who determine the annual quota for Namibian cattle imports to South Africa. Likewise, the production of karakul fur is a joint Namibian-South African industry in which these two countries together produce over half of the world's supply of the fur (with a ratio of 70 to 30 favoring Namibia). The karakul board represents both Namibian and South African producer-interests and controls Namibia's export of the pelts.

Closely associated with the integration of Namibia and South Africa's commercial livestock industries is the fact that ranchers in Namibia are recipients of generous subsidies from the South African state. South Africa maintains a network of highways and roads that offer ranchers easy, reliable access to their farmland and ranches and to urban centers where they conduct business. South Africa also provides a large but inexpensive veterinary and extension service to control disease and improve the quality of production. Practically all supplies for Namibian farmers come from South Africa. In addition, during periods of prolonged drought and depressed world prices for beef and karakul pelts, the state provides generous subsidies to the farmers.[20] Severe drought conditions in Namibia since 1978 have forced many ranchers to live on capital-reducing stock. The result is that white farmers may now be down to just over one million head of cattle (half of the mid-1970 level), and karakul sheep are down from 3.1 million in 1980 to 900,000 in 1984.

The combination of a six-year-long drought, rising costs, depressed beef and karakul prices (recovered in 1984), and the political uncertainty and insecurity arising from the war in Namibia has forced one-fourth of the white ranchers and farmers to abandon their land. Agricultural debt has risen from 30 million rands in 1980 to between 175 and 190 million rands in 1983 (Legum 1984a:B699). This situation has led to South African intervention to protect ranchers and farmers from further losses by reinstituting a major program of farm subsidies. In 1981/1982, for example, it was estimated that the government spent 55 million rands or 10,000 rands per white rancher in subsidy payments. The administrator-general of Namibia (virtually the governor) claimed that every rancher (white farmer) received 3,600 rands in state subsidies. This works out to about 150 million rands in subsidies to white ranchers per annum (*Africa Bureau Fact Sheet* 1982, and Legum 1984:3).

Another important form of state support for commercial farmers includes policies that guarantee cheap labor. This is particularly important for the ranches whose production and market prices are vulnerable to climatic changes and therefore whose profitability depends crucially upon state support. The importance of cheap labor to the ranching

---

[20] While South Africa heavily subsidizes white farmers and ranchers in Namibia in order to bolster the agricultural sector and to discourage the drift away from their land, it nevertheless restricts Namibians' access to South African markets in order to protect South African ranchers. Hence, Namibia is a residual source or "balance" for the South African market.

sector was evident in the lobbying efforts of the ranchers themselves, particularly at the Turnhalle Conference, which was convened in 1975.

In March 1976, the powerful white farmers' association, the South West Africa Agricultural Union (SWAAU), disassociated itself from the proposals advanced at the Turnhalle Conference to adopt a minimum monthly cash wage of 54 rands (or 106 rands including payments in kind). A measure of the commercial farmers' success in defeating efforts to adopt a minimum wage for their farm workers is evident in the eventual exclusion of agricultural workers from the minimum wage regulations that were adopted in July 1976. The upshot of this is that the majority of black farm workers receive substantially lower wages than miners and factory workers. The average inclusive wage for black miners at the Tsumeb, for example, was about U.S. $120, with U.S. $64 paid in cash monthly. In 1977, some clerks working at the British firm Metal Box reportedly earned about 86 rands per month. However, in February 1977, the chairman of the Agricultural Workers' Association (an affiliate of SWAAU) announced that the average cash wage for farm workers on cattle ranches was only 24.37 rands per month and 40.37 rands per month on sheep ranches (Cronje and Cronje 1979:43, 60, 66). Since 1977, mining wages have more than doubled, whereas ranching wages have not.

Unlike the mining and manufacturing sectors, low wages are essential for the profitability of the commercial farms and ranches. The black labor force in the modern agricultural sector is primarily a permanent work force, in contrast to the mining labor force, which is almost entirely contract migratory labor. The majority of agricultural workers on commercial farms and ranches live with their families on the farms where they work within the Police Zone. An estimated two-thirds of these regular laborers are noncontract workers. Cronje and Cronje (1979:64-65) estimate, for example, that less than 25 percent of the Ovambo contract workers are employed in the agricultural sector. Thomas (1978:286) estimates that of the 43,500 Ovambo contract workers in the early 1970s, only 10,000 were engaged in commercial agriculture. By extrapolation, it would mean that only 20 percent or 10,000 of the United Nations Institute for Namibia's estimate of the 50,000 black workers on commercial farms in 1977 were Ovambo.[21] This contrasts with Thomas's estimate of 12,000 Ovambo contract workers out of the United Nations' estimate of 19,000 black workers on the mines in 1977 (63 percent of the total black labor force).

The permanent black laborers on commercial farms and ranches on the whole tend to come from the regions where the farms and ranches on which they work are located. For example, Namas tend to predominate in the south, while Damaras provide the bulk of the labor force in the central region along with the Herero who are concentrated in the central and eastern areas of the country. The Rehoboth Baster are commercial farmers of some significance in the central part of Namibia, and the Bushmen tend cattle on the eastern borders and in the far north (see Map 15).

One reason for the relatively small number of Ovambo on the commercial farms and ranches is the low wages paid by the owners and the poor living conditions on the farms. This is not to say, however, that the number of migrant workers in the modern agricultural sector is negligible. To the contrary, there are estimated to be as many as

---

[21] Cronje and Cronje (1979:65) note, however, that some Ovambo have settled on farms and ranches as permanent laborers by disguising themselves as Damara or Herero, for example, and thereby obtaining a pass to be in the Police Zone as a local African. Green estimates that there are 10,000 Ovambo contract workers and up to an additional 10,000 noncontract Ovambo working "illegally" on Police Zone ranches. This higher estimate of Ovambo workers on agricultural farms and ranches would constitute about 40 percent of the total black labor force on commercial farms and ranches. (Private communication 1985.)

20,000 contract laborers working on the ranches in Namibia. However, since the 1971/1972 strike, which was interpreted as an "Ovambo strike," many commercial farmers and ranchers have refused to accept Ovambo contract workers.

Efforts to transform the commercial agricultural sector after independence will be politically explosive. The reason for this is that the major domestic threat to a unitary SWAPO-controlled independent Namibian state would likely emanate from the government's handling of the highly sensitive land reform issue.[22] In the event that SWAPO were to come to power, the government would immediately be faced with a major policy dilemma in dealing with the commercial ranching industry. Unlike the internal wing of SWAPO, the external branch has made land reform a central element in its political program for independent Namibia.[23]

[22] Chambers and Green (1981:227-258) have evaluated the major implications of agrarian reform of the commercial ranching sector of Namibia under the following five conditions: 1) the government of newly independent Namibia is committed to SWAPO's "Political Programme" and its "Programme of Action" (both drafted in Lusaka in 1976); 2) the transition to a SWAPO government occurs before 1985 and follows a negotiated transfer of power involving an election; 3) the commercial agricultural sector is largely intact; 4) significant numbers of white ranchers abandon their farms at or soon after independence; and 5) agricultural administrative, planning, and research services are in disarray.

[23] The external wing of SWAPO (which has functioned as a government in exile since its recognition by the United Nations and the OAU as the "sole authentic representative of the Namibian people") has taken a more doctrinaire position than the internal wing of the party in Namibia. Tactical considerations have largely determined the differences. The most obvious distinction is that, unlike the external wing which has carried out a guerilla war against the South African regime in Namibia, the internal wing has advocated a peaceful settlement of the conflict with South Africa. To do otherwise would have resulted in being declared an illegal party and would have forced the internal branch of the party to go underground. Second, the external wing's international recognition as the "sole representative" of the Namibian people rules out sharing political power with other Namibian groups in an independent Namibian state. The in-

The latter's national program of action under Section III headed "Economic Independence," includes the following precept:

> There shall be a land reform in Namibia, by which land will be given to the tillers. Those who have acquired land during colonial time—by either buying it or through the methods of shifting our people from one place to another, will be required by the Namibian People's Government to enter into new agreement which will define the terms by which such land or pieces of land could be owned.[24]

---

ternal wing, on the other hand, has taken the position that there are several other Namibian movements and groups who are entitled to have a voice in the constitutional settlement of the conflict. Tötemeyer (1977:68-69) notes, for example, that one serious split in the SWAPO leadership in May 1976 was over whether to collaborate with other political groups in Namibia in securing a constitutional settlement with South Africa. And, indeed, the internal wing of SWAPO actually entered into a political alliance with eight other political organizations who were opposed to continued South African occupation of Namibia. In addition to SWAPO (internal) other members of the National Convention (NC) of Freedom Parties formed in November 1971 included the National Unity Democratic Organization (NUDO), led by Chief Clemens Kapuuo, the South West Africa National Union (SWANU), led by Gerson Veii, the Rehoboth Volksparty, the Namib African People's Democratic Organization (NAPDO), the Herero Chiefs' Council, the Damara Tribal Executive (DTE), and the Democratic Cooperative Development party (DEMCOP). The NC was succeeded by the Namibia National Convention (NNC) in 1975, which excluded Kapuu's NUDO and his supporters but included the internal wing of SWAPO as well as SWANU. However, the external wing of SWAPO, led by President Sam Nujoma, refused to associate itself with the internal wing's efforts to form political alliances of Namibian political organizations, claiming to be the "sole authentic representative of Namibia."

[24] As quoted in Tötemeyer (1977:76-77). Just prior to the Turnhalle Constitutional Conference, which was convened in September 1975, the internal wing of SWAPO issued a document outlining its constitutional proposals for independent Namibia. The document made no mention of nationalizing land nor was there any preference indicated for a socialist or capitalist economy. The only specific reference to an economic policy

The party's commitment to eliminating unemployment and to distributing wealth equally to all regions of the country was also enunciated under Section III.

The external wing of SWAPO is firmly committed in principle at least to agrarian reform. Thus if SWAPO seeks to implement a major land reform program, they will be faced with a major policy dilemma. Since the bulk of the estimated 90 percent of usable land in the Police Zone is owned and worked by large commercial ranchers, the future of commercial ranching in independent Namibia will have to be decided.[25] Specifically, SWAPO will have to determine whether or not to retain Namibia's beef and karakul industries.

In order to appreciate the potential domestic political opposition to the party's agrarian reform program, it is necessary to examine the arguments for and against retaining commercial ranching under a SWAPO government. There are three main arguments for and three against it.

The first argument for retaining Namibia's commercial agricultural sector, albeit in a modified form, is its impor-

---

toward the agricultural sector was that of state support in subsidizing farmers to purchase equipment and fertilizers and build dams (ibid., pp. 72-74).

[25] Green points out in this regard that up to 20 percent of all ranches are abandoned due to the drought and the war, and an additional one-third to one-half of the remainder would be abandoned at or soon after independence regardless of what the newly independent government of Namibia said or did (private communication 1985). This would mean that between 46 and 60 percent of all ranches in the country would need to be "reformed" in one way or another and will be vacant. However, while Green's estimate of the number of white farmers abandoning their ranches may be correct, this does not rule out the possibility that "nonwhite" Namibians will take over the ranches nor does it remove the highly contentious issue of whether or not to continue state support for owner-operated commercial farms and ranches in the country after independence. In fact, in 1985 it was estimated that there were more Herero farmers and ranchers than white ones. Herero ranchers were estimated to produce approximately 33 percent of Namibia's total cattle exports (André du Pisani, private communication 1985).

tance to the economy. Except during years of serious drought or livestock disease, livestock farming contributes approximately 98 percent of the country's gross value of commercial agriculture. Cattle and karakul constitute about 80 percent of that figure. While agricultural products only contribute between 12 and 13 percent of total exports, roughly two-thirds of that export revenue derives from the sale of cattle and meat products and karakul sheep and wool by-products.

The second argument favoring continued state support for commercial ranching is that it provides an irreplaceable source of employment for roughly 50,000 black workers on the ranches. It also supplements the subsistence income of their families through wage remittances. Chambers and Green (1981:232) estimate, for example, that in 1977 to 1978 the wages paid to approximately 50,000 African workers (half in cash and half in kind) amounted to 15 million rands. An indication of how important this income is for the roughly 700,000 to 750,000 Africans in the subsistence or residual sector in the homelands is the fact that Namibia's entire migrant work force of 100,000 is estimated to remit to their families a total of only 15 or 20 million rands (Chambers and Green 1981:234).

The third major argument for retaining Namibia's commercial ranching industry relates to the country's fragile ecology. South Africa's homelands policy has created congestion of human and livestock population leading to overgrazing and the destruction of vegetation in the "reserves." Despite SWAPO's claim that the northern central areas (Ovambo and Kavango) are capable of producing enough food crops to feed the entire country, there is evidence to suggest otherwise (Thomas 1978:97). The soil is poor and overworked, and without expensive irrigation or dryland farming techniques it will be difficult to increase the present output. Only during good years are the northern African territories even self-sufficient in grains, for example. In bad years the government must provide large quantities of grains (primarily maize, millet, and sorghum) at heavily subsidized prices. The southern part of the country regularly receives the bulk of its maize from South Africa.[26]

It is only the commercial agricultural land in the Police Zone that although badly overgrazed is farmed according to scientific techniques. Because of the soil structure and delicate rainfall-ground water balance, it is essential to avoid overgrazing in order to prevent the permanent denuding of the land. Hence, the danger of resettlement programs as part of SWAPO's agrarian reform (projected to increase the existing population on white-owned farms during the first two years by 50 percent from 200,000 to 300,000—Gebhardt 1978) is that white-owned farms may be fragmented into subeconomic units. If the demand for the land exceeds the availability of land that was made possible through the departure of white farmers, inefficient or traditional African farmers may acquire the land. This would not only substantially lower the productive output of the ranches but it would further endanger the land's delicate ecological balance and threaten to turn productive land into unusable desert.

There are also three arguments against retaining Namibia's livestock industries. Critics of the existing system take the position that it is necessary to nationalize the ranching sector and replace it with state farms and cooperatives. The reason is that transferring ownership of white-owned farms and ranches to efficient and modern commercial Namibian farmers will simply create a privileged class of black owners. Thomas (1978:104) notes, for example, that if 2,000 of the existing 5,000 white owners were to subdivide and sell their land to 5,000 black Nami-

[26] Green notes, for example, that in the Otavi Highlands, South African subsidies to Namibia's cattle producers have tilted the balance against crop production (private communication 1985).

bians, it would simply increase the membership of the exclusive class of owner-ranchers by 3,000 to 8,000 and would produce little or no change in the present highly unequal distribution of wealth in the agricultural sector. This is evident in the so-called "big house and hovel" analogy in which the white rancher's net income ranges from between 5,000 and 20,000 rands while their Africans workers receive between 200 and 500 rands annually (in cash and kind). Chiefs and their headmen have amassed large herds of cattle as a reward for supporting the homelands policy.[27] Herero and Rehoboth ranchers have sought to mimic white ranchers in terms of life style and social attitudes. These developments have given substance to the debate.

A second argument against maintaining the existing ranching sector after independence is that the livestock industry requires heavy state subsidies[28] that will be more critically needed to finance SWAPO's post-independence rehabilitation programs designed to achieve food self-suf-

[27] This was made possible by the large budget allocations for the eleven ethnic second-tier governments in Namibia. This was not only consistent with South Africa's "homelands" policy but it was designed to build an internal Namibian political infrastructure that could form the basis of an anti-SWAPO political alliance. The ethnic second-tier authorities were one of the major expenditure items in the 1984 budget, constituting 272 million rands out of a total budget of 1.18 billion rands. The SWA government has been described as a "national industry" that absorbs 75 percent of the country's budget and employed 44,629 people out of an economically active population of 196,000 in 1983 (SAIRR 1984:606, and *African Business* 1984u:52).

[28] Chambers and Green (1981:233) point out the fact that Namibia's ranching industry operates within a dense state supporting system. For example, the government does the planning for the ranchers and pays 50 percent of their capital costs. In addition, the state regulates an estimated 80 percent of all cattle that is shipped to South Africa, and the purchase and exportation of karakul sheep and wool products is handled through South Africa by firms that are based there. All agricultural inputs, land and water management, transportation, and communication services are provided and maintained by South Africa.

ficiency and to resettle people displaced by the war. State subsidies are also needed to accommodate those who migrate from the congested homelands to the less populated central and southern regions. Namibia presently imports approximately 75 percent of its fruit and vegetable requirements in addition to large amounts of grain from South Africa. The large-scale population migration that is expected after independence will create an immediate and substantial food requirement, which must be imported. If SWAPO carries out its income distribution policy of egalitarian grassroots development (using Ujamaa as one possible model) in the commercial agricultural areas, it may well reduce the output of agricultural production.[29] This places an ever greater burden upon the state if it decides to support the ranching industry.

The third argument against maintaining the existing ranching sector is that it is an integral part of South Africa's livestock industry, and for reasons of profitability ranches in Namibia are labor-saving enterprises. This mitigates against SWAPO's policy of full employment. For example, Thomas (1978:105) points out that the increasing costs of labor to white commercial farmers led to a shift toward less labor-intensive products, that is, away from dairy farming toward karakul and toward labor-saving farming techniques (extensive grazing rather than intensive feeding). In addition, some commercial farmers have abandoned their farms or used them for hunting or tourist purposes, which has forced African workers off the farms and out of employment. These actions are particularly crucial since agriculture employs about one-half of the economically active population of Namibia, and the employment-absorbing possibilities are extremely limited in the

---

[29] Green argues, however, that with the same labor force and the same support services, cooperatives should produce the same output as the white commercial ranches (private communication 1985).

mining and manufacturing sectors.[30] The large-scale resettlement and rural-urban migration that is expected immediately following independence will make the question of
labor-absorption in the agricultural sector extremely sensitive. In this regard, critics of the livestock industries argue for severing the ties between Namibia's and South Africa's integrated industry, taking the view that it is not
amenable to the full employment and income redistribution objectives of a SWAPO government.[31]

Opposition to Agrarian Reform

In the event that a SWAPO-controlled government does attempt to implement a "radical" agrarian reform program,
the implications for Africans who are directly affected (la-

[30] Fishing is Namibia's only major manufacturing industry, accounting
for roughly one-half of the total employment in the manufacturing sector.
There are about 5,000 black workers in the industry, which is located at
Walvis Bay (the only important industrial town in the country), and most
of the workers are contract laborers from Ovambo. Due to overfishing,
however, within and outside of the twelve-mile limit, the industry is in
serious decline. Manufacturing, in general, is in its infancy in Namibia.
Although it contributes approximately 10 percent of GDP and provides
about 10,000 jobs, it is based almost entirely upon processing local raw
materials. Essentially, it is an extension of Namibia's fishing, agriculture,
and mining sectors. It is so highly dependent upon the primary sectors
that there is little chance of its becoming the leading sector of the economy, at least in the near future.

[31] Green points out that since about one-half of all commercial ranches
will be vacant within six months after achieving independence, the government of Namibia will be faced with the decision of what to do with
this land. They could simply allow laissez faire squatting, set up state
ranches, establish cooperatives, or allow commercial ranches based upon
the present experienced labor force. In the case of the last option, since
large commercial ranches require support services that are among the
most costly anywhere in the world, the government's inability to provide
those services (with or without white farmers) may result in the collapse
of the sector. However, technical assistance and aid from South Africa
and Western aid donors could prevent this collapse. (Private communication 1985.)

borers and farmers on or adjacent to the farms) will be profound.

An estimated two-thirds of all permanent nonwhites working on the commercial ranches originate from within the Police Zone. Bryan O'Linn, the leader of the Federal party of SWA/Namibia (comparable to the Progressive Federal party of South Africa) has made an interesting analysis of population distribution using the official 1970 population statistics (Serfontein 1976:17). O'Linn compared the number of each ethnic or language group in the homelands with those who live in the Police Zone. An estimated 49,000 Herero were said to be distributed as follows: 18,000 in their homeland, 9,000 in other homelands, and 22,000 in the white areas. Of 65,000 Damara, 7,000 lived in their homeland, while an estimated 57,000 lived in the white areas. Only the Rehoboth Baster had more people living in their homeland—an estimated 12,000 compared with 4,000 living in the white areas.

By contrast, the situation in the three northern homelands was entirely different. O'Linn found that almost 100 percent of the Caprivi, Kavango, and Kaoko lived in their designated homelands. Just over 80 percent of the Ovambo lived permanently in their homeland, while an estimated 50,000 male Wambo worked in the white areas on a temporary basis as contract workers before returning home for short periods. O'Linn concluded that while the northern areas were almost 100 percent black, the nonwhites outnumbered the whites in the so-called white areas. For example, in the white (urban) areas, whites were outnumbered by nonwhites by 119,000 to 67,000. The margin was even greater in the white (rural) areas where there were estimated to be 67,500 permanent nonwhites to only 24,000 whites.

Ovambo migrant workers (a principal source of SWA-PO's support) are a minority of the total black labor force in the commercial ranching areas. In the national labor strike of 1971 to 1972, the non-Ovambo black workers on the ranches and farms did not join the strike, which was largely led and supported by Ovambo contract workers. Voipio (1981:130) explains the absence of Herero and Damara support for the strike in terms of their noninvolvement in the migratory labor system.

SWAPO is the only mass political movement in Namibia with national support. In addition to the Ovambo migrant workers, it also has support from some non-Ovambo (particularly among younger elites in black and brown political groups). However, it is estimated that as much as 90 percent of SWAPO's political support comes from Ovambo inside and outside of the Ovambo homeland (Tötemeyer 1977:62-63, and Serfontein 1976:159). In fact, African groups in central and southern Namibia have a long history of opposition to SWAPO, with many regarding the organization as an expression of Ovambo domination.

These groups emphasize the point that unlike the Ovambo (Kavango and Caprivi) who did not lose their traditional land to the Germans and the South Africans, the central and southern groups lost heavily. The Herero, Nama, Baster, and the Damara all forfeited their traditional lands to the colonizing powers (du Pisani 1977:91).

In addition, these groups are predominately pastoralists specializing in cattle raising. For example, before their uprising against the Germans in 1904, the Herero numbered an estimated 70,000 and were known for their fine cattle. After the uprising, the Herero were reduced to about 20,000 and were virtually cattleless. The Germans took the Herero hardveld land where the pasture and browse are nutritionally satisfactory and where the land has proven ground water and forced the people onto the dreaded expanses of the omaheke—the sandveld, where there is poor ground water, deep sand, and a deficiency of essential nutrients in the grasses for cattle raising. After the South Africans took control of SWA under the League Mandate, South Africans ("poor whites") took possession of Herero farmland that was formerly occupied by the Germans. This arrangement was formalized by the South African government with the creation of the Herero homeland, three-quarters of which is waterless except for panwater for a few weeks after the rains. The Herero homeland is almost entirely on the sandveld.

The other central and southern groups have had similar experiences. After the decimation of the Herero, the Damara became the principal source of farm labor in the territory. The Odendaal Commission estimated that there were 44,000 Damara farm laborers. An estimated 19,000 Nama were also employed on the white farmlands. Despite the decimation of the Herero, they gradually recouped their numbers. By 1965 it was estimated that 11,000 lived in the rural areas primarily as cattle herdsmen with another 16,000 living in their homeland where they were trying to rebuild their herds in the hopes of reacquiring their lost land when Namibia achieved independence under a black nationalist regime. The Bushmen numbered about 8,000 working as farm laborers. The Rehoboth Baster also aspire to have successful "white farms" and life styles, and many of them have, in fact, rented their farms to whites and coloreds (Wellington 1965:43-47).

The central and southern groups have figured prominently in South Africa's strategy of forging a Namibian anti-SWAPO alliance. The fear of SWAPO domination has been the basis of several such alliances. One of the first and to date the most effective was the National Convention (NC) of Freedom Parties, which was formed in 1971.[32] The

---

[32] A more recent political alliance of central and southern Namibian political organizations that were opposed to both South African and SWAPO domination was the Namibian National Front (NNF), which sought to perform the role of a middle alternative between the so-called right (the Democratic Turnhalle Alliance—DTA) and the so-called left (SWAPO). Membership in the NNF included SWANU, the Damara Advisory Council (under Chief Justus Garoëb), the National Independence party (coloreds), the Mbanderu group (Herero), the Damara Council, the Federal party (under Bryan O'Linn), and SWAPO-Democrats led by Andreas Shipanga. Although the NNF was too small to be a real contender

NC represented nine political groups that were opposed to South African occupation of Namibia as well as to SWA-PO's claim to be the "sole representative" of the Namibian people.

An intense rivalry for leadership of the NC emerged, focusing on the leader of the NC, Clemens Kapuuo, and on the failure of the United Nations and the OAU to accord recognition to the NC comparable to their recognition of SWAPO. This led to a split in the alliance. In March 1975, the Herero leader, Kapuuo, and his political organization, the National Unity Democratic Organization, along with the Herero Chief's Council and the Nama Chief's Council decided to continue their association with the NC despite the withdrawal of the other groups. At the third session of the Constitutional Conference in Windhoek in March 1976, the NC put forth constitutional proposals for a future government of independent Namibia.

While not all of the central and southern political groups agreed with the NC's proposed constitution, elements of the constitution, particularly those concerning their fear of SWAPO domination and the return of, or compensation for, the "theft" of their historic lands, did have general support.

---

in national elections, it hoped it could play the role of balancer of power comparable to the role of the small Free Democrat party in West German elections. A recent South African attempt to forge an anti-SWAPO Namibian political alliance was the formation of the so-called Multiparty Conference (MPC) in November 1983. Included among the six major groups that comprised the MPC were the Rehoboth Liberation Front, the predominately Herero/Mbanderu South West Africa National Union, and the Damara Council. The Damara Council later defected from the MPC, and SWANU split in its support for it. However, their original motivation in agreeing to form the alliance was to gain support from the Western Contact Group for their demand that all Namibian political parties (including SWAPO) must negotiate an agreed constitutional solution to the country's independence. They took the position that SWAPO's unwillingness to negotiate with other Namibian political groups was a major stumbling block to achieving Namibian independence. See Kozonguizi (1985) and du Pisani (1984) for a discussion of the dispute.

Briefly, the constitutional proposals called for proportional representation in Namibia's parliament. They also called for two chambers of the parliament, one representing the northern party (meaning the Ovambo) and one for the southern-central areas of the country to prevent the "domination of the Parliament by any single population group." On the sensitive issue of land the proposals called for a "Bill of Rights" that included the following section.

Therefore, we propose that, as part of the completion and final adoption of the constitution and the Bill of Rights therein, a settlement be negotiated and arrived at by mutual agreement between the present holders of the lands and the group which suffered the deprivation on the other hand, providing for the return and/or the paying of compensation with respect to these lands. (Tötemeyer 1977:144)

While the NC, the NNC, NNF, and the MCP have been unable to subordinate their ethnic and leadership rivalries to the overriding threat of potential SWAPO domination and South African occupation,[33] their mutual interest in reclaiming historic lands continues to dominate their concerns.

A major area of potential political conflict, therefore, between a SWAPO-controlled government of Namibia and the central and southern political groups centers on a policy toward large white-owned commercial ranches and farms. SWAPO favors a "land to the tiller" policy of allocating land to workers on the ranches. While it has not elaborated a program for transfering control of the land to workers, the party is explicit about avoiding the re-crea-

[33] For an exchange of views concerning the source of interethnic rivalry in the NNF, see Katjivongua (1979) and O'Linn (1979). As in the case of the NNF as well as all previous and subsequent efforts to form an anti-SWAPO and anti-South African alliance of central and southern groups, efforts have foundered on accusations of Herero domination of the other groups.

tion of large commercial "black boer" ranches. This position conflicts with the interests of important central and southern parties who favor the subdivision and transfer of ranches and farms to "owner-occupiers" by resale through a development bank. In other words, they favor a land reform that enables them to reclaim their historic lands.[34]

For as long as South African domination of Namibia obscures the threat of SWAPO domination, the central and southern political groups can be expected to lend at least nominal political support to SWAPO.[35] However, after achieving independence and after the South African presence is removed, the situation may change dramatically. The historic rivalry between SWAPO and SWANU and other Herero groups plus non-Herero central and southern political groups will likely surface. The extent to and speed with which SWAPO implements a radical land reform policy that does not accommodate the historic rights and claims which central and southern groups have to the land will be critical. It will undoubtedly be a major factor in determining the nature and extent of domestic political opposition to a SWAPO-controlled state of Namibia.

[34] Green argues that SWAPO's land reform policy conflicts only with the Herero desire to reclaim pre-German areas. Moreover, he maintains that granting the Herero land that they claim as a matter of historic right would not be in the interest of the Damara nor Ovambo workers who are presently on the land. Green appears to view this problem in terms of class conflict, with the interests of the workers being in opposition to the interests of the large ranchers. However, as Green himself notes, whether Herero, Damara, and other non-Ovambo workers on the ranches see the problem in these terms is unclear. (Private communication 1985.)

[35] In mid-1984, for example, the Damara Advisory Council, SWANU, the Mbanderu Faction, and the Christian Democratic party all associated themselves with SWAPO.

THE PERSPECTIVE adopted in this study of the politics of the Southern African regional economy has two important advantages over conventional approaches. First, it distinguishes between state action and the regional economy; second, it emphasizes the importance of domestic national politics for interpreting the significance of regional economic relationships.

STATE ACTION AND THE REGIONAL ECONOMY

A major contribution of the present study is the differentiation of state action and the regional economy. Most writing and commentaries on Southern Africa fail to make this important distinction. It is assumed that regional economic ties constrain state action to the point where there is little, if any, room for political strategies in the manipulation of economic ties to serve domestic and foreign policy objectives. It is usually taken for granted, for example, that regional economic relationships tend to strengthen the South African state regardless of the policies and strategies followed by the regime. This notion so thoroughly dominates discussions of Southern African politics that the only issue in question is how to increase neighboring black African governments' ability to survive a severance of economic ties with South Africa.

Likewise, it is usually assumed that regional economic relationships only constrain and limit black African states' freedom of action regardless of the leaders of these regimes or their policies. This approach to the politics of regional economics removes leadership and political action as significant factors. Therefore, little attention is given to determining the actual freedom of action that exists among states in the region. The tendency is to assume that black African states are forced to maintain their economic relationships with South Africa because they have no alternative. It is also assumed that South Africa maintains its economic ties with states in the region because they are beneficial and do not incur any serious political costs to the regime. Therefore, regional economic relationships are presumed to have an independent force above and transcending political leadership, ideology, and the domestic politics of the states in the region.

A moment's reflection, however, should suggest that this cannot be. A state's external economic relationships are intimately related to its domestic politics. Southern Africa is no exception to this. While the regional economy predated state formation in a number of countries of the region, the importance of regional economic ties to these states is largely determined by the ruling parties or groups in these countries.

The approach I have presented takes into account autonomous state action in relation to the regional economy. For my purposes, leadership, ideology, and domestic policies are integral to an understanding of economic relationships among states in the region. This approach also allows for feedback upon a state's domestic policies stemming from its efforts to manipulate regional economic ties. Invariably this has an impact upon a state's domestic economy and its politics.

Without a distinction between state action and the regional economy we are left with simply observing regional economic relationships. This can tell us little about the importance of these relationships to ruling parties or groups nor will it tell us much about the consequences to ruling groups of their strategies to manipulate regional economic ties.

It is necessary to go beyond simply describing these relationships to examine precisely how a state's involvement in the regional economy affects its domestic politics and vice versa. As my analysis has demonstrated, state action in the regional economy can have both positive and negative effects upon state power. However, the balance between positive and negative effects shifts in terms of how effectively ruling groups manipulate regional economic ties to cope with domestic political threats. The balance depends upon both the political strategies for manipulating regional economic relationships and upon the nature of the domestic political threats to these regimes.

In some cases such as Malawi, Mozambique, Zambia, and Zaire, state strategies toward the regional economy tend to bolster rather than weaken domestic political support for the regimes in power. In other states such as South Africa, Zimbabwe, and Tanzania, political strategies have tended to weaken rather than strengthen domestic political support. And in still other states such as Botswana, Lesotho, and Swaziland, they have had the ambivalent consequence of equally supporting and undermining state power.

However, there is nothing inexorable or irreversible about this process. As major changes occur in the nature of domestic political opposition in regional states, the political significance of regional economic ties to these states will change. Likewise, as major changes occur in the regional economy, the domestic political support for the regimes in power will change. Both changes will require alterations in state strategies for manipulating regional economic relationships.

THE AUTONOMY OF POLITICS

Conventional approaches to the political economy of Southern Africa do not take adequate account of the importance of domestic politics in regional economic relationships. The purpose of the present study is to partially fill this lacuna. My approach is to evaluate the politics of regional economic relationships primarily from the perspective of the ruling parties or groups in countries that are involved in the regional economy. Table 7.1 illustrates the relationships between regionally oriented and domestically oriented interests in each state in the region. It reveals three patterns of regional-domestic political economy relationships: conflictive, supportive, and ambivalent.

Conflictive regional-domestic relationships are evident in the cases of South Africa, Zimbabwe, and Tanzania where these relationships tend to weaken domestic political support for the regimes in power. In the case of South Africa and Zimbabwe, state alliances with transnational corporations have contributed to political opposition from major domestic interests. In the case of Tanzania, its liberation commitment to provide Zambia with an alternative "economic lifeline" to the north not only involved heavy economic costs but has opened the country to competitive economic threats from the southern regional economy. The effect of Tanzania's involvement in the regional economy, therefore, has been to further erode the ruling party's declining political support.

Supportive regional-domestic relationships are present in Malawi, Mozambique, Zambia, and Zaire. In each of these countries, state strategies have been successfully employed to use the regional economy in order to boost domestic political support for the rulng parties or groups in power. In Malawi, President Banda has used regional economic inputs primarily from South Africa to help create a personal base of power comprised of agricultural estate owners and traditional rural elite on which his regime depends to rule the country. In Mozambique, the ruling party, Frelimo, depends heavily upon earnings from its South African-oriented migrant labor, transport, and port facilities to fulfill its principal domestic political goal of securing national control of the country. In Zambia, the ruling party, UNIP, depends upon the support of its South African-dominated mining sector in which the trade unions

Table 7.1 Regional-Domestic Political Economy Relationships in
Southern Africa

	Regional Interests	Domestic Interests
CONFLICTIVE		
South Africa	Transnational corporations	Alienates Afrikaner working class and state bureaucracy.
Zimbabwe	Transnational corporations	Alienates populist faction of ruling party (ZANU).
Tanzania	Service sector (TANZAM road, TAZAMA oil pipeline, and the TAZARA) and port (Dar es Salaam)	Erodes ruling party's (CCM) political support.
SUPPORTIVE		
Malawi	Estate sector and rural elites	Constitutes the president's personal base of political support.
Mozambique	Urban service sector (ports, railways, tourism, hydroelectric power)	Finances the national independence goals of the ruling party (Frelimo).
Zambia	Mining sector, trade unions, and urban middle class	Economic base of support for the ruling party's (UNIP) principal political constituency.
Zaire	Mining sector	Strengthens Zaire's ruling class.
AMBIVALENT		
Botswana	Mining-urban sector	Principal source of state financing but undermines the ruling party's (BDP) rural base of political support.
Lesotho	Migrant laborers	Principal source of state financing and is also the social base of political opposition to the ruling party (BNP).

Table 7.1 (*cont.*)

	Regional Interests	Domestic Interests
Swaziland	Modern-urban sector	Principal source of state financing but undermines the chieftaincy's peasant base of political support.
Namibia	Mining-ranching sectors	Principal source of state financing and employment, but disruption of ranching sector by an independent SWAPO government will alienate central and southern pastoral groups.

and urban middle class are concentrated to remain in power. And in Zaire, the decision to rely upon South African transport and ports for the shipment of its vital mineral exports and for industrial and consumer imports has stabilized the regime's principal source of economic surplus, which the ruling class needs to remain in power.

Regional states that have a more ambivalent pattern of regional-domestic political economy relationships include Botswana, Lesotho, Swaziland, and Namibia (under a unitary SWAPO-controlled state). The ruling parties or groups in Botswana and Swaziland rely primarily upon rural political support that, however, is being eroded by regionally stimulated urban growth and migratory labor, which functions as an integral part of the South African economy. In the case of Lesotho, its migratory labor force (primarily in the South African mines) is a major source of revenue, foreign exchange earnings, and employment, and yet it constitutes the principal source of support for the political opposition to the ruling party. In Namibia, the South African-based mining industry is the country's principal source of revenues and foreign exchange, while the South African-oriented ranching and cattle industries are a major source of wage employment. While the mining industry in Namibia does not appear to conflict with SWAPO's program for creating a "socialist state," the large "white-owned" commercial ranches do conflict. Therefore, if SWAPO carries out a program of socialist land reform as advertised and ignores the historic rights and claims of central and southern pastoral groups, the latter will likely emerge as a major source of potential political opposition to a SWAPO-controlled state.

The Limits of South African Domination

It is widely assumed that the economic "backwardness" of South Africa's black neighbors gives South Africa political leverage over these states and is, therefore, the basis of its regional domination. Proponents of Western "constructive engagement" in Southern Africa have elaborated an argument for the peaceful transition to majority rule in South Africa based upon this assumption. They argue that economic development is the overriding concern of the leaders of black African states in the region. Leaders of these states are described as "pragmatic" and therefore receptive to expanding economic linkages with South Africa. Hence, Western engagement in the region was said to help expand the process of regional economic cooperation and thereby to create a climate of compromise and accommodation. According to this logic, political turmoil threatens all countries in the region. By implication, the expansion of economic ties is said to benefit all countries in the region. This was said to have made the peaceful transfer of power in Zimbabwe compelling and the peaceful transfer of power in Namibia and South Africa essential.

The exponents of Western "disengagement" from South Africa also base their argument on the assumption of South African regional economic hegemony. They argue that

South Africa's regional economic ties strengthen its economy. The stronger the South African economy, the greater the surplus that is available to the regime for the purpose of reinforcing or "modernizing" the apartheid regime. Therefore, in order to overthrow apartheid, the South African economy must be weakened. This is to be achieved by isolating South Africa economically, politically, and socially. However, in order to effectively isolate South Africa, massive Western assistance to black African states in the region is required to help stabilize their economies.

Since both arguments ignore the political limits of South Africa's economic hegemony, they are flawed. Regional economic ties are not the only, nor even the primary, focus of the leaders of black African states because their countries are economically "backward." Likewise, regional economic ties are not the only, nor even the primary, focus of South Africa because they strengthen its economy. The political significance of these economic relationships is far more specific and limited and is largely determined by the political strategies of the ruling parties or groups in these countries.

Therefore, while South Africa's economic ties with neighboring African states remained largely unchanged during the 1970s and early 1980s, the country's political strategies for manipulating regional economic ties to achieve domestic and foreign policies did change. There are significant differences between the dialogue and détente policies of the 1970s and the Constellation of Southern African States policy of the 1980s. One of the most important differences is that the ruling party under President P. W. Botha sought to form a political alliance with transnational corporations based in South Africa in order to deal with internal and external threats to the regime. Hence, in contrast to dialogue and détente strategies, the CONSAS strategy increased the regime's vulnerability to external pressure upon South African-based transnational corporations, which occupied a strategic role in the state's survival strategy under the Botha regime.

This would suggest that the Western antiapartheid disinvestment campaign, for example, is likely to have a greater impact upon the Botha regime in accelerating domestic reforms than under previous governments. How significant this reform is likely to be, however, will be largely determined by the importance of these corporations in the state's political strategy. Hence, the more important transnational corporations are to the South African state in carrying out domestic and foreign policies, the more vulnerable the regime will be to external economic pressure upon these corporations.

Adherence to the notion of unqualified South African regional economic domination has also tended to obscure our understanding of the political significance of economic relationships with South Africa to the leaders of black African states. It is simplistic in the extreme to assume that any abstract notion of development is uppermost in the concerns of these leaders or that that concern compels them to maintain their economic ties with South Africa.

Like the South African regime, the ruling parties or groups in black African states in the region are primarily oriented toward maintaining themselves in power. Also like South Africa, the ruling parties of black African states have political strategies for manipulating their economic ties with states in the region to serve their own interests. Therefore, the political significance of their regional economic ties must be evaluated primarily in terms of how the ruling parties or groups perceive their ability to use their ties with South Africa, for example, to achieve domestic political objectives.

Most discussions of the Southern African Development Coordination Conference—a group of nine black-ruled states in Southern Africa—completely ignore national state strategies. It is assumed that these states have an overriding commitment to develop their resources and markets on a regional scale in order to reduce the threat of South African economic pressure. However, this overlooks the fact that domestic political problems in a number of these countries are at least as threatening to the regimes in power as the South African economic threat. Indeed, in some cases their economic ties with South Africa play an important role in enabling the ruling groups in these countries to cope with internal political threats.

INNOVATION OF THE APPROACH

Conventional approaches to the study of the political economy of Southern Africa make two interrelated assumptions that are challenged by the present study. The first assumption is functionalism and the second is dependency.

The functionalist assumption stresses the interdependence of patterns and institutions in the Southern African region. Since South Africa is the center of the regional economy, any strengthening of South Africa's economy is assumed to increase its domination of the regional economy. Likewise, any strengthening of the regional economy is assumed to strengthen South Africa. It is also assumed that South Africa's economic strength in the region automatically gives it political leverage over regional states. Therefore, South Africa's economic strength is assumed to increase its foreign policy leverage, particularly in the region. The implication of this assumption is that the stronger the South African economy is, the greater its political leverage is over states in the region.

For example, it is commonly believed that there is a direct correlation between South Africa's trade with states in the regional economy and its political influence in the region. Hence, the volume of South Africa's trade with states in the region is said to be inversely correlated with the level of political-military tension there. The implication of this is that an increase in the volume and value of South African trade with states in the region tends to reduce political tension and thereby mitigates political opposition to the apartheid regime and vice versa. This is the logic behind recommendations for reducing African states' trade with South Africa. Reduced trade implies reduced South African political leverage.

It is also assumed that functional economic cooperation with South Africa gives the regime political leverage over states in the region. For example, the involvement of African states in regional transport, hydroelectric power, water, and migratory labor is assumed to strengthen the regional "subsystem." According to this logic, since South Africa dominates the subsystem, regional cooperation makes the cooperating states vulnerable to South African pressure. Projects such as the Cabora Bassa Dam in Mozambique and the Oxbow Dam in Lesotho, for example, are assumed to give South Africa political leverage over those states.

The obverse is also believed to be true. For example, the construction of the Tanzania-Zambia Railway line completed in 1976 that linked Zambia to the port of Dar es Salaam in Tanzania was viewed as having a profound political significance for Southern Africa. It was interpreted as representing a challenge to South Africa's domination of regional states that formerly were forced to rely upon transport routes through South Africa. TAZARA has even been described as a "black-dominated transport system" that challenged the South African-dominated regional transport system. The implication of this interpretation is that "disengagement" from functional cooperation in the regional economy diminishes South Africa's political domination of states in the region.

Economic cooperation in the form of migrant labor from African states to South Africa is also said to contribute to South Africa's domination of regional states. The flow of migrant laborers is usually portrayed as a source of South

African political leverage against labor-exporting countries. The rationale behind this assumption is that labor-exporting states depend upon the earnings of their migrant workers for national income, budget revenues, and foreign exchange. In addition, since the countries that export labor to South Africa do not have alternative employment opportunities, any major interruption in the flow of migrant labor to South Africa will contribute to social unrest in these countries.

The second major assumption of conventional approaches to the study of Southern Africa's political economy is dependency. Dependency theory assumes that South Africa has a fundamental economic, political, and strategic position in the capitalist imperialist system. Its position is that of an intermediate semiperipheral economy that functions as a subimperialist power within the Southern African subcontinent. Three reasons are usually given for South Africa's unique position within the imperialist system. The first is that the country produces about 80 percent of the capitalist world's gold, and thus its financial importance to the system is great. The second reason is that South Africa is a major producer and exporter of strategic minerals that are of importance to the Western world. The third reason for South Africa's special position in the imperialist system is its strategic location between the Indian and Atlantic oceans through which the petroleum transport routes pass from the Middle East to Europe and the United States.

South Africa's industrial development was made possible by large-scale inflows of Western capital and by low wages in the agricultural, mining, and industrial sectors. The country is said to be an attractive place for capitalist investment because of the superexploitation of black workers (enforced through apartheid and repression) that enables foreign investors to earn higher rates of profit than in almost any other place in the world. Therefore, imperialist capital (British, American, German, French, Japanese, and others) is allied to South African capital, which occupies a subordinate position, and to the South African state, which "superexploits" blacks. Herein lies the central concern of the dependency approach to the region's political economy. The low wages for black workers produces a highly unequal distribution of income, with the white minority monopolizing national income. This has blocked the formation of a mass market of sufficient size to sustain industrial expansion.

A resolution of this problem is said to lie behind South Africa's efforts to establish "dialogue" with African states. Since it is politically unfeasible, at least at present, to dismantle apartheid in order to expand the internal South African market, the regime has been forced to export its industrial production to African countries, particularly within its region.

Dependency analysis seeks to explain regional economic relationships primarily in terms of South Africa's role as a subimperialist power attempting to penetrate regional markets and control the economies of African states. Hence, the focus of attention is upon the degree to which African states in the region have opened their economies to trade and investment from South Africa. Since most regional states trade in one way or another with South Africa, since most have substantial investment from South Africa, and since many export labor there, they are all considered to be willing or unwilling collaborators with the apartheid regime. From this point of view the only difference among African states concerns matters of degree and style. For example, Zambia's effort to shift away from its southern economic orientation has been praised, while Malawi's policy of openly trading with South Africa has been condemned. Nevertheless, the results are the same. They both help South Africa to circumvent the internal blockage of industrial growth by providing external markets for its production.

In fact, in the dependency approach the denial of markets in Southern Africa and the denial of necessary regional economic inputs such as cheap migrant labor that can be "superexploited" in South Africa are assumed to be the only counterpressures African states have to use against South African subimperialism. The threat of being shut out of the regional economy is also said to lie behind imperialist business interests such as Anglo American Corporation and other transnational corporations with regional headquarters in South Africa pressing the South African regime for some relaxation of apartheid. For example, this threat is said to be the primary impetus behind the Riekert and Wiehahn Commission recommendations to allow black workers to unionize and to relax the hated pass laws that regulate the movement of the black population.

In this conceptualization, South African regional subimperialism reduces neighboring African states to veritable political impotence. Thus it has been argued that despite Mozambique's "liberationist duty" toward South Africa, it was forced to offer its rail and port facilities and sell its electricity from the Cabora Bassa Dam to South Africa. Likewise, despite Zambian President Kenneth Kaunda's commitment to the liberation of South Africa, his country has been forced to cooperate with South Africa in order to avert an economic crisis.

The functionalist and dependency assumptions underlying conventional approaches to the study of Southern Africa's political economy are incomplete. They exaggerate the power of economic relationships to explain political events in the region. The functionalist assumption tends to overlook conflicts of political interest within national political systems and conflicts within the regional subsystem by stressing its generalized capacity for cooperation and integration. Dependency theory tends to overlook the political motivation behind South African regional subimperialism. Both assumptions lead to oversimplifications of complex political relationships.

In contrast, my approach emphasizes the autonomous

role of domestic national politics in evaluating the political significance of regional economic relationships. It leads to major revisions in conventional perceptions of the region's political economy. For example, my conceptualization suggests that in addition to the political leverage that South Africa enjoys as a result of its penetration of regional markets, there are major political costs to the regime arising from this trade. The penetration of regional markets that was made possible by South African state support for transnational corporations has not only not reduced tension in the region but it has contributed to divisions within the ruling National party. In other words, South Africa's trade with regional states has been a source of internal political disunity as well as a source of political leverage over neighboring African states.

Likewise, the conventional assumption that economic cooperation of African states with South Africa weakens them politically and opens them up to blackmail and intimidation by South Africa requires revision. In the case of Mozambique, for example, Frelimo's national independence goals, including, ironically, their antiinsurgent war against South African-backed guerillas, have been advanced by economic cooperation with South Africa. While Frelimo's foreign policy objectives are in conflict with South Africa's objectives, economic cooperation with South Africa serves the party's overriding domestic political objectives. Similarly, in the case of Zambia, the regime's foreign policy goals of "disengaging" from its economic ties with Rhodesia and South Africa ultimately gave way to the overriding domestic political necessity of cooperating economically with the minority regimes. While Zambia's commitment to the "liberation" of Rhodesia, Namibia, and South Africa did not change, the importance of cooperating economically with Rhodesia and South Africa was reevaluated in the light of domestic political threats to the ruling party. Zambia's decision to reopen the border with Rhodesia and to continue economic cooperation with

South Africa therefore served the interests of the ruling party by increasing domestic political support for the regime.

While migrant labor represents an important source of state revenues for labor-exporting countries, it also constitutes a major source of radicalization and political recruitment for opposition movements in most states. In several labor-exporting countries, for example, migrant laborers constitute a powerful political force in opposition to the ruling parties or groups. This presents a far more complicated situation for both labor-exporting and labor-importing countries than is usually portrayed in conventional treatments of the subject. The migrant labor system, for example, constitutes at least as great if not a greater threat to South Africa than it does to neighboring African states. The specter of a political conflict in a bordering state spilling over into the mines and factories in the strategic industrial Witwatersrand area haunts the South African leadership. Therefore, migrant labor in Southern Africa is not simply a source of South African political leverage against neighboring states.

The approach I have proposed for the study of the regional political economy should help to compensate for several major shortcomings in conventional approaches to the subject. It provides a framework of analysis for evaluating the political stakes to ruling parties and groups stemming from their countries' involvement in the regional economy. It should also help to explain the political consequences to each state in the region resulting from economic disruption of regional economic ties that are imminent in the growing political struggle over South Africa's future.

BIBLIOGRAPHY

Adam, Heribert. 1978. "Interests behind Afrikaner Power." *Social Dynamics* 4, no. 2.

————, and Giliomee, Hermann. 1979. *Ethnic Power Mobilized: Can South Africa Change?* New Haven and London: Yale University Press.

Adelman, Kenneth L. 1978. "Old Foes and New Friends." *Africa Report*, January-February.

————. 1978a. "Zaire's Year of Crisis." *African Affairs* 77, no. 306.

Africa. 1984. "Economic Challenges." No. 158, October.

————. 1984a. "Foreign Investment: Pretoria's Achilles' Heel." No. 158, October.

————. 1984b. "Interview: Prime Minister Salim Ahmed Salim." No. 154, June.

————. 1984c. "Mozambique/South Africa: Diplomacy and Destabilization." No. 151, March.

————. 1984d. "Opposition Unites against Mobutu." No. 149, January.

————. 1984e. "Tanzania-Malawi: Highway Politics." No. 156, August.

————. 1984f. "The Train with Good News." No. 149, January.

————. 1984g. "Zimbabwe: The Problems of Resettlement." No. 152, April.

————. 1981. "UNIP versus the Unions." No. 115, March.

————. 1980. "Benguela Railway's Uncertain Future." No. 109, September.

————. 1980a. "Maputo—Port of Southern Africa." No. 107, July.

————. 1980b. "Zambia's Strategy for Full Stomachs." No. 108, August.

————. 1978. "New Sales Strategy for Intra-African Trade." No. 83, July.

————. 1978a. "South Africa's African Connection." No. 78, February.

————. 1977. "Dr. Banda's Medicine." No. 72, August.

Africa. 1977a. "Mozambique: Socialism in the Face of White Domination." No. 72, August.

———. 1977b. "Tanzania and the Community." No. 66, February.

———. 1974. "Life with 'Big Brother.' " No. 39, November.

Africa Bureau Fact Sheet. 1982. January/February.

———. 1982a. "Namibia's Political Economy." No. 69, September/October.

Africa Confidential. 1984. June 6.

Africa Insight. 1984. "The Legacy of Sobhuza." Vol. 14, no. 1.

———. 1983. Vol. 13, no. 1.

African Business. 1985. "Maputo Seeks a Deal on Gold Miner's Pay." January.

———. 1985a. "There May Yet Be an IMF Deal—Eventually." January.

———. 1985b. "Zambia Reinstates Free Collective Bargaining." January.

———. 1984. "Big Spending Threatens Development Strategy." July.

———. 1984a. "Botswana Survey: High Exports the Key to Growth." September.

———. 1984b. "Botswana Survey: Labour Market Set for Slow Development." September.

———. 1984c. "Debt and Price Burdens Sap Selebi-Phikwe." January.

———. 1984d. "The Great Grain Success Story." September.

———. 1984e. "IMF Agreement Needed to Stave Off Disaster." February.

———. 1984f. "Jwaneng's Diamond Output Exceeds All Expectations." July.

———. 1984g. "Lack of Commitment Prevents PTA Progress." February.

———. 1984h. "Leaked Documents Spark CDM Diamond Controversy." November.

———. 1984i. "A Little Warmth amid Cold Realities." May.

———. 1984j. "Mobutu's Belgian Visit Marks Renewed Ties." September.

———. 1984k. "A More Hopeful Future for TAZARA?" June.

———. 1984l. "Mozambique: 'Iron Discipline' First; Elections Later." July.

———. 1984m. "Msuya Unveils Desperation Budget." August.

———. 1984n. "Namibia's Financial Legacy." October.

———. 1984o. "Optimism May Not Last All Next Year." December.

———. 1984p. "Regional Rail Effort Needs More Funding." June.

———. 1984q. "SA's Black Middle Class: Traitors or Saviors?" September.

———. 1984r. "Some Zambian Workers Are Going Unpaid." September.

———. 1984s. "South Africa Profits From Mozambique Aid Trade." September.

———. 1984t. "Tibyo Head Is the New Swazi Finance Minister." January.

———. 1984u. "Tough Budget Underlines Economic Problems Ahead." September.

———. 1984v. "Transport Costs Set to Rise." March.

———. 1984w. "US Aid Axe Falls on Zimbabwe." February.

———. 1984x. "Where Zambia Stands after 20 Years." October.

———. 1984y. "Zaire's Mobutu Circles Globe to Discuss Debts." November.

———. 1984z. "Zambia-Zimbabwe Trade Fails to Pick Up." February.

———. 1984aa. "Zimbabwe Budget Charts Economic Stagnation." September.

———. 1983. "Botswana: Austerity Pays Off—Helped by Diamond Revival." April.

———. 1983a. "Import Surcharge Cut Seems Likely." April.

———. 1983b. "Karakul's Decline Symbolises Economy's Ruin." February.

———. 1983c. "SA Lures Two Companies to Bantustans." April.

———. 1983d. "Tanzania and Zambia Choose Barter." March.

———. 1982. "Industry Faces the Hard Realities." May.

———. 1982a. "Riddell Spells Out Drawbacks of IMF Financing." April.

———. 1981. "Bad Years Cause Radical Economic Reforms." August.

———. 1979. "An Assessment of Ujamaa." July.

———. 1979a. "Punishing Port Charges for Zambian Exporters." March.

Africa News. 1983. "Malawi: Focus on Banda's Malawi." May 16.

———. 1983a. "Three-Nation Summit Ends." July 11.

Africa Research Bulletin. 1984. June 1-30.

————. 1984a. August 1-31.

————. 1983. July 15-August 14.

————. 1982. August 15-September 14.

————. 1982a. November 15-December 14.

Africa South of the Sahara, 1984-85. 1984. 14th ed. London: Europa Publications, Ltd.

Africa South of the Sahara, 1980-81. 1981. 10th ed. London: Europa Publications, Ltd.

Amin, Samir. 1976. *Unequal Development.* New York: Monthly Review Press.

————. 1972. "Underdevelopment and Dependence in Black Africa." *Journal of Modern African Studies* 19, no. 4.

Anglin, Douglas. 1983. "Economic Liberation and Regional Cooperation in Southern Africa: SADCC and PTA." *International Organization* 37, no. 4.

Arnold, Guy. 1979. *African Business,* no. 6, January.

Arrighi, G. 1970. "Labour Supplies in Historical Perspective: A Study of the Proletarianization of the African Peasantry in Rhodesia." *The Journal of Development Studies* 6, no. 3.

Association of Rhodesian Industries. 1965. "Rhodesia Economy Could be Crippled by U.D.I." *East Africa and Rhodesia,* May 20.

Azevedo, Mario J. 1981. "A Sober Commitment to Liberation?" *African Affairs,* October.

Bailey, Martin. 1977. 'Vorster Bids to Break Isolation with South American Connection," *New African,* February.

————. 1976. *Freedom Railway: China and the Tanzania-Zambia Link.* London: Rex Collings.

Barker, Jonathan, S. 1974. "Ujamaa in Cash Crop Areas of Tanzania: Some Problems and Reflections," *Journal of African Studies* 1, no. 4.

Baylies, C. 1978. "The State and Class Formation in Zambia," Ph.D. dissertation, University of Wisconsin-Madison.

Bender, Gerald; Coleman, James; and Sklar, Richard, eds. 1985. *African Crisis Areas and U.S. Foreign Policy.* Berkeley: University of California Press.

————. 1983. "Angola: The Continuing Crisis and Misunderstanding." *Current History* 82, no. 482.

Biersteker, Thomas J. 1980. "Self-Reliance in Theory and Practice in Tanzanian Trade Relations," *International Organization* 34, no. 2.

Bobb, F. Scott. 1979. "Another Rescue Operation," *Africa Report*, March-April.

Boeder, Robert B. 1984. "Malawian Labour Migration and International Relations in Southern Africa," *Africa Insight* 14, no. 1.

Böhning, W. R. 1977. "Black Migration to South Africa—What Are the Issues?" Geneva: International Labour Organization.

Bonner, Phillip. 1983. *Kings, Commoners and Concessionaires.* Ravan: Johannesburg.

Botha, P. W. 1979. Opening address in "Towards a Constellation of Southern African States." Meetings between the prime minister and business leaders, Carlton Centre, Johannesburg, November 22. Pretoria: Information Service of South Africa.

Botswana Daily News. 1975. July 31.

Botswana, Republic of. 1984. *1981 Population and Housing Census.* Gaborone: Central Statistics Office.

Botswana, Republic of. 1976. *Rural Income Distribution Survey.* Gaborone: Central Statistics Office.

Bowman, Larry W. 1971. *South Africa's Outward Strategy: A Foreign Policy Dilemma for the United States.* Athens: Ohio University Press.

———. 1968. "The Subordinate State System of Southern Africa," *International Studies Quarterly* 12, no. 3.

Bozzoli, Belinda. 1981. *The Political Nature of a Ruling Class.* London: Routledge & Kegan Paul.

Bratton, Michael. 1978. *Beyond Community Development: The Political Economy of Rural Administration in Zimbabwe.* London: Catholic Institute for International Relations.

Brecher, Michael. 1963. "International Relations and Asian Studies: The Subordinate State System of Southern Asia," *World Politics*, vol. 15, January.

Breytenbach, W. J. 1975. *Crocodiles and Commoners in Lesotho.* Pretoria: The African Institute of South Africa.

"British-Canadian Report on an Engineering and Economic Feasibility Study of a Proposed Zambia-East Africa Rail Link." 1966. London: Maxwell Stamp Associates and Canairo.

Brits, R. N. 1969. "The Marketing of South African Maize." *The South African Journal of Economics* 37, no. 3.

Bryceson, Deborah Fahy. 1982. "Peasant Commodity Production in Post-Colonial Tanzania." *African Affairs* 81, no. 325.

Business and Finance. 1978. Johannesburg, January 9.

Callaghy, Thomas M. 1984. *The State-Society Struggle.* New York: Columbia University Press.

————. 1983. "Absolutism and Apartheid: Relations between Zaire and South Africa." In *South Africa in Southern Africa,* edited by Thomas M. Callaghy. New York: Praeger Publishers.

Chamber of Mines of South Africa. 1985. *Ninety-Fifth Annual Report, 1984.* Johannesburg.

————. 1984. *Ninety-Fourth Annual Report, 1983.* Johannesburg.

Chambers, Robert, and Green, Reginald H. 1981. "Agrarian Change." In *Namibia: The Last Colony,* edited by Reginald H. Green, Kimmo Kiljunen, and Marja-Liisa Kiljunen. Essex: Longman Group, Ltd.

Chilivumbo, Alifeyo. 1977. "On Rural Development: A Note on Malawi's Programmes of Development for Exploitation." Paper presented at the Southern African Universities Social Science Conference, University of Zambia, Lusaka, Zambia, May 12-16.

Christiansen, Robert E. 1984. "Financing Malawi's Development Strategy." Paper presented at the conference "Malawi—An Alternative Pattern of Development," University of Edinburgh, May 24-25.

————, and Kydd, Jonathan G. 1983. "The Return of Malawian Labour from South Africa and Zimbabwe." *The Journal of Modern African Studies* 21, no. 2.

Christopher, A. J. 1976. *Southern Africa: Studies in Historical Geography.* Hamden: Archon Books.

Clayton, M. J. 1976. "Foreign Aid Helps Rebuild Mozambique Economy." *African Development* 10, no. 11.

Cliffe, Lionel. 1980. "Zambia in the Context of South Africa." *The Evolving Structure of Zambian Society.* Proceedings of a seminar held in the Centre of African Studies, University of Edinburgh, May 30-31.

————; Mpofu, Joshua; and Munslow, Barry. 1980. "Nationalist Politics in Zimbabwe: The 1980 Elections & Beyond." *Review of African Political Economy,* May-August.

Cobbe, James H. 1983. "The Changing Nature of Dependence: Economic Problems in Lesotho." *The Journal of Modern African Studies* 21, no. 2.

———. 1977. "Wage Policy Problems in the Small Peripheral Countries of Southern Africa, 1967-1976." *Journal of Southern African Affairs* 2, no. 4.

———, and Bardill, John. 1985. *Lesotho.* Boulder, Colo.: Westview Press.

Cohen, Dennis L. 1979. "The Botswana Political Elite: Evidence from the 1974 General Election." *Journal of Southern African Affairs* 4, no. 3.

Cohen, Neal P. 1984. "Estimates of Rural and Urban Income." *ECONEWS* 2, no. 2, SSRU, University of Swaziland.

Coker, Christopher. 1981. "The South African Elections and Neo-Apartheid." *The World Today*, June.

Colclough, Christopher, and McCarthy, Stephen. 1980. *The Political Economy of Botswana.* London: Oxford University Press.

Committee for Action and Solidarity for Southern African Students (CASSAS). 1979. *The Vanguard* (Roma), no. 5, December.

Commonwealth Secretariat. 1978. *The Front-Line States: The Burden of the Liberation Struggle.* London: Marlborough House.

Cornwell, Richard. 1982. "Botswana: Ripples in a Mill-Pond." *Africa Insight* 12, no. 3.

Coulson, Andrew. 1982. *Tanzania: A Political Economy.* Clarendon: Oxford University Press.

The Courier. 1985. "Botswana Meat Commission: 18 years of Service." No. 90, March-April.

———. 1985a. "A Deep-Pile Carpet of Minerals under the Kalahari." No. 90, March-April.

Cronje, Gillian, and Cronje, Suzanne. 1979. *The Workers of Namibia.* London: International Defence and Aid Fund for Southern Africa.

Crush, Jonathan. 1980. "The Colonial Division of Space: The Significance of the Swaziland Land Partition." *The International Journal of African Historical Studies* 13, no. 1.

———. 1980a. "The Genesis of Colonial Land Policy in Swaziland." *The South African Geographical Journal* 62, no. 1.

Crush, Jonathan. 1979. "The Parameters of Dependence in Southern Africa: A Case Study of Swaziland." *Journal of Southern African Affairs*, no. 4.

———, and Wellings, Paul. 1983. "The South African Pleasure Periphery, 1966-83." *The Journal of Modern African Studies* 21, no. 4.

Curtis, D. 1972. "The Social Organization of Ploughing." *Botswana Notes and Records* vol. 4. Gaborone: The Botswana Society.

Dale, Richard. 1978. "The Challenges and Restraints of White Power for a Small African State: Botswana and Its Neighbors." *Africa Today*, July-September.

———. 1972. "Botswana." In *Southern Africa in Perspective: Essays in Regional Politics*, edited by Christian P. Potholm and Richard Dale. New York: The Free Press.

Daniel, John. 1982. "The Political Economy of Colonial and Post-Colonial Swaziland." *South African Labour Bulletin* 7, no. 6.

Davies, Robert H., and Fransman, Martin. 1978. "Labour Supply Trends in the Supplier Economies in Southern Africa." Paper presented at the Economic Commission for Africa, Lusaka, Zambia, April 4-8.

———, and O'Meara, Dan. 1985. "Total Strategy in Southern Africa: An Analysis of South Africa's Regional Policy since 1978." *Journal of Southern African Studies* 2, no. 2.

Depelchin, Jacques. 1981. "The Transformation of the Petty Bourgeoisie and the State in Post-Colonial Zaire." *Review of African Political Economy*, no. 22, October-December.

de Vletter, Fion. 1984. "Economy." In *Africa South of the Sahara, 1984-85*. 14th ed. London: Europa Publications, Ltd.

———. 1982. "Labour Migration in Swaziland: Recent Trends and Implications." *South African Labour Bulletin*, no. 7.

Dimsdale, J. 1982. "Two Roads to Socialism." *Africa Report* 27, no. 5.

du Pisani, André. 1984. "SWA/Namibia Update: 1981 to April 1984." *Africa Insight* 14, no. 3.

———. 1977. 'Reflections on the Role of Ethnicity in the Politics of Namibia." *Plural Societies* 8, no. 3/4.

du Plessis, J. C. 1965. "Investment and the Balance of Payments." *The South African Journal of Economics*, December.

du Plessis, R. G. 1978. "Concentration of Economic Power in the

South African Manufacturing Industry." *The South African Journal of Economics* 46, no. 3.

East Africa and Rhodesia. 1964. "Outlook for Rhodesian Industry." Salisbury, March.

————. 1962. Salisbury, March.

————. 1961. "Mr. Paul Gillet on the Situation in Katanga." Salisbury, June 8.

The Economist. 1983. "Tanzania's Socialist Safari is Lost in the Bush." London, June 11.

————. 1985. Vol. 294, no. 7387. March 30.

The Economist Intelligence Unit (EIU). 1986. *Quarterly Economic Review of Zimbabwe, Malawi.* No. 1. London: The Economist Publications, Ltd.

————. 1985. *Quarterly Economic Review of Tanzania, Mozambique.* Annual Supplement. London: The Economist Publications, Ltd.

————. 1984. *Quarterly Economic Review of South Africa.* No. 4. London: The Economist Publications, Ltd.

————. 1983. *Quarterly Annual Review of Tanzania, Mozambique.* Annual Supplement. London: The Economist Publications, Ltd.

————. 1981. *Zimbabwe's First Five Years: Economic Prospects Following Independence.* Special Report No. 111. London: The Economist Publications, Ltd.

————. 1980. Quarterly Economic Review of Zimbabwe, Malawi. Annual Supplement. London: The Economist Publications, Ltd.

————. 1979. *Quarterly Economic Review of Tanzania, Mozambique.* Annual Supplement. London: The Economist Publications, Ltd.

Emmanuel, Arghiri. 1972. *Unequal Exchange.* New York: Monthly Review Press.

Fair, T.J.D. 1981. *Towards Balanced Spatial Development in Southern Africa.* Pretoria: Africa Institute of South Africa.

————; Murdoch, G.; and Jones, H. M. 1969. *Development in Swaziland.* Johannesburg: Witwatersrand University Press.

Farnie, D. A. 1956. "The Mineral Revolution in South Africa." *The South African Journal of Economics* 24, no. 2.

Finance Week. 1985. Johannesburg, August 14.

Financial Mail. 1981. Johannesburg, February 6.

———. 1979. "SWA Economy on Ice." Johannesburg, August 17.

———. 1978. Johannesburg, June 23.

———. 1977. "Moving Away from Maputo." Johannesburg, January 21.

———. 1977a. Johannesburg, June 10.

Financial Times. 1983. Johannesburg, February 2.

Fitzpatrick, J. 1981. "The Economy of Mozambique: Problems and Prospects." *Third World Quarterly* 3, no. 1.

Frank, Andre Gunder. 1981. *Crisis: In the Third World.* London: Heinemann Educational Books, Ltd.

Fransman, Martin. 1978. "The State and Development in Swaziland, 1960-1977." D. Phil. Thesis, University of Sussex.

Freund, W. M. 1981. "Class Conflict, Political Economy and the Struggle for Socialism in Tanzania." *African Affairs* 80, no. 321.

Gebhardt, F. B. 1978. "The Socio-Economic Status of Farm Labourers in Namibia." *South African Labour Bulletin* 4, nos. 1 and 2.

Geldenhuys, Deon. 1984. *The Diplomacy of Isolation: South African Foreign Policy Making.* New York: St. Martin's Press.

———, ed. 1984a. "South Africa's Regional Policy." In *Regional Co-Operation: The Record and Outlook.* Braamfontein: The South African Institute of International Affairs.

———. 1982. "What Do We Think? A Survey of White Opinion on Foreign Policy Issues." Braamfontein: The South African Institute of International Affairs.

Gertzel, Cherry. 1975. "Labour and the State: The Case of Zambia's Mineworkers Union—A Review Article." *The Journal of Commonwealth and Comparative Politics* 13, no. 3.

Gervasi, Sean. 1971. "The Nature and Consequences of South Africa's Economic Expansion." *The Societies of Southern Africa in the 19th and 20th Centuries.* Collected Seminar Papers, vol. 2. University of London: Institute of Commonwealth Studies, October 1970-June 1971.

Giliomee, Hermann. 1983. "The Disintegration of the Nationalist Movement, ca. 1965-1983." Manuscript.

Gillet, Simon. 1973. "The Survival of Chieftancy in Botswana." *African Affairs* 72, no. 287.

Gould, David J. 1979. "The Administration of Underdevelopment." In *Zaire: The Political Economy of Underdevelopment*, edited by Guy Gran. New York: Praeger Publishers.

Gramsci, Antonio. 1973. *Letters from Prison.* New York: Harper & Row.

———. 1968. *The Modern Prince, and Other Writings.* New York: International Publishers.

Green, Reginald H. 1977. *Toward Socialism and Self-Reliance: Tanzania's Striving for Sustained Transition Projected.* Uppsala: Scandinavian Institute of African Studies.

———, and Kiljunen, Kimmo. 1981. "The Colonial Economy: Structures of Growth and Exploitation." In *Namibia: The Last Colony*, edited by Reginald H. Green, Kimmo Kiljunen, and Marja-Liisa Kiljunen. Essex: Longman Group, Ltd.

Grundy, Kenneth. 1979. "Economic Patterns in the New Southern African Balance." In *Southern Africa: The Continuing Crisis*, edited by Gwendolen M. Carter and Patrick O'Meara. Bloomington: Indiana University Press.

———. 1973. *Confrontation and Accommodation in Southern Africa.* Berkeley: University of California Press.

Guelke, A. 1974. "Africa as a Market for South African Goods." *Journal of Modern African Studies* 12, no. 1.

Hackland, Brian. 1980. "The Economic and Political Context of the Growth of the Progressive Federal Party in South Africa, 1959-1978." *Journal of Southern African Studies* 7, no. 1.

Halpern, Jack. 1965. *South Africa's Hostages: Basutoland, Bechuanaland and Swaziland.* London: Harmondsworth.

Hanekom, D. 1982. "The Spatial Structure of an Economic System." Paper read at a conference in Pretoria.

Hanlon, Joseph. 1984. *Mozambique: The Revolution under Fire.* London: Zed Books, Ltd.

Harris, Laurence. 1980. "Agricultural Co-Operatives and Development Policy in Mozambique." *The Journal of Peasant Studies* 7, no. 3.

Hawkins, Anthony M. 1976. "The Economy: 1924-1974." In *Rhodesia: Economic Structure and Change*, edited by G.M.E. Leistner, Pretoria: The Africa Institute.

Heisler, Helmuth. 1971. "The Creation of a Stabilized Urban Society: A Turning Point in the Development of Northern Rhodesia/Zambia." *African Affairs* 70, no. 279.

Henderson, Robert D'A. 1983. "The Food Weapon in Southern Africa." *International Affairs Bulletin* 7, no. 3.

————. 1978. "Principles and Practice in Mozambique's Foreign Policy." *The World Today* 34, no. 7.

Henriksen, Thomas H. 1978. "Marxism and Mozambique." *African Affairs* 77, no. 309.

————. 1978a. *Mozambique: A History*. London: Rex Collings, Ltd.

The Herald. 1981. Harare, September 24.

Hill, Christopher R. 1972. "Independent Botswana: Myth or Reality?" *The Round Table*, no. 245, January.

Hirschman, David. 1979. "Changes in Lesotho's Policy towards South Africa." *African Affairs* 78, no. 310.

Hodges, Tony. 1977. "External Threats and Internal Pressures." *Africa Report*, November-December.

————. 1977a. "Zambia: Agonies of a Frontier State." *New African*, November.

Holleman, J. F., ed. 1964. *Experiment in Swaziland*. Durban: University of Natal Press.

Holm, John D. 1972. "Rural Development in Botswana: Three Basic Political Trends." In *African Rural Development: The Political Dimension*, vol. 18, edited by Fred M. Hayward and Clyde R. Ingle. The African Studies Center: Michigan State University.

Houghton, D. Hobart. 1976. *The South African Economy*. 4th ed. Cape Town: Oxford University Press.

————. 1973. *The South African Economy*. 3d ed. Cape Town: Oxford University Press.

Humphrey, D. H. 1973. "Malawi's Economic Progress and Prospects." *Eastern African Economic Review* 5, no. 2.

Hyden, Goran. 1980. *Beyond Ujamaa in Tanzania: Underdevelopment and an Uncaptured Peasantry*. Berkeley: University of California Press.

Innes, Duncan. 1983. "Monopoly Capitalism in South Africa." In the South African Research Service's *South African Review* 1, edited and compiled by the South African Research Service. Johannesburg: Ravan Press.

————. 1981. "South African Capital and Namibia." In *Namibia: The Last Colony*, edited by Reginald H. Green, Kimmo Kiljunen, and Marja-Liisa Kiljunen. Essex: Longman Group, Ltd.

————, and Malaba, Luke. 1978. "The South African State and Its Policy towards Supplier Economies." Paper presented at the Economic Commission for Africa Conference on Migratory Labour in Southern Africa, Lusaka, Zambia, April 4-8.

International Bank for Reconstruction and Development (IBRD). 1977. *Zambia: A Basic Economic Report.* Washington, D.C.: Eastern Africa Regional Office.

International Labour Office (ILO). 1977. *Reducing Dependence: A Strategy for Productive Employment and Development in Swaziland.* ILO: Addis Ababa.

International Monetary Fund (IMF). 1985. *Direction of Trade Statistics Yearbook.* Washington, D.C.: International Monetary Fund.

————. 1981. *Direction of Trade Statistics Yearbook.* Washington, D.C.: International Monetary Fund.

Isaacman, Allen. 1985. "Mozambique and South Africa, 1900-1983: Tugging at the Chains of Dependency." In *African Crisis Areas and U.S. Foreign Policy,* edited by James Coleman, Gerald Bender, and Richard Sklar. Berkeley: University of California Press.

————, and Isaacman, Barbara. 1980. "On the Road to Economic Recovery." *Africa Report,* May-June.

Isaacman, Barbara, and Isaacman, Allen. 1982. "A Socialist Legal System in the Making: Mozambique before and after Independence." In *The Politics of Informal Justice,* edited by R. L. Abel. New York: Academic Press.

James, Jeffrey. 1978. "Conditions of Agricultural Employment and Effects of Foreign Workers in South African Agriculture." Paper presented at the Economic Commission for Africa Conference on Migratory Labour in Southern Africa, Lusaka, Zambia, April 4-8.

Kabwit, Ghislain. 1979. "Zaire: The Roots of the Continuing Crisis." *The Journal of Modern African Studies.* 17, no. 3.

Kalter, Joanmarie. 1984. "Lesotho: The Economic Squeeze." *Africa Report,* September-October.

Kane-Berman, John. 1972. *Contract Labour in South West Africa.* Johannesburg: South African Institute of Race Relations.

Kaniki, M.H.Y., ed. 1980. *Tanzania under Colonial Rule.* London: Longman Group, Ltd.

Kaplan, Irving, ed. 1979. *Zaire: A Country Study.* Washington, D.C.: The American University.

Karl-I-Bond, Nguza. 1981. "The Situation in Zaire." *African Report,* November-December.

Katjivongua, Moses K. 1979. "An Open Letter to All South West African (Namibian) Patriots." *Windhoek Observer,* July 28.

Kauseni, Max. 1977. "A Quarter of the Workers Jobless." *New African.* February.

Kazadi, F.S.B. 1981. "Recovery or Relapse?" *Africa Report,* July-August.

Keenan, Jeremy. 1982. "Black Earnings: Changing Contemporary Patterns." African Studies seminar paper presented at the African Studies Institute, University of Witwatersrand, May.

Kiljunen, Marja-Liisa. 1981. "The Land and Its People." In *Namibia: The Last Colony,* edited by Reginald H. Green, Kimmo Kiljunen, and Marja-Liisa Kiljunen. Essex: Longman Group, Ltd.

Kofi, T. A. 1981. "Prospects and Problems of the Transition from Agrarianism to Socialism: The Case of Angola, Guinea-Bissau and Mozambique." *World Development* 9, no. 9/10.

Kozonguizi, Jariretundu. 1985. "Namibian Independence: What is the Goal and How Can We Achieve It?" *South African International* 15, no. 3.

Krogh, D. C. 1960. "The National Income and Expenditure of South West Africa (1920-1950)." *The South African Journal of Economics* 28, no. 1.

Kuper, Adam. 1970. *Kalahari Village Politics: An African Democracy.* London: Cambridge University Press.

Kuper, Hilda. 1980. *An African Aristocracy: Rank among the Swazi.* New York: Africana Publishing Co.

———. 1978. *Sobhuza II: Ngwenyama and King of Swaziland.* London: Duckworth.

———. 1963. *The Swazi: A South African Kingdom.* New York: Holt, Rinehart and Winston.

Kydd, Jonathan. 1984. "Malawi in the 1970s: Development Policies and Economic Change." Paper presented at the conference "Malawi—An Alternative Pattern of Development," University of Edinburgh, May 24-25.

————, and Christiansen, Robert. 1982. "Structural Change in Malawi since Independence: Consequence of a Development Strategy Based on Large-Scale Agriculture." *World Development* 10, no. 5.

Lagden, Sir G. 1909. *The Basutos*. Vol. 1. London: Hutchinson.

Legum, Colin. 1984. "Third World Reports. Namibia: The Expensive War." August 17.

————, ed. 1984a. *Africa Contemporary Record: Annual Survey and Documents*. New York: Africana Publishing Co.

Leistner, G.M.E. 1983. "Lesotho and South Africa: Uneasy Relationship." *Africa Insight* 13, no. 3.

————. 1981. "Economic Relationships among Southern African States." *GeoJournal*, Supplementary Issue 2. Wiesbaden: Akademische Verlagsgesellschaft.

————. 1981a. "Towards a Regional Development Strategy for South Africa." *The South African Journal of Economics* 49, no. 4.

————. 1976. "Southern African Community of Interests—A South African Viewpoint." *South African Journal of African Affairs*, nos. 1 and 2.

————. 1972. "Public Finance in South West Africa, 1945/46 to 1969/70." *The South African Journal of Economics* 40, no. 1.

————, and Smit, P. 1969. *Swaziland: Resources and Development*. Pretoria: African Institute of South Africa.

Levin, Richard M. 1984. "Traditional Rulers or Bourgeoisie: Class and Ideology in Swaziland." Liverpool Papers in Politics, University of Liverpool.

Leys, Roger. 1979. "Lesotho: Non-Development or Underdevelopment." In *The Politics of Africa: Dependence and Development*, edited by Timothy M. Shaw and Kenneth A. Heard. New York: Dalhousie University Press.

————, and Tostenson, Arne. 1982. "Regional Co-operation in Southern Africa: The Southern African Development Coordination Conference." *Review of African Political Economy*, January-April.

Libby, Ronald T. 1984. "Developmental Strategies and Political Divisions within the Zimbabwean State." In *The Political Economy of Zimbabwe*, edited by Michael Schatzberg. New York: Praeger Press.

Libby, Ronald T. 1983. "Transnational Class Alliances in Zambia." *Comparative Politics* 15, no. 4.

———. 1980. *Toward an Africanized U.S. Policy for Southern Africa.* Berkeley: Institute of International Studies, University of California.

———. 1977. "The Frontline States of Africa: A Small Power Entente." Paper presented at the University of Zambia.

———, and Woakes, Michael E. 1980. "Nationalization and the Displacement of Development Policy in Zambia." *African Studies Review*, vol. 23, April.

Lipton, Merle. 1980. *Optima* 29, no. 2/3. Special Issue on Migrant Labour in South Africa.

Lofchie, Michael F. 1978. "Agrarian Crisis and Economic Liberalisation in Tanzania." *The Journal of Modern African Studies* 16, no. 3.

Lombard, J. 1984. "Power in the Market Economy." *Focus on Key Economic Issues*, no. 34. Johannesburg: Mercabank.

McMaster, Carolyn. 1974. *Malawi: Foreign Policy and Development.* London: Julian Friedman.

MacQueen, Norman. 1984. "Mozambique's Widening Foreign Policy." *The World Today* 40, no. 1.

Maina, Geoffrey M., and Strieker, Gary G. 1971. *Customary Land Tenure and Modern Agriculture on Swazi Nation Land.* Mbabane: Ministry of Agriculture.

Makgetla, Neva, and Seidman, Ann. 1980. *Outposts of Monopoly Capitalism: Southern Africa in the Changing Global Economy.* Westport: Laurence Hill and Co.

Malawi—An Alternative Pattern of Development. Centre of African Studies. Edinburgh: University of Edinburgh. Forthcoming.

Malawi, Republic of. 1977. *Population Census.* Zomba: Governmental Statistical Office.

———, Reserve Bank of. 1980. *Financial and Economic Review* 12, no. 3.

Marais, G. 1981. "Structural Changes in Manufacturing Industry 1916 to 1975." *The South African Journal of Economics* 49, no. 1.

Markovitz, Irving Leonard. 1977. *Power and Class in Africa: An Introduction to Change and Conflict in African Politics.* Englewood Cliffs, N.J.: Prentice-Hall.

Martin, David. 1975. "Tan-Zam Railway, Iron Links." *Africa*, no. 47, July.

Matsebula, J.S.M. 1976. *A History of Swaziland*. 2d ed. Cape Town: Longmans.

Mboukou, Alexandre. 1982. "An African Triangle." *African Report*, September-October.

Metzger, Dorothea. 1978. "How the Mining Companies Undermine Liberation." *Review of African Political Economy*, no. 2. May-August.

Meyns, Peter. 1981. "Liberation Ideology and National Development Strategy in Mozambique." *Review of African Political Economy*, no. 22, October-December.

Milazi, Dominic. 1978. "Malawi (Part III): Country Case Study." Paper presented at the Conference on Migratory Labour, Lusaka, Zambia, April 4-8.

Mittelman, James H. 1978. "Mozambique: The Political Economy of Underdevelopment." *Journal of Southern African Affairs* 3, no. 1.

Molteno, Robert. 1971. *Africa and South Africa*. London: Africa Bureau.

Mondlane, Eduardo. 1969. *The Struggle for Mozambique*. Baltimore: Penguin.

Moody's International Manual. 1984. Vol. 2. New York: Moody's Investment Service.

Morgan, E. Philip. 1979. "Botswana: Development, Democracy and Vulnerability." In *Southern Africa: The Continuing Crisis*, edited by Gwendolen M. Carter and Patrick O'Meara. Bloomington and London: Indiana University Press.

Mozambique, People's Republic of. 1984. *Economic Report*. Maputo: National Planning Commission.

Mpakati, Attati. 1973. "Malawi: The Birth of a Neo-Colonial State." *The African Review* 3, no. 1.

Munslow, Barry. 1984. "State Intervention in Agriculture: The Mozambican Experience." *The Journal of Modern African Studies* 22, no. 2.

————, and O'Keefe, Phil. 1984. "Energy and the Southern African Regional Confrontation." *Third World Quarterly* 6, no. 1.

Murray, Roger. 1979. "Namibia: Breaking South Africa's Economic Stranglehold." *African Business* (London), January.

Mwanza, Jacob M. 1979. "Rural-Urban Migration and Urban Employment in Zambia." *The Developing Economies* 17, no. 2.

Myers, Desaix, III; Propp, Kenneth; Hauck, David; and Liff, David M. 1980. *U.S. Business in South Africa.* Bloomington and London: Indiana University Press.

Nattrass, Jill. 1981. *The South African Economy.* Cape Town: Oxford University Press.

Nchanga Consolidated Copper Mines, Ltd. (NCCM). 1975-1978. *Annual Reports.*

Nedbank Group, Ltd. 1983. *South Africa: An Appraisal.* Johannesburg: Nedbank Group Economic Unit.

New African. 1984. "Bombings in Kinshasa." June.

———. 1984a. "Does East Africa Have a Future?" August.

———. 1984b. "Facing the Economic Crunch." October.

———. 1984c. "The Guide with Wobbly Feet." September.

———. 1984d. "Swaziland's 'Worst Disaster.' " April.

———. 1983. "On the Brink." July.

———. 1983a. "13 MPs Get the Mobuto Medicine." October.

———. 1981. September.

———. 1980. "Plan for Prosperity." June.

———. 1980a. December.

———. 1979. "Lid of the Tea Estates." July.

———. 1977. "S. African Firm Will Ship Zaire Copper." March.

New York Times. 1986. January 21.

———. 1985. September 15.

———. 1985a. December 5.

Novicki, Margaret A. 1983. "Zimbabwe: The Economic Outlook." *Africa Report* (New York) 28, no. 1.

Nyathi, V. M. 1974. "South Africa's Imperialism in Southern Africa." Mimeographed.

Nzongola, Georges N. 1970. "The Bourgeoisie and Revolution in the Congo." *Journal of Modern African Studies* 8, no. 4.

Nzongola-Ntalaja. 1984. "Bureaucracy, Elite, New Class: Who Serves Whom and Why in Mobutu's Zaire?" *Canadian Journal of African Studies* 18, no. 1.

O'Linn, Bryan. 1979. "An Open Letter to All South West Africans (Namibians) in Reply to the So-Called Open Letter by Mr. Moses K." *Windhoek Observer*, August 11.

O'Meara, Dan. 1983. *Volks-Kapitalisme: Class, Capital and Ide-*

ology in the Development of Afrikaner Nationalism, 1934-1948. Cambridge: At the University Press.

Palmer, Robin, and Parsons, Neil, eds. 1977. *The Roots of Rural Poverty in Central and Southern Africa*. Berkeley: University of California Press.

Parson, Jack. 1983. "The Trajectory of Class and State in Dependent Development: The Consequences of New Wealth for Botswana." *The Journal of Commonwealth and Comparative Politics* vol. 21, November.

————. 1981. "Cattle, Class and the State in Rural Botswana." *Journal of Southern African Studies* 15, no. 4.

————. 1977. "Political Culture in Rural Botswana: A Survey Result." *Journal of Modern African Studies* 15, no. 4.

Peemans, J. Ph. 1975. "Social and Economic Development of Zaire." *African Affairs* 74, no. 295.

Plaut, Martin. 1984. "Changing Perspectives on South African Trade Unions." *Review of African Political Economy*, no. 3, September.

Potholm, Christian P. 1972. *Swaziland: The Dynamics of Political Modernization*. Berkeley: University of California Press.

Price, Robert M. 1980. "Apartheid and White Supremacy: The Meaning of Government-led Reform in the South African Context." In *The Apartheid Regime: Political Power and Racial Domination*, edited by Robert M. Price and Carl G. Rosberg. Berkeley: Institute of International Studies, University of California.

Prinsloo, Wilhelm. 1984. "Political Restructuring, Capital Accumulation, and the 'Coming Corporatism' in South Africa: Some Theoretical Considerations." *Politikon* II, no. 1.

Pritchard, J. M. 1971. *Africa: The Geography of a Changing Continent*. New York: Africana Publishing Co.

Proctor, J. H. 1973. "Traditionalism and Parliamentary Government in Swaziland." *African Affairs* 72, no. 288.

————. 1969. "Building a Constitutional Monarchy in Lesotho." *Civilisations* 19, no. 1.

————. 1968. "The House of Chiefs and the Political Development of Botswana." *The Journal of Modern African Studies* 6, no. 1.

Rand Daily Mail. 1985. March 19.

The Report of the Study Commission on U.S. Policy toward

South Africa (Rockefeller Report). 1981. *South Africa: Time Running Out*. Berkeley: University of California Press.

Reynders, H.J.J. 1977. "Black Industrial Entrepreneurship." *Southern African Journal of Economics* 45, no. 3.

————, and van Zyl, J. C. 1973. "Foreign Trade Policy." In *Economic Policy in South Africa: Selected Essays*, edited by J. A. Lombard. Cape Town: Citadel Press.

Rich, Tony. 1982. "1980 Elections in Midlands." *Africa* 52, no. 3.

Riddell, Roger. 1984. "Zimbabwe: The Economy Four Years after Independence." *African Affairs* 83, no. 333.

————. 1977. "Alternatives to Poverty." London: Catholic Institute for International Relations.

Ross, Andrew. 1967. "White Africa's Black Ally." *New Left Review*, no. 8, September-October.

Rothchild, Donald. 1972. "Rural-Urban Inequities and Resource Allocation in Zambia." *Journal of Commonwealth Political Studies*, vol. 10.

Rweyemamu, Justinian. 1973. *Underdevelopment and Industrialization in Tanzania*. Nairobi: Oxford University Press.

Rymenam, Jean. 1977. "Comment le régime Mobutu a sappé ses propres fondements." *Le monde diplomatique*, May.

Samoff, Joel. 1981. "Crises and Socialism in Tanzania." *The Journal of Modern African Studies* 19, no. 2.

Saul, John S., and Gelb, Stephen. 1981. *The Crisis in South Africa*. New York: Monthly Review Press.

Savage, Mike. 1984. "Ownership and Control in South Africa." Paper presented at the ASSA Conference in Johannesburg.

Schatzberg, Michael G. 1980. *Class and Politics in Zaire*. New York: Africana Publishing Co.

————. 1980a. "The State and the Economy: The Radicalization of the Revolution in Mobutu's Zaire." *Canadian Journal of African Studies* 14, no. 2.

Schlemmer, Lawrence, and Welsh, David. 1982. "South Africa's Constitutional and Political Prospects." *Optima* 30, no. 4.

Seidman, Ann, and Seidman, Neva. 1977. *U.S. Multinationals in Southern Africa*. Dar es Salaam: Tanzania Publishing House.

Serfontein, J.H.P. 1976. *Namibia?* Randburg: Fokus Suid Publishers.

Seushi, I., and Loxley, John. 1974. "Financing Ujamaa—State Resources and Cooperative Development." Cited in Jonathan S.

Barker, "Ujamaa in Cash Crop Areas of Tanzania: Some Problems and Reflections," *Journal of African Studies* 1, no. 4.

Shaw, Timothy M. 1974. "Southern Africa: Co-Operation and Conflict in an International Sub-system." *The Journal of Modern African Studies* 12, no. 4.

———, and Heard, Kenneth A., eds. 1977. *Cooperation and Conflict in Southern Africa: Papers on a Regional Sub-System.* Washington, D.C.: University Press of America.

Shivji, Issa G. 1976. *Class Struggle in Tanzania.* London: Monthly Review Press.

———. 1973. "Tanzania: The Silent Class Struggle." In *The Silent Class Struggle.* Dar es Salaam: Tanzania Publishing House.

Short, Philip. 1974. *Banda.* London: Routledge & Kegan Paul.

Skocpol, Theda. 1979. *States and Social Revolutions: A Comparative Analysis of France, Russia, and China.* Cambridge: At the University Press.

The South Africa Foundation News. 1985. Vol. 11, no. 8.

———. 1978. Vol. 4, no. 3.

———. 1976. Vol. 2, no. 11.

South African Commissioner of Customs and Excise. 1985. *Monthly Abstract of Trade Statistics.* January-December 1984. Pretoria.

South African Institute of Race Relations (SAIRR). 1985. *Survey of Race Relations in South Africa.* Johannesburg: SAIRR.

———. 1984. *Survey of Race Relations in South Africa.* Johannesburg: SAIRR.

———. 1978. *Survey of Race Relations in South Africa.* Johannesburg: SAIRR.

———. 1977. *Survey of Race Relations in South Africa.* Johannesburg: SAIRR.

South African Observer. 1982. August.

South Africa, Republic of. 1984. *Bulletin of Statistics.* Vol. 18, December. Pretoria: Central Statistical Services.

Southall, Roger. 1985. "Monopoly Capital and Labour's Response: Emergent Unionism in the South African Motor Industry." Manuscript.

———. 1984. "Botswana as a Host Country for Refugees." *Journal of Commonwealth and Comparative Politics* 22, no. 2.

Southall, Roger. 1982. "Botha Reformism, the Bantustan Strategy and the Marginalization of the South African Periphery." *Labour Capital and Society*, November.

———. 1980. "African Capitalism in Contemporary South Africa." *Journal of Southern African Studies* 7, no. 1.

Southern African Development Coordination Conference (SADCC). 1984. *Drought*. Lusaka, Zambia, February 2-3.

———. 1984a. *SADCC Agriculture toward 2000*. Rome: Food and Agriculture Organization of the United Nations.

Spence, J. E. 1965. *Republic under Stress*. London: Oxford University Press.

Standard Chartered Review. 1982. London, September.

———. 1981. London, March.

The Star. 1985. Johannesburg, September 9.

Stevens, Richard P. 1967. *Lesotho, Botswana, and Swaziland*. New York: Frederick A. Praeger.

Sunday Times. 1980. Johannesburg, November 23.

Swaziland, Kingdom of. 1984. *Annual Statistical Bulletin, 1982*. Mbabane: Central Statistical Office.

———. 1983. *Annual Statistical Bulletin, 1981*. Mbabane: Central Statistical Office.

———. 1974. *Second National Development Plan, 1973-1977*. Mbabane: Swaziland Printing & Publishing Company, Ltd.

Szeftel, Morris. 1978. "Conflict, Spoils and Class Formation in Zambia." Ph.D. dissertation, University of Manchester.

Tanganyika Industrial Development. 1961. Dar es Salaam: Arthur D. Little, Inc.

Thomas, Simon. 1975. "Economic Developments in Malawi since Independence." *Journal of Southern African Studies* 2, no. 1.

Thomas, Wolfgang H. 1978. *Economic Development in Namibia*. Munchen: Matthias-Gruenwald-Verlag Mainz and Chr. Kaiser Verlag.

Times of Swaziland. 1982. February 17.

———. 1982a. June 24.

———. 1981. October 9.

Tordoff, William. 1974. "Local Administration in Botswana—Part II." *Journal of Administration Overseas* 13, no. 1.

———. 1973. "Local Administration in Botswana—Part I." *Journal of Administration Overseas* 12, no. 4.

Tötemeyer, Gerhard. 1977. *South West Africa/Namibia.* Randburg: Fokus Suid Publishers.

Trapido, Stanley. 1971. "South Africa in a Comparative Study of Industrialization." *Journal of Development Studies* 7, no. 3.

Tregenna-Pigott, J. V. 1980. "The Welfare Cost of Monopoly in South African Manufacturing Industry." *The South African Journal of Economics* 48, no. 2.

United Nations. 1983. *Statistical Yearbook.* 32d issue. New York: United Nations Statistical Office.

United Nations Centre on Transnational Corporations (UNCTC). 1980. *The Activities of Transnational Corporations in the Industrial, Mining and Military Sectors of Southern Africa.* New York: United Nations. ST/CTC/12.

United Nations Conference on Trade and Development (UNCTAD). 1981. *Monthly Digest of Statistics,* July.

United Nations Development Program (UNDP). 1976. *A Profile of the Zambian Economy.* Lusaka: UNDP.

United Nations General Assembly (UNGA). 1982. *Review Mission to Zimbabwe* (August 22-27). A/37/139, Thirty-Seventh Session, Agenda Item 74(b), October 14.

United Nations Institute for Namibia (UNIN). 1979. "Agrarian and Land Reform Programmes for an Independent Namibia." Seminar Report. Lusaka: United Nations Institute for Namibia.

———. 1978. *Towards Manpower Development for Namibia—Background Notes.* Lusaka: United Nations Institute of Namibia.

United States Agency for International Development (USAID). 1977. *Transition in Southern Africa: Botswana.* Washington, D.C.: USAID.

———. 1977a. *Transition in Southern Africa: Lesotho.* Washington, D.C.: USAID.

———. 1977b. *Transition in Southern Africa: Malawi.* Washington, D.C.: USAID.

———. 1977c. *Transition in Southern Africa: Mozambique.* Washington, D.C.: USAID.

———. 1977d. *Transition in Southern Africa: Namibia.* Washington, D.C.: USAID.

———. 1977e. *Transition in Southern Africa: Swaziland.* Washington, D.C.: USAID.

United States Agency for International Development. 1977f. *Transition in Southern Africa: Zimbabwe.* Washington, D.C.: USAID.

Vail, Leroy, and White, Landeg. 1984. "Variations on the Theme of Ethnicity: The Malawian Experience." Paper presented at the conference "Malawi—An Alternative Pattern of Development," University of Edinburgh, May 24-25.

———. 1980. *Capitalism and Colonialism in Mozambique.* Minneapolis: University of Minnesota Press.

Venter, Denis, and du Pisani, André. 1978. "SWA/NAMIBIA: Prospects for Coalition-Formation." Pretoria: Africa Institute of South Africa.

Voipio, Rauha. 1981. "Contract Work through Ovambo Eyes." In *Namibia: The Last Colony,* edited by Reginald H. Green, Kimmo Kiljunen, and Marja-Liisa Kiljunen. Essex: Longman Group, Ltd.

Wallis, Malcolm, and Henderson, Robert D'A. 1983. "Lesotho 1983: Year of the Election?" *The World Today* 39, no. 5.

Weber, Max. 1983. *Max Weber on Capitalism, Bureaucracy, and Religion: A Selection of Texts.* Edited by Stanislav Andreski. Boston: Allen & Unwin.

Weisfelder, Richard F. 1981. "The Basotho Nation-State: What Legacy for the Future?" *The Journal of Modern African Studies* 19, no. 2.

———. 1972. *The Basotho Monarchy: A Spent Force or a Dynamic Political Factor?* Africa Series No. 16, Ohio University, Center for International Studies.

———. 1972a. "Lesotho." In *Southern Africa in Perspective,* edited by C. P. Potholm and R. Dale. New York: The Free Press.

Wellings, Paul. 1985. "Lagging behind the Bantustans: South African Corporate Investment in Lesotho." *Journal of Contemporary African Studies,* forthcoming.

———. 1985a. "The 'Relative Autonomy' of the Basotho State: Internal and External Determinants of Lesotho's Political Economy." Manuscript.

Wellington, J. H. 1965. "South West Africa: The Facts about the Disputed Territory." *Optima* 15, no. 1.

Whitaker, Sylvester C. 1970. *The Politics of Tradition: Continuity and Change in Northern Nigeria, 1946-1966.* Princeton, N.J.: Princeton University Press.

Wield, David. 1981. "Manufacturing Industry." In *Zimbabwe's*

Inheritance, edited by Colin Stoneman. New York: St. Martin's Press.

Wiese, Bernd. 1981. *Seaports and Port Cities of Southern Africa*. Wiesbaden: Steiner Verlag.

Williame, Jean-Claude. 1984. "Reflexions sur l'etat et la société civile au Zaire: de l'illusion à la réalité." Paper presented at the workshop "State Penetration at the Local Level in Modern Africa," Antwerp, December 20-21.

Williams, T. David. 1978. *Malawi: The Politics of Despair*. Ithaca: Cornell University Press.

Winter, Isobel. 1978. "The Swazi State." *Review of African Political Economy*, no. 9, May-August.

Wiseman, John A. 1978. "Conflict and Conflict Alliances in the Kgatleng District of Botswana." *Journal of Modern African Studies* 16, no. 3.

Wolpe, Harold. 1983. "Apartheid's Deepening Crisis." *Marxism Today* 26, no. 1.

―――. 1972. "Capitalism and Cheap Labour Power in South Africa: From Segregation to Apartheid." *Economy and Society* 1, no. 4.

Woodward, Calvin. 1982. "Not a Complete Solution: Assessing the Long Years of Foreign Aid to Lesotho." *Africa Insight* 12, no. 3.

World Bank (IBRD). 1984. *Toward Sustained Development in Sub-Saharan Africa*. Washington, D.C.: IBRD.

―――. 1979. *The Manufacturing Sector of Zaire*. Report No. 2212-ZR, October 29.

―――. 1978. *Staff Appraisal Report: Malawi*. Report No. 2075-MAI, November 13.

X-Ray. 1982. "Current Affairs in Southern Africa." May/June.

―――. 1981. "Current Affairs in Southern Africa." May/June.

―――. 1979. "Current Affairs in Southern Africa." July/August.

Young, Crawford. 1984. "Zaire: Is There a State?" *Canadian Journal of African Studies* 18, no. 1.

Zambia, Republic of. 1984. *Monthly Digest of Statistics* 20, nos. 7-9. Lusaka: Central Statistical Office.

―――. 1984a. *Economic Report 1983*. Lusaka: National Commission for Development Planning.

―――. 1979. "Budget Address by the Minister of Finance, the Hon. M. J. Lumina, MP." Lusaka.

Zambia, Republic of. 1978. *Monthly Digest of Statistics* 14, nos. 7-9. Supplement. Lusaka: Central Statistical Office.

―――. 1974. *Transport Inventory Series*, vol. 3, *Zambia's External Transportation by Routes, 1969-74*. Lusaka: Ministry of Power, Transport and Works.

Zimbabwe, Republic of. 1984. *Quarterly Digest of Statistics* (December). Harare: Central Statistical Office.

―――. 1983. *Quarterly Digest of Statistics*. Harare: Central Statistical Office.

―――. 1981. "Growth with Equity." Salisbury, Cmd. R.Z.4.

―――. 1981a. *Report of the Commission of Inquiry into Incomes, Prices and Conditions of Service* (The Riddell Report). Salisbury.

LIBRARY OF CONGRESS CATALOGING-IN-
PUBLICATION DATA

Libby, Ronald T.
The politics of economic power in southern Africa.

Bibliography: p.   Includes index.
1. Africa, Southern—Foreign economic relations—South Africa.
2. South Africa—Foreign economic relations—Africa, Southern.
3. Africa, Southern—Economic conditions. 4. Africa, Southern—
Economic policy. 5. Africa, Southern—Politics and government.
I. Title.
HF1613.3.Z4S65   1987   337.68   87-2406
ISBN 0-691-07723-1 (alk. paper)
ISBN 0-691-02256-9 (pbk.)